Royal Society of Tasmania

**Papers and Proceedings of the Royal Society of Tasmania**

Royal Society of Tasmania

**Papers and Proceedings of the Royal Society of Tasmania**

ISBN/EAN: 9783337161491

Printed in Europe, USA, Canada, Australia, Japan

Cover: Foto ©Suzi / pixelio.de

More available books at **www.hansebooks.com**

# ROYAL SOCIETY
OF
## TASMANIA

# PAPERS & PROCEEDINGS

OF THE

# ROYAL SOCIETY

# OF TASMANIA

FOR THE YEAR

# 1921

(With 30 Plates and 5 Text Figures)

ISSUED 28th FEBRUARY, 1922

PUBLISHED BY THE SOCIETY

The Tasmanian Museum, Argyle Street, Hobart
1922

*Price: Ten Shillings*

# ROYAL SOCIETY OF TASMANIA

The Royal Society of Tasmania was founded on the 14th October, 1843, by His Excellency Sir John Eardley Eardley Wilmot, Lieutenant Governor of Van Diemen's Land, as "The Botanical and Horticultural Society of Van Diemen's Land." The Botanical Gardens in the Queen's Domain, near Hobart, were shortly afterwards placed under its management, and a grant of £400 a year towards their maintenance was made by the Government. In 1844, His Excellency announced to the Society that Her Majesty the Queen had signified her consent to become its patron; and that its designation should thenceforward be "The Royal Society of Van Diemen's Land for Horticulture, Botany, and the Advancement of Science."

In 1848 the Society established the Tasmanian Museum; and in 1849 it commenced the publication of its "Papers and Proceedings."

In 1854 the Legislative Council of Tasmania by "The Royal Society Act" made provision for vesting the property of the Society in trustees, and for other matters connected with the management of its affairs.

In 1855 the name of the Colony was changed to Tasmania, and the Society then became "The Royal Society of Tasmania for Horticulture, Botany, and the Advancement of Science."

In 1860 a piece of ground at the corner of Argyle and Macquarie streets, Hobart, was given by the Crown to the Society as a site for a Museum, and a grant of £3,000 was made for the erection of a building. The Society contributed £1,800 towards the cost, and the new Museum was finished in 1862.

In 1885 the Society gave back to the Crown the Botanical Gardens and the Museum, which, with the collections of the Museum, were vested in a body of trustees, of whom six are chosen from the Society. In consideration of the services it had rendered in the promotion of science, and in the formation and management of the Museum and Gardens, the right was reserved to the Society to have exclusive possession of sufficient and convenient rooms in the Museum, for the safe custody of its Library, and for its meetings, and for all other purposes connected with it.

In 1911 the Parliament of Tasmania, by "The Royal Society Act, 1911," created the Society a body corporate by the name of "The Royal Society of Tasmania," with perpetual succession.

The object of the Society is declared by its Rules to be "the advancement of knowledge."

His Majesty the King is Patron of the Society; and His Excellency the Governor of Tasmania is President.

# ROYAL SOCIETY OF TASMANIA

## PAPERS AND PROCEEDINGS, 1921

### CONTENTS

# PAPERS

OF THE

# ROYAL SOCIETY OF TASMANIA

## 1921

---

NOTOTHERIA AND ALLIED ANIMALS—

A REJOINDER.

By

H. H. Scott, Curator Launceston Museum,
and
Clive E. Lord, Curator Tasmanian Museum.

Plates I.-III.

(Read 14th March, 1921.)

Before presenting to the Royal Society of Tasmania our notes upon the extinct Marsupial Rhinoceros, *Nototherium mitchelli*, [1] we cast them into such a form as to embrace extreme osteological details upon the one hand, and the widest taxonomical scope upon the other. This latter item. in fact, had its entire origin in the circumstances incidental to the super-imposition of the Rhinoceros trend upon the more or less generalised Marsupial races of geological periods long since past. Any criticism of our work or methods should therefore, in justice, take note of this duality, or to descend to details—deductions made from the wide scope of the trend should not be quoted in terms of that man-made taxonomy that is enthralled within the iron bands of genus, species, and variety. Again, to quote backwards from the living—and largely fixed—marsupials of to-day, to plastic, rapidly evolving generalised types, is to throw ourselves open to contradiction by the very next discovery that fortune places at our disposal. Accordingly, we used considerable caution in this respect, but, as it now appears, stand charged with an under-estimation of the values of the evidence yielded by a study of the Nototherian and modern marsupial premolars. (1920, pp. 13, 17, and 76.)

---

[1] Pap. and Proc. Roy. Soc. Tas. 1920.

A

We therefore desire to add the present note to our previous papers in order to reply to certain remarks made by Mr. Heber Longman in his recent interesting contribution to the memoirs of the Queensland Museum, [2] on *Euryzygoma dunense.* (1920, p. 65.)

The extent to which generalisation obtained among Nototherian animals can only be appreciated by those who have for some reason or other paid special attention to the matter, and, therefore, we must be pardoned for giving in detail the following item of cranial morphology.

The zygomatic arch of a Nototherium such as that of *Nototherium tasmanicum* leaves the occiput under conditions that are not exactly repeated by either *Macropus* (Kangaroos), *Phascolomys* (Wombats), or *Phascolarctus* (Native Bears), but upon the whole they are those of *Macropus.* It descends into the orbit at a vertical line at least 50 mm. in advance of the premasseter process (not so in *N. mitchelli*), while in the Kangaroo this process outwardly underprops the posterior third of the orbit. It does not reach it by 8 mm. in the Native Bear and 10 mm. in the Wombat. Owing to the heavy developed premasseter process the morphology of the orbit here departs from that of the Kangaroo, misses the Wombat outline, but with generic characteristics assumes in exaggeration that of the Native Bear, which it continues to follow with added closeness to the end of the skull, including the lateral incisors, but not the nasal regions. Here, then, in a few inches of space we have the characters of three modern animals in generalised association in the skull of a single Nototherium, and might we not then expect that equally generalised creatures of the same age should show intergrading dental characters that would render the strictest terms of modern classification untenable?

Our use of the word *Phascolonus* was intended to imply that the jaws called *Nototherium dunense* conformed even more strongly to the *Phascolonian* type than they did to the *Nototherian.* In other words we considered the Wombat characters so accentuated in this mandible that it would be eventually classified with a type more generalised than *Nototherium*, and one that more closely approached the common progenitor of gigantic Wombats and Nototheria. Others besides ourselves have found such a creature thinkable; for instance, the late Richard Lydekker wrote thus of the family *Nototheridæ*:—"This family connects *Phascolomyidæ* with the

(2) Heber A. Longman. A New Genus of Fossil Marsupials. Mem. Qld. Mus. Vol. VII., pt. II.

"*Diprotodontidæ*. . . . It is easy to see how the structure of "the cheek teeth could pass into that of the *Phascolomyidæ;* "and it is not improbable that the two families may have "diverged from a common ancestor." [3] (1887, Vol. 5.)

That was our thought at the time of writing, and Mr. Longman's association of these jaws, almost immediately afterwards, with a more aberrant type of cranium than anything that had hitherto come to light, shows that our diagnosis was not misplaced.

Anybody who will carefully read our notes cannot fail to see how highly we estimated De Vis' work, and we regret to stand charged with any unfairness to him. We, therefore, take the first opportunity of saying that nothing was farther from our thoughts. Our general perusal of De Vis' works left the definite impression upon our minds that he looked to *Sceparnodon* to clear up some outstanding puzzles in regard to these generalised creatures, of which (as the future may yet prove) he visualised at least eight groups. In effect our reference simply meant this—*Sceparnodon*, having been shown by Stirling to be a synonym of *Phascolonus*, was eliminated *ipso facto* as a possible generalised animal, and this, in our opinion, left its generalised connection to the Wombat stirp pure and simple. Unfortunately (so hard is it to kill "genus," "species," and "variety"), the word "genus" crept in here, although the wider sense of the word is quite manifest when the sentence enclosing it is taken in conjunction with the full context.

Mr. Longman's criticism therefore pivots upon the single word "genus." Nature never produced animals ready made to genus, species, or variety, although she may have produced them in groups, and we yet hope to see these Nototherian groups with their sex, age, and individual variations clearly defined.

As, however, this was not a *fait accompli* when our notes were in course of compilation, and very much printer's ink had already been used over the dentition by those who had gone before us, we decided to seek the effects produced by the super-imposition of the Rhinoceros trend upon this section of the *Marsupialia*, rather than re-list the variation of the premolars; some of which mutations are dangerously close to the morphological minutiæ inseparable from diphyodont succession. That any marsupial group should have taken on the Rhinoceros trend would, in the fact itself, introduce

---

(3) Lydekker. Cat. Fossil Mammalia, Brit. Mus. Vol. 5, 1887.

an enormous element of variation, from which the teeth, in addition to the other parts of the skeleton, could hardly escape the process of remoulding, and in the absence of a complete series of such changes, even in one group of animals, quite apart from the sum total, we tentatively classified known material in terms of the most obvious trend characters. If all extinct creatures had first been classified in groups, and as knowledge increased genera and species had been eventually created within the groups, how much confusion would have been avoided!

All classification is man-made, and in essence chiefly intended to avoid ambiguity when the name of an animal is mentioned. Most of us admit this, and yet rise up in arms immediately we are asked to act upon our conviction. Accordingly, we did not expect a ready acceptance of our group taxonomy, yet nevertheless it is as sound as if we had called the White Rhinoceros of to-day "A large-horned Rhinoceros" and the Chittagong animal a "Small-horned Rhinoceros."

## RECAPITULATION.

(1) We are convinced that the several groups of more or less generalised animals lived in the Australian Zoogeographical province and that the names *Diprotodon*, *Nototherium*, *Phascolonus*, *Euryzygoma*, etc., stand as outpost flags to a largely unexplored realm.

(2) That De Vis' estimate of seven or eight groups may yet prove to be feasible.

(3) That the most generalised groups have yet to be re-constructed.

(4) That in view of these facts it is better to seek the elucidation of the groups than it is to argue over the sub-divisions of such groups. Accordingly, we write, and always have written, in that spirit, and without any desire to under-estimate the works of others.

## EXPLANATIONS OF PLATES.

### PLATE I.

Side view of the articulated skeleton of *Nototherium mitchelli*. The specimen, although not perfect in all details, shows, for the first time, the general outline of this animal.

Plate I.

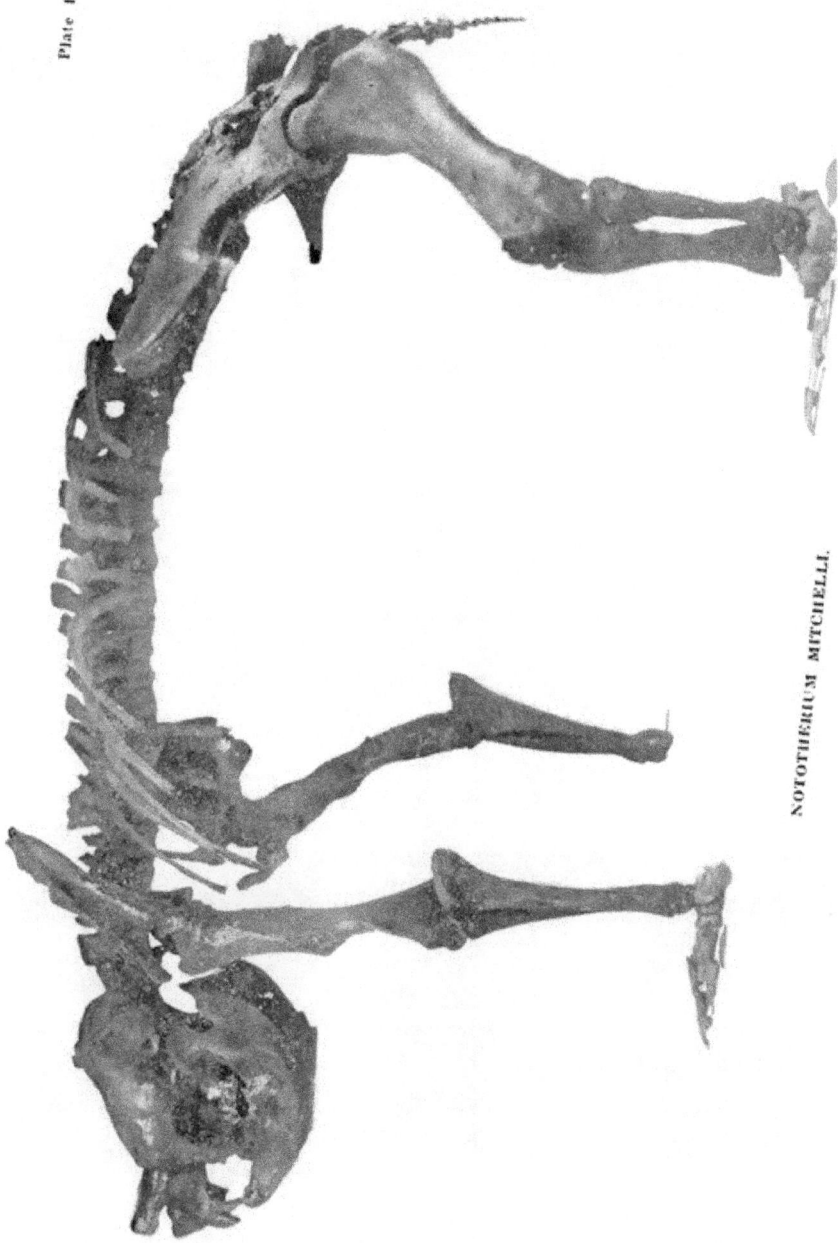

NOTOTHERIUM MITCHELLI.

P. & P. Roy. Soc. Tas., 1921.

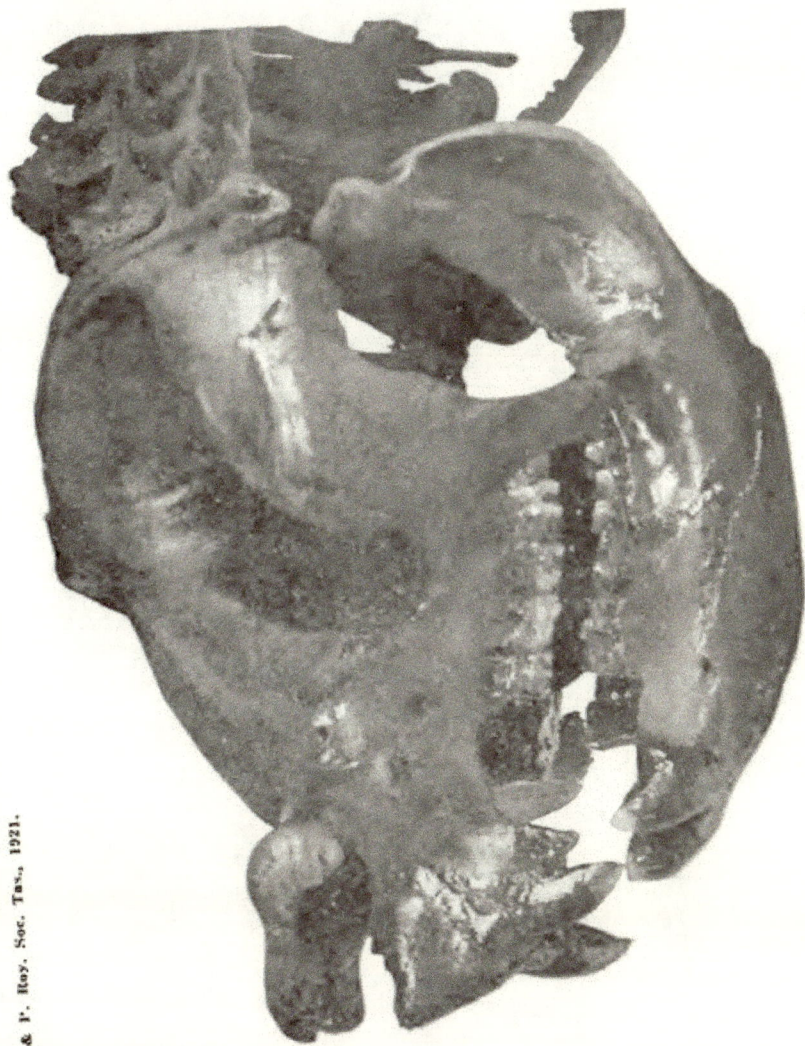

SKULL OF NOTOTHERIUM MITCHELLI.

## PLATE II.

This aspect shows the aggressive, bulldog-like character of the fighting *Nototherium*.

## PLATE III.

This view is specially arranged to show the pugnacious type of skull incidental to the evolution of the Rhinoceros trend among the Marsupials.

## LIST OF WORKS REFERRED TO.

Longman, Heber A., 1920.—A New Genus of Fossil Marsupials. Memoirs of the Queensland Museum, Vol. VII., Pt. II., pp. 65-80.

Lydekker, R., 1887.—British Museum Catalogue of Fossil Mammalia, Part V.

Scott, H. H., and Clive Lord, 1920.—Studies in Tasmanian Mammals. Papers and Proceedings of the Royal Society of Tasmania, 1920.

# STUDIES IN TASMANIAN MAMMALS, LIVING AND EXTINCT.

## Number IV.

## THE CAVE DEPOSITS AT MOLE CREEK.

By

H. H. Scott, Curator, Launceston Museum,

and

Clive Lord, Curator, Tasmanian Museum.

(Read 13th June, 1921.)

Through the courtesy of the Director of the Tasmanian Government Tourist Bureau (Mr. E. T. Emmett), we have recently had the opportunity of visiting two of the caves at Mole Creek, and obtaining a number of specimens relating to the mammalian fauna of Tasmania. Higgins and Petterd (1883) drew attention to the osteological remains in these caves, and they were later noted by Johnston (1888). Very little attention appears to have been paid to this locality by subsequent investigators, and we, therefore, desire to submit this short preliminary note to the Society in the hope that further investigations will be made. In the near future we hope to obtain a second and deeper series of specimens, and then to transmit to the Society a paper dealing with the material in general. Until we obtain a longer and older series of specimens than we have at present, we prefer to treat the matter on very general lines.

The two caves visited were Baldock's Cave and King Solomon's Cave. In the latter there are many specimens. The more recent are quite free, but the older ones have become encrusted with a thick limestone stalactitic coating, or else have become completely covered. In some cases the floors of certain of the caverns are practically bone breccia. Careful research may yield much of interest, for it is not improbable that some remains of *Thylacoleo* should be in these caves, if that marsupial lion ever inhabited Tasmania. Considering the knowledge we have recently gained in relation to the habitats of *Nototherium*, there is no reason to exclude the possibility of *Thylacoleo* being found.

We have only had time to examine a small section of the caves mentioned, and that only in a very superficial manner. When we consider that the Mole Creek district is honeycombed with limestone caves, and that only a few have been explored, and these only to a very limited extent, we can form some idea of the work that remains to be done in carrying out a systematic examination of the locality. Much information concerning the mammalian fauna of Tasmania is doubtless to be gained by an examination of the fossil remains in these caves, and our present note is merely to call attention to the need for this work to be carried out. In illustration of the possibilities for useful scientific research that these caves hold out to us, we may mention that during December, 1914, we induced Mr. E. C. Clarke, of Liena, to collect osteological specimens from such caves as were immediately available to him, with the following results:—

(1) From a mass of material—amounting in the total to two sack loads—we, after the laborious process of sorting and classifying, were able to show that the conditions obtaining in these caves in times past were similar to those of the great bone caves of England and France.

(2) That almost every animal living in Tasmania to-day was represented by osteological remains, in the upper strata of these limestone caverns.

(3) That such evidence as the collection yielded all tended to suggest that the Carnivorous marsupials had dragged the Herbivorous animals into the caves to feast upon their remains. In addition, the well-like openings of certain of the caves doubtless served as an effective trap, as any animals accidentally falling down these would have no hope of returning to the surface.

(4) The deepest strata investigated supplied evidence of a Wombat very closely akin to the Hairy-nosed Wombat of South Australia.

(5) Eye rings of an Owl showed that these birds found homes in the caves, and doubtless joined issue with the Carnivora in picking the bones.

Some caves on Flinders Islands were (at our suggestion) partly explored by Mr. Henwood in 1917, with the result that such evidence as the material yielded proved to be exactly similar data to that obtained at Mole Creek, and suggested a common date of deposition of the superficial strata.

As already said, the real problem of the future is to penetrate the upper layers of bone deposits, and seek for remains of the more ancient Pleistocene giants, and in this search any, or all, of the Mole Creek Caves may prove important sites.

## LIST OF WORKS REFERRED TO.

Higgins and Petterd (1883).—Papers and Proceedings of the Royal Society of Tasmania, 1883.

Johnston, R. M. (1888).—Systematic Account of the Geology of Tasmania.

# NEW SPECIES OF FOSSIL SHELLS FROM TABLE CAPE.

## By W. L. May.

### Plate IV.

(Read 13th June, 1921.)

The following nine species here described were mostly collected by the late E. D. Atkinson, so widely known for his interest in the Table Cape fossils, and who probably did more collecting in these beds than any other worker. Shortly before his lamented death he placed most of these specimens in my hands for description, he being particularly desirous that the two large *Turridæ* should be described and named. I have therefore felt it a duty devolving upon me to carry out my friend's wishes, to the best of my ability.

The five species of *Marginella* here described, together with the four already recorded, make up the goodly number of nine species of these interesting forms, and show that the genus was well represented in Tertiary times in our seas, as well as being so abundant in recent times. All the figures are drawn from the types, which will be presented to the Tasmanian Museum.

### *Marginella atkinsoni*, Sp. nov.

Shell broadly fusiform, smooth, white and shining. Whorls four, much rounded; spire exsert, about one-third the length of the shell; broadly shouldered but tapering narrowly anteriorly. Aperture rather narrow; columella slightly concave, bearing four strong plaits, the anterior one being almost vertical, the second less so, the upper two very transverse, the highest of all being at right angles to the pillar. Outer lip curved, very heavily thickened, crenulated on the inner edge by about a dozen rather irregular denticles.

Long. 5, lat. 3 mill.

This species, which is common at Table Cape, is very similar to *M. wentworthi*, Ten.-Woods, but is a much broader shell, with rounder whorls, and a more curved, and far more heavily varixed outer lip.

Named after the late E. D. Atkinson.

Pl. IV., fig. 1.

### *Marginella corpulenta*, Sp. nov.

Shell very broadly pyriform, with an elevated pyramidal spire and mammillated apex. Whorls four, well rounded;

very broadly shouldered.  Aperture large; columella very convex above, excavate below, where it bears four rather thin plications, of which the anterior is almost vertical, the others being more transverse.  Outer lip very rounded in outline much thickened, slightly corrugated within.

Long. 5, lat. 3.3 mill.

Table Cape, 2 examples.

Related to the last, but is a much broader shell, of different appearance, and lacks the strong toothing on the lip.

Pl. IV., fig. 2.

### *Marginella subquinquidens*, Sp. nov.

Shell smooth, shining, broadly fusiform, with a prominent blunt topped spire.  Whorls four, rounded; not shouldered above the aperture.  Aperture rather narrow, widening towards the front.  Columella nearly straight, bearing five plaits, which are massive and broad, and practically all on the same slant.  The fourth plait varies in different individuals, from being nearly as strong as the others, to less and less prominence, until in some specimens it is absent; hence the name.  Outer lip rather rounded, strongly thickened, smooth within.

Long. 5, lat. 3 mill.

Common at Table Cape.

Pl. IV., fig. 3.

### *Marginella rotunda*, Sp. nov.

Shell very small, roundly pyriform, spire scarcely exserted.  Aperture about as high as the shell, curved, narrow above, but widening towards the front, which is somewhat produced.  Columella very roundly convex, with three moderate-sized teeth, and two or three minute denticles above.  Outer lip moderately thickened, unarmed.

Long. 2.5, lat. 2 mill.

Table Cape, 3 specimens.

This may resemble in form *M. octoplicata*, Ten.-Woods, of which he gives no measurements, but it is separated from that species by its smooth outer lip.

Pl. IV., fig. 4.

### *Marginella altispira*, Sp. nov.

Shell broadly fusiform, with a tall, blunt-topped spire.  Whorls four, moderately rounded; the spire and aperture are

Plate IV.

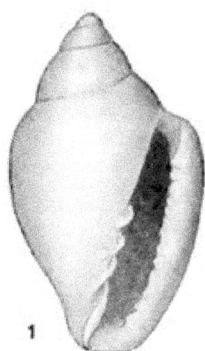
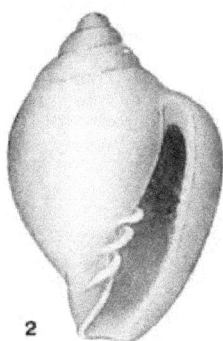
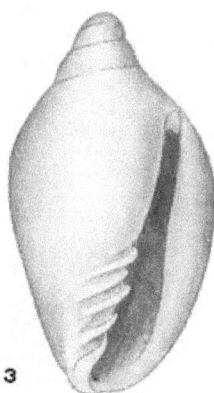

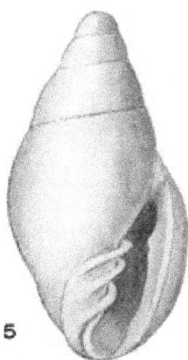

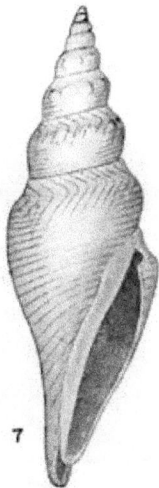

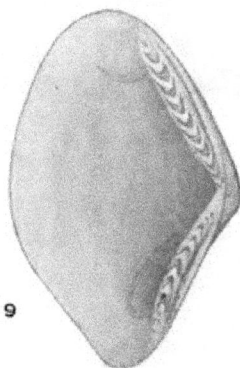

Fig. 1.
*Marginella atkinsoni.*
Fig. 4.
*Marginella rotunda.*
Fig. 7.
*Turris conspicua.*

Fig. 2.
*Marginella corpulenta.*
Fig. 5.
*Marginella altispira.*
Fig. 8.
*Turris altispira.*

Fig. 3.
*Marginella subquinquidens.*
Fig. 6.
*Haurakia crassicosta.*
Fig. 9.
*Nuculana rhomboidea.*

of about equal length. Aperture small; columella concave, bearing four strong teeth, which extend about two-thirds up the pillar, and extend well out on to the base of the shell; outer lip very massively thickened, much rounded, with a strong tubercle within, placed near the upper third.

Long. 5, lat. 3 mill.

Table Cape, several specimens.

Remarkable in the genus for its tall spire and small short aperture. It makes some approach to the recent *M. allporti*, Ten.-Woods.

Pl. IV., fig. 5.

### *Haurakia crassicosta*, Sp. nov.

Shell minute, broadly turbinate. Whorls five, the two apical smooth and polished; suture well impressed. The first adult whorl has about 9 to 10 closely set axial ribs in a half turn; the second has 6 to 7 much stronger ribs; and the body whorl about 5 strong rounded ribs, separated by deep furrows of equal width; these ribs cease near the centre of the whorl, the base being quite smooth. Aperture roundly-oval; columella very convex.

Long. 2, lat. 1.5 mill.

Table Cape, 2 specimens.

This resembles *H. tateana*, Ten.-Woods, in size and general appearance, but has much fewer and stronger ribs.

Pl. IV., fig. 6.

### *Turris conspicua*, Sp. nov.

Shell very large, fusiform, spire and aperture about equal. Whorls about eight, rounded; suture impressed. Aperture narrow. The sculpture indicates a fairly deep sinus immediately below the suture. The upper whorls are faintly coronate at the angle, and ridged by lines of growth; and are concentrically finely lirate all over.

Long. 83, lat. 24 mill., or 3¼ x 1 inches.

Table Cape, two examples.

This is a very fine conspicuous form, and must be extremely rare, as these were the only specimens taken by Mr. Atkinson during many years' collecting.

It would seem to approach the Turrid genus *Genota*.

Pl. IV., fig. 7.

### *Turris altispira*, Sp. nov.

Shell narrowly fusiform, with a very high attenuate spire, which is nearly twice the length of the aperture. Whorls about 13, rounded, suture impressed, with a broad groove, or hollow immediately below it. The ornament consists of well developed axial ribs, about six on a half-turn; these are crossed on the lower half of the whorl by four spirals, which nodulate the ribs; the upper slope being nearly smooth, but showing the growth-lines of the sinus which occupied this position; the spiral liræ continue on the base. Aperture narrow, contracted anteriorly into a canal; outer lip imperfect.

Long. 28, lat. 9 mill.

Table Cape, two examples only.

Probably related generically to the last.    Remarkable for its tall attenuate spire and small aperture.

Pl. IV., fig. 8.

### *Nuculana rhomboidea*, Sp. nov.

Shell minute, smooth, white and shining, rhomboidal, rounded in front, narrowly produced behind into a short beak.    Hinge line arcuate, bearing arrow-shaped teeth, strong on the anterior slope, but less so posteriorly.

Breadth 2, height 1.3 mill.

Table Cape, fairly common.

A very solid little shell, easily distinguished from associated species by its minute size, shape, and smooth polished exterior.

Pl. IV., fig. 9.


## EXPLANATION OF PLATE IV.

Fig. 1.   *Marginella atkinsoni.*

Fig. 2.   *Marginella corpulenta.*

Fig. 3.   *Marginella subquinquidens.*

Fig. 4.   *Marginella rotunda.*

Fig. 5.   *Marginella altispira.*

Fig. 6.   *Haurakia crassicosta.*

Fig. 7.   *Turris conspicua.*

Fig. 8.   *Turris altispira.*

Fig. 9.   *Nuculana rhomboidea.*

# STUDIES IN TASMANIAN MAMMALS, LIVING AND EXTINCT.

## Number V.

### *Zaglossus harrissoni*, Sp. nov.

By

H. H. Scott, Curator of Launceston Museum,

and

Clive Lord, Curator of the Tasmanian Museum, Hobart.

Plate V.

(Read 13th June, 1921.)

Among some fossil bones recently recovered by Mr. K. M. Harrisson, from a swamp upon King Island, we have found evidence of a giant Ant Eater, that exceeded very considerably in point of size the modern *Monotreme.* The evidence is furnished to us in the form of a nearly perfect right femur, and a very small portion of the proximal end of a humerus. We fortunately possess several femora of the modern animals, collected by Mr. L. L. Waterhouse in January, 1916, during a visit to King Island upon Geological Survey Work, and are therefore enabled to make a direct comparison between the Pleistocene, and the more recent Monotremes of that locality. We are evidently dealing with a smaller animal than *"Zaglossus hacketti,"* of Western Australia, since that animal was fully double the size of the modern Monotreme, in point of femoral and humeral length, in addition to an added robustness of the skeleton generally, but the extent to which it overtopped the Ant Eaters of modern King Island will be appreciated by the following table of measurements.

| FEMUR OF GIANT. | FEMUR OF MODERN MONOTREME. |
|---|---|
| Total length = 72 mm. (2 13-16 inches). | Total length = 53 mm. (2⅛ inches). |
| Proximal width = 30 mm. (1⅛ full). | Proximal width = 18 mm. (¾ approx.). |
| Distal width = 35 mm. (1⅜ inches). | Distal width = 19 mm. (¾ full). |
| Thickness of shaft = 10 mm. (7-16 full). | Thickness of shaft = 5 mm. (3-16). |

In life, this Pleistocene Ant Eater was, by estimation, some twenty-six inches in length (660 mm.) and more robust, in proportion, to the largest Tasmanian *Tachyglossus* of to-day.   In view of the fact that isolation from mainland climatic conditions almost certainly enabled the Pleistocene animals to survive, and vary, upon King Island and Tasmania, after their extinction elsewhere, we feel justified in segregating this animal to specific distinction, and have much pleasure in naming it after Mr. K. M. Harrisson, of Smithton, who has manifested such a keen interest in the extinct animals of Tasmania, and generously presented his specimens to our Museums.

## DESCRIPTION OF THE FEMUR.

The shaft of the femur is nearly flat, as obtains in the *Monotremata* generally, and the head is devoid of an articular attachment for a ligamentum teres, thereby agreeing with mammals as high in the scale as the *Nototheria* from the same locality.   The trochanter major is missing, but it evidently did little more than bound the epitrochanterian surface, since its muscular attachment functions are largely carried out by the extensive ridge extending for 35 mm. down the shaft.   Both sides of the shaft indicate great muscular conditions, the popliteal fossa is enormous, its crescent shaped area taking the full mass of a large human thumb to fill it, when the latter is strongly pressed to the diaphysis.   The rotular trochlea is 25 mm. wide, well marked, and curved only in the vertical direction.   The intercondylar fossa is 10 mm. wide, and 9 mm.   The lina aspera is similar to that of the modern animal, as also are the proportions existing between the internal and the external condyles.

A complete skeleton of one of these animals, obtained from a swamp that has undergone fewer mutations than the King Island lagoons appear to have suffered, would be a welcome addition to our knowledge, and for this desideratum we may yet turn to the Mowbray Swamp at Smithton, and meet with success.

The portion of the humerus is too fragmentary for detailed description or even photographic reproduction.   The evidence relating to gigantic Monotremes is largely contained in the following archives:—

## CLASSIFICATION AND NOMENCLATURE.

Ann. Record Science and Industry, 1876, Page clxxi., in which Gills' use of the name *Zaglossus* predates Gervais' term *Proechidna.*

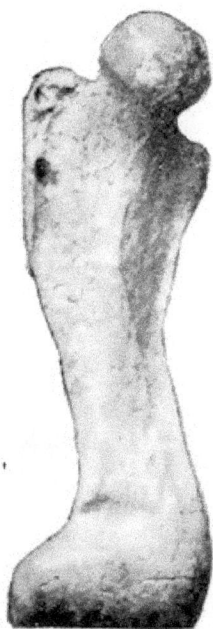

*Femur of*
*Tachyglossus aculeata*
*(Enlarged).*

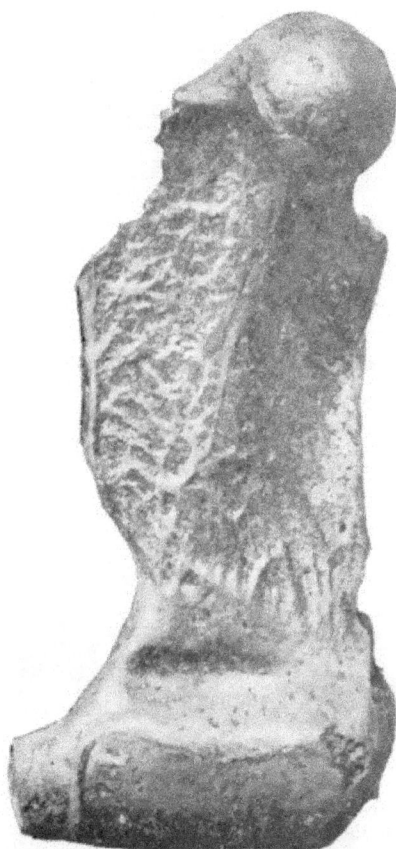

*Femur of*
*Zaglossus harrissoni*
*(Scott and Lord. 13/6/1921).*
*(Enlarged).*

Osteog. Monot. viv. et foss., Page 43, in which Gervais uses the term *Acanthoglossus*.

Bull. Soc. Zool. France, 1881, No. 6, Pages 267-270, in which Dubois uses the name *Bruijinia*.

## CHIEFLY DESCRIPTIVE.

Krefft, 1868.    Ann. Mag. Nat. Hist., Vol. I., Page 113.

Krefft, 1884.    Phil. Trans., Page 273.

W. S. Dun, 1895.    Rec. Geol. Surv., N.S. Wales, Vol. 4, Part 3, Page 121.

L. Glauert, F.G.S., 1914.    Records of the W.A. Museum, Vol. I., Part 3, Pages 244-248, gives Bibliography, Taxonomy, and detailed description of *Zaglossus hacketti*.

## DESCRIPTION OF PLATE V.

Femur of Giant Ant Eater, *Zaglossus harrissoni* (Scott and Lord, 13/6/1921), from the Pleistocene formation of King Island, contrasted with the femur of a sub-fossil specimen of *Tachyglossus aculeata*, from the sand blow at Cape Wickham, King Island, collected by L. L. Waterhouse, Assistant Government Geologist, 19th January, 1916.

# A PRELIMINARY SKETCH OF THE GLACIAL REMAINS PRESERVED IN THE NATIONAL PARK OF TASMANIA.

By A. N. Lewis, M.C.

Plates VI.-XIV.

(Read 11th July, 1921.)

## INTRODUCTORY REMARKS.

This paper is offered as a preliminary and very general sketch of the district described, upon which more detailed examinations of separate sections may be based. The author cannot at present offer a complete geology of the National Park of Tasmania. Its size, ruggedness, and general inaccessibility, aided by the usually inclement weather of the mountains, make the task difficult, and demand a far greater expenditure of time than has been available up to the present. Much of the Park is still unexplored, and parts were first visited that some of the information contained in this paper might be gleaned. But an outline description is urgently needed, firstly as a frame into which more detailed investigations may be fitted, secondly, for the information of visitors, who, in annually increasing numbers, spend holidays on the Park's highlands, and also as an assistance to the parties who are now inspecting this region in connection with water supply questions.

The author also offers the information as a small contribution to the Geology of Tasmania, information which, in the absence of local text books, it is hoped will be of assistance both to students and teachers. Tasmania is our home. It provides us with wonderful examples of every geological phenomenon. These are of living interest to us. Let us rather study them, and know our own home, than seek our geology from books published about distant countries describing objects that are mere names to us.

As far as can be ascertained, the glacial remains on the Mt. Field ranges have never been described. They do not appear to have been observed, or at least their existence recorded, before the proclamation of the area as a National Park. There is, therefore, no previous literature on the subject to which to refer.

# AN OUTLINE SKETCH OF THE GEOLOGY OF THE
## NATIONAL PARK OF TASMANIA.

The National Park of Tasmania is located about 50 miles from Hobart, among the Mt. Field ranges, on the northern slope of the Russell Falls River, a tributary of the Derwent. It comprises some 38,500 acres of wild mountain tops and dense forests, and contains the most varied scenery within a day's trip of Hobart. The Park was originally set aside in an endeavour to preserve some native fauna and a little of the romantic virgin bush from the depredations of a misguided civilisation, but with the opening up of the area it has been discovered that there are contained within its boundaries geological features of considerable interest.

Topographically the Park is a portion of the very much dissected Central Plateau of Tasmania, itself cut off from the remainder of the plateau, and isolated by the valleys of the Derwent and the Russell Falls Rivers. The smaller plateau so formed is itself a dissected tableland. This tableland consists of diabase that intruded into the older strata of most of Tasmania during the Cretaceous period, and the general topography conforms to the outline of this diabase. Probably the area was raised to its present height in one uplift by this diabase, contemporaneously with the elevation of the Mt. Wellington Range to the south and the Central Plateau to the north. Any overlying rocks carried up by the intrusion have since been removed by erosion.

In the past the Mt. Field Range has been considered a portion of the Mt. Wellington Range. This appears to me to be stretching the term mountain range too far. The diabase is undoubtedly of the same age, but the Mt. Field Range is separated from the Mt. Wellington Range by the Tyenna Valley. This valley is not entirely waterworn. The West Coast rocks extend into it at an altitude of less than 1,000 feet, and Ordovician limestones circle round from the Florentine Valley to the Junee. Above these, large beds of Permo-Carboniferous and Trias-Jura sediments bound the western face of Mt. Field West, and the entire northern slope of the Tyenna Valley. and there is no surface connection between the diabase of Tyenna Peak and that of

B

Mt. Mueller. We are, therefore, bound to conclude that the diabase intrusion raised the country from Mueller to Styx to an elevation of 4,000 feet, and similarly raised the Mt. Field plateau, but left the valley of Tyenna-Westerway at an altitude of less than 1,000 feet above sea level.

From the Tyenna Valley, through which flows the Russell Falls (or Tyenna or Crooke) River, the edge of this diabase mass rises rapidly, attaining an altitude of 4,000 feet in a mile or so. The backbone of the range extends roughly east and west from Mt. Mawson, through Mt. Monash, and Seager's Look-Out, to Mt. Field East, to which the land rises steeply from the Tyenna Valley on the south. From Mt. Field East and Mt. Mawson two large parallel ranges stretch away slightly west of north, reaching to the southern edge of the Derwent Valley, about 10 miles farther north, and maintaining an elevation of over 3,000 feet. Between these runs the deep valley of the Broad River.

To the west of this system stands the third parallel chain of the Tyenna Peak—Mt. Field West Range, a western outlier from the main diabase mass, to which it is connected by K. Col. The wonderful escarpment on the west of this range, dropping nearly sheer to the Florentine Valley, 3,000 feet below, represents the western edge of the diabase upthrust in this part of Tasmania.

These three great mountain ridges show the form of the diabase intrusion. Sedimentary rock skirts the lower slopes of the mountains from Mt. Field East to Mt. Mawson. It then runs a mile or more up the valley of the Humboldt Creek, and back round the end of Tyenna Peak, and right across the western face of Mt. Field West. Undoubtedly, the intrusive diabase took the form we now see it in, and erosion has worn out the softer sedimentary rocks between the lines of intrusion, forming the valleys now existing. If any further proof were required that such was the case, and not that water has worn the valleys out of a plateau of solid diabase, we can find it in the Lake Hayes Valley, where the face of the valley is lined with sandstone.

Of course, erosion has affected the diabase mountain tops to a certain extent, but the great valley regions of the Park are caused by the absence of diabase there. The columnar cliffs so common near the tops of all the mountain ranges in this area probably represent the edges of laterally intruded sills of diabase.

Time has not allowed a detailed examination of the
sedimentary rocks of the Park. Near the entrance, and extending for some distance up the Tyenna Valley, are beds
of Permo-Carboniferous lime—and mud—stones. These are
overlaid by over a thousand feet of sandstone in huge, com-
pact beds, in which strata can be scarcely distinguished.
From general observations, all these sandstones appear to
be of the Trias-Jura age, similar to the Knocklofty series so
well known in Southern Tasmania. These beds have been
distinguished by Mr. Loftus Hills at the foot of Mt. Field
West in the Florentine, but their age requires confirmation elsewhere.

The drainage is typical of the stage known as juvenile,
and most of the streams are mere mountain torrents. During the Pleistocene times, the cycle of river erosion was in-
terrupted by glaciers in the higher altitudes. These have
widened many of the valleys and dammed them in places.
forming lakes and causing the streams to meander over an
almost level bed. The Upper Broad River has the appearance of being in the mature stage, but it is really cutting
through a valley not of its own making, and from which
it has not yet had time to remove the remains of the
glacier. In a day's walk along this valley, the student can
see every form of river erosion.

The glaciers which caused this, and the way they have
moulded the topography of the plateau, it is now the main
purpose of this paper to describe.


## THE COURSE OF THE PLEISTOCENE GLACIERS.

At the same time as the western half of Tasmania
was more or less under ice, and from the same cause, snowfields accumulated on the Mt. Field Plateau, and glaciers
flowed a little way down the valleys. It is well known that
the Pleistocene Ice Age was not of uniform coldness. During periods of milder climate the glaciers shrank towards the
mountain tops, and in intervals of intense cold they pushed
out down the valleys. Unfortunately, a glacier tends to
erase all traces of earlier action by its latest flow, but still
we can see to what point the glacier reached, and trace the
stages of its final retreat.

During the period of maximum glaciation, a permanent
snow cap covered the entire top of the Mt. Field Plateau, and

probably extended down the sides to an altitude of 3,000 feet. The great snowfields that accumulated on the more level portions of the highlands fed glaciers that pushed down the valleys.

The chief of these ice rivers flowed down the Broad River; one branch fed by the snowfields extending from Mt. Monash to Mt. Mawson pushed straight down the valley. It was soon joined by a second flow of equal size from Lake Seal Valley, fed by accumulations of snow on the ridges above that lake, and later by a third branch flowing down from Lake Newdegate to Lake Webster. Together, these pushed four or five miles farther down the valley of the Broad River, and during its prime the glacier must have been seven miles in length, and over half a mile wide, and 300 feet deep. It extended to a point 2,400 feet above sea-level, where it melted, and the water was carried off down the Broad River to the Derwent. In the track of this glacier we find the most extensive evidences of ice action to be found in the Park.

On each side of this considerable glacier existed a group of smaller ice-streams. To the east, growing from snowfields on Mt. Field East, Kangaroo Moor, and on the eastern side of Wombat Moor, a glacier flowed down the valley now occupied by Lake Fenton, breaking up at about 3,000 feet above sea-level, not far below the present shore of Lake Fenton, at about the six mile peg on the track from the entrance to the Park.

Farther to the east, under the slope of Mt. Field East, two other glaciers developed. The larger, flowing southeast, was responsible for Lake Nicholls and Lake Rayner, and the other flowed south-west over the present site of Beattie's Tarn. Neither of these reached much lower than 3,000 feet, and both were small, as they were situated on the eastern, and, therefore, the dry and warm, side of the ranges.

The western group comprised two glaciers of considerable extent flowing in opposite directions, one southward through the Belcher-Belton Valley, and the other north through the Hayes Valley. These were fed by the snow from the lofty crags that surrounded them. The Belcher-Belton glacier was a composite one, and flowed for about two miles down the valley of the Humboldt Creek to an altitude of about 2,900 feet. The other was only about a mile in length, and reached to about the 3,000 feet level.

It must be borne in mind that the erosion of the various creeks working up their valleys may have destroyed traces of ice action lower down than the altitudes mentioned, but this cannot have happened to any great extent, as the erosion has had little effect on other glacial remains in other parts equally exposed, so short has been the time since the disappearance of these glaciers.

Up to the present, there have been found in this part of Tasmania no indications calculated to throw any light on the age of this glacial period, but the remains are of most recent age, and evidences elsewhere in Tasmania place the occurrence in the Pleistocene period. The glaciers in the National Park were contemporaneous with those elsewhere, and strong evidence to the contrary would have to be deduced to alter the settled opinion that these glaciers belong to the Pleistocene.

Unfortunately, the entire area affected by this agency is of diabase. This makes it impossible to observe different kinds of rock in the moraines or to guess where the materials came from. Also the diabase weathers too rapidly to retain any trace of striæ. This is also the case with very much harder rocks. "It must be borne in mind that weather-"ing agencies have been at work so long and disintegrational "forces so active, that all positive traces on the rock sur-"faces would have been destroyed in the case of such rock "as granite." (Waterhouse, 1916.) "The Conglomerate" (West Coast Series Conglomerates of the Cambrian system, one of the hardest of rocks) "does not possess the requisite "texture for the preservation of the striations which almost "invariably have been effaced by exposure to the weather." (Reid, 1918.) Perhaps glaciated pebbles that have been protected from weathering processes by clay or sand may yet be found in the National Park with signs of striations.

Time and weather have prevented a complete exploration of the National Park, and other regions of glaciation may yet be found, especially north of Mt. Field East, and between the valleys of the Broad River and Bunyip Creek, and even over the shoulder between Mt. Field West and the Florentine Peaks. There is still ample scope for the enthusiast. The author can only hope that this paper may be of some assistance.

## DESCRIPTIVE ACCOUNT OF THE GLACIAL REMAINS.

### I. THE BROAD RIVER VALLEY (See Plates VI. and VIII.)

#### (a) Below Lake Webster.

The whole seven miles of the Upper Broad River Valley is a typical glacial trough, most markedly U-shaped, straight, and devoid of spurs. The floor, averaging half a mile in width, is quite flat, and the sides, gently sloping at first, rise abruptly 500 feet in a slope that is often precipitous. At the top of these sides depressions and spurs have begun to appear, but these have been shorn off lower down.

Glacial remains can be traced over four miles below Lake Webster. In this distance, the floor of the valley is nearly level, dropping only 150 feet. It is covered with button-grass growing on a stiff clay, and crossed at intervals by definitely marked and easily visible moraines. The Broad River winds through these button-grass plains, and cuts through the moraines first on one side, then on the other, and where it does so it drops quickly in a succession of stony rapids, passing out again on to the flats hardly to drop at all until the next moraine is reached. The river has cut down in places to a depth of six feet below the surface of this plain, and there you can see what underlies the vegetation.

Evidently, the glacier deposited in its retreat the various moraines which have successively blocked the valley from side to side. Behind these dams, large, shallow lakes were once banked up. The glacier dropped the larger boulders, as it melted, in the spot where we now see them as moraines, while the water escaping from the melting ice carried the finer materials out into these lakes as silt, and formed great beds of clay and sand on their floors. Across the surface of the lakes floated blocks of the glacier as icebergs, and dropped stones and pebbles into the clay. A large volume of water was liberated as the glacier melted, and these lakes overflowed at the lowest side of the moraine. In time this overflow cut away the loosely knit material of the dam, and eventually drained the water from the lakes, leaving the peculiarly level beds of clay we now

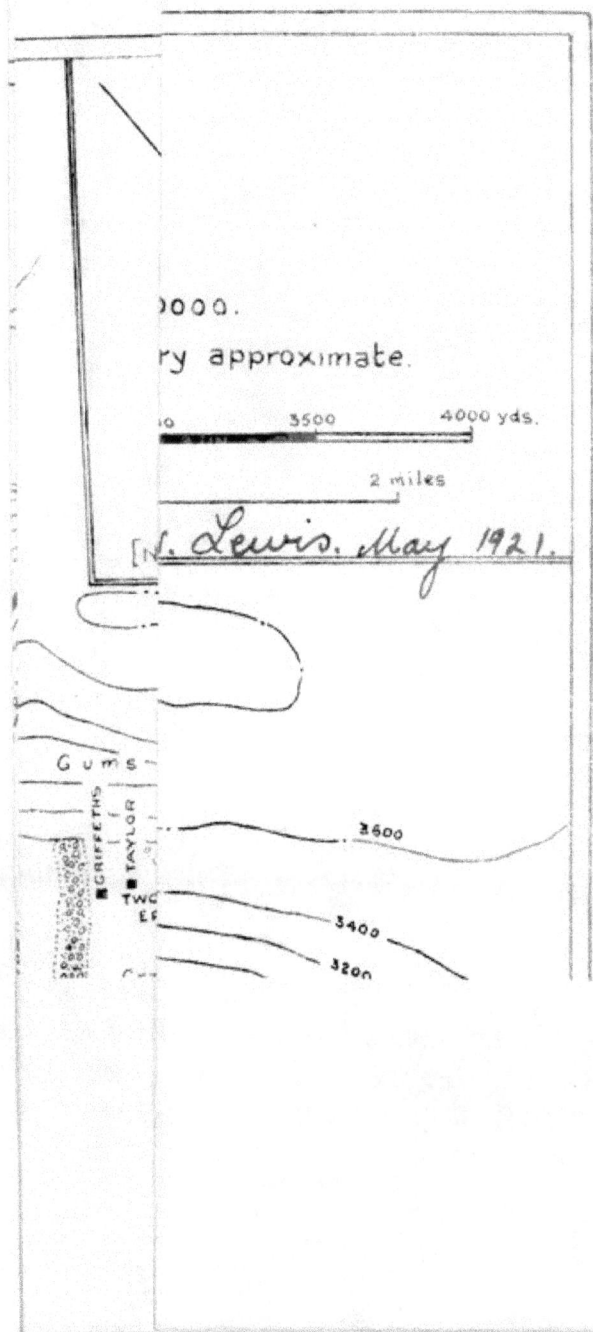

Plate VI.

)000.

ry approximate.

3500        4000 yds.

2 miles

[N. Lewis. May 1921.

Gums

GRIFFETHS
TAYLOR
TWO
E

3600

3400

3200

see covered with button-grass. Lake Webster and the watery marsh half a mile lower down the valley are all that are now left of a line of at least five lakes. Each lake must have been at least 30 feet lower than its higher neighbour. Perhaps they did not exist contemporaneously.

By following the course of the Broad River, it can be seen that the present floor of the valley consists of a fine grained, almost greasy, clay, usually of a yellow ochre colour, but also varying from light yellow to brown. It is never red, and iron deposits do not appear to exist in it. Boulders measuring a few feet in diameter are common throughout this clay, more particularly on the edges. In some places it can be clearly seen that stones have been dropped into the sediment from ice by the bending of the layers of the clay immediately below them, and here and there stones can be seen that are standing up on edge in the clay. In some places there are thin but extensive layers of gravel, suggesting a change of conditions, such as a flood; in other places there are layers of water-worn flaked cobbles, suggesting a wind-swept beach. In a few spots there exist considerable beds of sand and fine conglomerate, which here and there has already solidified into a rock of some hardness. These, however, are only occasional in the lower reaches of the glacial valley, the clays predominating.

Nearer Lake Webster, sand, gravel, and more typical glacial till increases in proportion until the clays vanish at about the confluence of the Broad River and the outlet of Lake Webster.

The entire deposit shows the characteristic confusion of a glacial deposit, except perhaps, where the stream has recently accumulated piles of alluvial drift. These are few, and confined to the river bed, and no notice is to be taken of them when studying the glacial deposits.

From these beds of clay rise at intervals masses of morainal debris, in some cases stretching in thin belts right across the valley, and in others standing in groups promiscuously dotted about in the button-grass flats. These rise to any height up to twenty feet above the floor of the valley. They consist of a brown earth and gravel freely mixed with oblong slabs of diabase, and containing many boulders of all sizes, up to 10 feet in diameter. Rain has washed the lighter material off the top of these piles of boulder clay, and the larger rocks stand out predominantly, but their entire section can be studied where the river has cut through any one of these banks.

These were formed where the glacier halted for an interval during its retreat, from the debris tumbled out of the melting ice. We see them to-day just as the rocks and finer materials fell in a heap off the end of the glacier. Owing to their elevation above the surrounding flats, they are well-drained, and trees, chiefly dwarfed swamp gums, cover them, giving a rough guide to their whereabouts.

Probably there existed a small moraine below the place where the glacial remains now appear to end, at the spot at which the Broad River turns from north-west to north, and drops into a narrow V-shaped water-worn gorge, as lacustrine clays continue below the last remaining moraine. Once past these glacial flats, the river drops rapidly, and so has greater cutting power. Perhaps in the future further traces of glacial moraines will be found on the side of this water-worn valley, but this is doubtful.

The lowest of the remaining moraines can be clearly distinguished by the belt of trees growing on it. It is not very clearly defined, rising some five feet above the button-grass plain above it, and about twenty feet above the lower flat below. It averages fifty yards in width.

The next two moraines up the valley in the direction of Lake Webster are most distinct. The northern one of the pair has two large erratics standing about 50 yards from its north-west corner. These blocks (see Pl. XIV., Fig. 3) are roughly square, and measure 10 feet by 15 feet, and are resting on the clay beds of the button-grass swamp. From this point upwards nearly to Lake Webster lateral moraines on both sides of the valley can be traced, although they only stand a few feet from the surrounding country, but are marked by many large boulders. Both these moraines rise some 15 feet from the button-grass on the upper side, and about 30 feet on the lower. They both stretch from one side of the valley to the other in a wonderfully straight line. The lower one averages 200 yards in width, while the upper of the pair, which is the best example of a moraine in the Park, is only about 20 yards in width.

From a spot about 2,000 yards below Lake Webster, and a little distance below the considerable marsh that lies some way below that lake, this country of definite moraines, separated by beds of lake-formed clay, gives place

to a confused bed of glacial till, rising more quickly, and covering the whole floor of the valley. Evidently, here the glacier receded with an even movement, distributing its terminal moraine equally over an area of country extending up to Lake Webster.

### (b) Lake Webster to Lake Seal, Including the Tarns.

### (See Plates VI. and VII.)

From a point somewhere about the junction of the Broad River with the outlet from Lake Webster, up the valley to about level with the end of Lake Seal, it is difficult to trace any definite movements of the ice-river. The whole valley is strewn with accumulations of morainal material of unknown depth. The surface of the ground is rendered very uneven by lines of this moraine in every direction, and at all angles, and by the many boulders scattered over the surface of the till.

Lake Webster lies in a depression in this moraine. It is a shallow lake seldom exceeding 10 feet in depth, and overflowing over the lower slope of the morainal mass. The Broad River flows down the eastern side of the valley, and is slightly lower than the lake, from which it is separated by a considerable ridge of glacial till running parallel to the course of the river and the side of the lake.

Three ice streams met in the vicinity of Lake Webster to form the great Broad River glacier. From the amount of work done, it appears that the glacier that flowed down the Lake Seal Valley was the most considerable. Rising in the great cirque that stands at the head of Lake Seal, and fed by ice flows from the higher ridges behind, some of which excavated the tarns, it conformed to the curve of the valley where now Lake Seal lies, and flowing round the eastern foot of Mt. Bridges until it emerged into the Broad River Valley, where it was joined by a second ice river flowing straight down the valley from the snowfield on the ridge between Mt. Monash and Mt. Mawson. Together, these glaciers passed on for a short distance, till they were met by a smaller flow descending from Lake Newdegate, and the ridges beyond, and joining the main flow at the site where we now see Lake Webster. The jumbled nature of the morainal deposits in this area probably reflects the confusion which this junction of three great glaciers caused in their component ice flows.

On the east of Lake Webster there are ridges running parallel with the sides of the valley, which may be medial moraines formed on the larger glacier from the laterals of the tributaries. But the traces are too confused to allow certainty on this subject, and signs of the erosive effect of the volumes of water that escaped from the glacier and flowed over this newly-formed bed of till can be seen everywhere.

The great gorge running west from Lake Webster, half a mile into the hills, shows most typically the sculpturing work of the glacier. It is decidedly U-shaped, with sides rising 1,000 feet nearly sheer, and it finally ends in a perfect cirque over which the outlet from some of the tarns and Lake Newdegate falls in cascades hundreds of feet in height.

Passing from Lake Webster to Lake Seal, you rise 200 feet in under half a mile. The surface of this rise consists entirely of glacial till, which runs out in a ridge or series of ridges already mentioned lying between Lake Webster and Lake Seal. This rise is probably a great moraine blocking the Lake Seal Valley completely, making the floor of Lake Seal on approximately the same level as Lake Webster. This could only be verified by soundings, and if it is not the case, Lake Seal could only be a wonderful example of hanging and overdeepened valley, but this latter view is unlikely.

Following up the outlet of Lake Seal, just after leaving the shore of Lake Webster, you cross a large transverse ridge of morainal material, through which the stream from Lake Seal has cut, and behind which run tributary streams. Past several more ridges the ground rises abruptly to the shore of Lake Seal. This slope consists of glacial till containing boulders of all sizes, set in red or brown earth and gravel, the typical decomposition product of diabase. Huge boulders rest on the surface of this lying tilted at the angle of the slope, evidently toppled off the edge of the glacier, melting just above, at the present shore of the lake. The outlet of Lake Seal falls over this moraine in a series of pretty cascades, and has cut a small valley in the glacial till, but nowhere in its course can solid rock be seen. The glacier was not confined to the gully of this outlet, but spread at least 400 yards wide right across the valley of the lake, and thus swung round into the Broad River Valley.

Plate VIII.

P. & P. Roy. Soc. Tas., 1921.

Lake Webster, National Park, Tasmania.

Lake Seal lies in a long, deep valley, decidedly U-shaped, which is blocked by the moraine at the eastern end of the lake. The top of this stands 200 feet above Lake Webster, but has been much worn down near its junction with the solid rock of Mt. Bridges. Farther east it is at least another hundred feet higher. This as it stands represents the largest specimen of a moraine in the Park. The moraine bounds the eastern edge of the lake, and curves round the southern shore, abutting on to a ridge running down past Platypus Tarn from a shoulder of Mt. Mawson. The shore of the lake on this moraine is bordered by a beach of water-worn cobbles, testifying to the force of the waves churned up by the winter hurricanes.

On the Broad River, opposite the end of this lake, can be seen half a mile of diabase outcrops rising 100 feet abruptly from the river, but on the Lake Seal side these rocks are covered with glacial till of the moraine just discussed, and are invisible. It was here that the glacier turned north. The depth of ice must have been tremendous, perhaps 1,000 feet. One of the most useful pieces of investigation in the Park would be to ascertain the height on each side of Mt. Bridges to which the glacier extended, and to ascertain the depth of Lake Seal by a series of soundings.

The line of glacial till extends over the whole slope from the Broad River to Lake Seal, reaching its highest point some six hundred yards south-east of the lake, whence it drops sharply to the southward into the gully of an un-named tributary of the Broad.

A spur bounds Lake Seal on the southern side, gradually rising until it becomes part of the configuration of Mt. Mawson. This doubtless has a core of solid diabase, although it is deeply overlaid with glacial till. Along this ridge south of the lake, and parallel to the shore, run lines and ridges of this morainal material, perhaps representing lines of lateral moraines, but more probably ridges caused by lateral pressure of the ice. Some of the hollows between them contain ponds. Some of these hollows may have been formed by the imprisoning of large masses of ice in the moraine, the melting of which has caused the surface of the ground to sink. Among these ridges lie whole lines of huge boulders, many exceeding 20 feet in every measurement, and often piled on top of each other. Nowhere in the Park are there finer examples of erratics. In one place the author saw two stones measuring 6 feet by 2 feet sticking on their ends out of the ground at different angles, and balanced across them lay a flat boulder, with a diameter of about 6 feet and a thickness of 1 foot. These deposits descend to the shore of Lake Seal, 200 feet below, and it is impossible to tell the depth of the deposit on this side, but on the edge of the Broad River Valley they soon disappear. They extend westward beyond Platypus Tarn, which lies in a hollow in this till.

From the centre of this ridge the morainal deposits curve round the top of the steep gully immediately to the south, and run past Eagle Tarn to the eastern shore of Lake Dobson. They appear to keep the same level at which we saw them on the ridge, not stretching far down the gully, and they do not extend far up the slopes of Mt. Mawson.

At the western end of Lake Seal there can be seen a most perfect specimen of the glacial phenomenon known as a cirque. The glacier has eaten the foot of the hill away until the lake now ends in a wall 1,000 feet high, consisting of a series of rugged cliffs. The glacier has cut farther in to the north-west corner, and here formed a smaller cirque within the greater feature, making, indeed, a nail-shaped valley, a common feature in glaciated country.

The ice fed by the snow on the ridge above the tarns flowed in a sheet down the slope until it hit the ridge on which the tarns are now to be seen, which appears to run right round the eastern face of Mt. Mawson, a common feature on diabase mountains. Here its pace was checked, but it pushed on, until divided by the shoulder of Mt. Bridges, one half dropped over into the Lake Seal cirque, and the other into the cirque at the head of the valley leading to Lake Webster.

Where it hit the ledge of rock in its descent it ground great basins out of the solid rock, and it polished and rounded the outer portion of the ledge. In these rock basins water has accumulated which we now know as the six tarns, and between them and the edge of the two cirques —only a matter of fifty yards in the case of Robert Tarn— the diabase has been rounded and smoothed into waves of *roches moutonnees*, very distinct towards the southern end of the line of tarns. Many huge erratics stand on these and lie scattered over the country side, and towards Lake Newdegate there are considerable deposits of morainal material.

The size of these cirques has probably been increased by
later action of frost, but undoubtedly the ice is responsible
for the outline of this rugged stretch of country. Lateral
expansion of the Lake Seal glacier, and the upward movement of its lead as it swung round Mt. Bridges, also had
something to do with the forming of its wonderful valley.

### (c) The Head of the Broad River Valley.

Returning to the third branch of the main glacier, the
one flowing straight down the trough of the Broad River.
To the east of Lake Webster the river now flows on the
east of the lines of ridges of glacial till already described,
and for which the Lake Seal glacier was probably responsible. Shortly after passing the level of the end of Lake
Webster, the glacial deposits in the actual valley of the
Broad disappear, and within the general U-shaped valley
the river runs for over half a mile down a typical water-
worn gully over a series of pretty cascades. On both sides
of this gully native diabase outcrops, and no signs of
glaciation exist in the bed of the creek or further east,
although a mile to the west, and 400 feet up the side
of Mt. Mawson, we see the ridge of glacial till already
mentioned, and glacial deposits abound above this gully
as below. Evidently here, with a more abrupt slope in
the floor of the glacial valley, the river has had more cutting
power, and has cut a small valley of its own out of the
floor of the larger valley, a floor probably largely composed of loose materials, and cut by the considerable flow
of water escaping from the melting glacier, thus giving
us an example of a valley within a valley. It does not
appear reasonable to suppose that the glacier never pushed
down over this section of the valley, and that the glacier
lower down came entirely from the Lake Seal Valley, but
rather that all traces just here have been removed by subsequent water action.

Once this short stretch is passed, the Broad River Valley assumes again an appearance somewhat similar to that
below Lake Webster. But here the bottom of the valley is
not so flat nor so wide as in the lower reaches, and is clearly
the work of a smaller ice-river. The whole floor is covered
with till consisting of earth, a quantity of clay, and a high
proportion of boulders, especially towards the sides. These
erratics increase in size and frequency until the Broad
bends west to its source in Lake Dobson.

Just beyond this bend is a large bed of ice-borne erratics lying so thickly as to resemble a "ploughed field" of a mountain top rather than the bottom of a wide valley. The head of the glacier rested on the ridge connecting Mt. Monash to Mt. Mawson, where it has developed a broad but shallow and "young!" cirque. This valley head is shaped somewhat like a nail head, too.

Lake Dobson lies in the western side of the head of the Broad River Valley. It is a shallow sheet, lying behind a slight moraine, which its outlet has cut through in a deep channel. To the east of the lake rises a high ridge completely covered by, if not entirely composed of, glacial till, which circles west past Eagle Tarn, and then east, joining the ridge south of Lake Seal, already described. The lateral creases are continued across this ridge, especially in the vicinity of Eagle Tarn, the outlet of which, cutting through several ridges, drains through a pretty gully to Lake Dobson. This whole ridge, with that nearer Lake Seal, appears to be a great pressure ridge formed in the V between the Broad River Valley glacier and the Lake Seal Valley glacier, and was doubtless largely formed by lateral pressure from both great flows.

The moraine that dams up Lake Dobson, and the deposits that run from there a few hundred yards into the Broad River Valley, appear to be the work of the last phase of the glaciers, and to have been caused by a small flow from the slopes of Mt. Mawson.

This whole valley of the Broad River can be traversed in an easy day's walk from Lake Fenton, and it would be difficult to imagine a locality of equal size that can provide such a series of points of interest to a student of nature or of pleasure to the picnicker.

## II. THE EASTERN GLACIAL GROUP.—(See Plates IX. and X.).

### (a) The Lake Fenton Valley.

To-day the country east of the Broad River Valley is drier, and the climate milder than the country farther west, and we may presume that during the ice age this condition prevailed in proportion  So we see few glaciers on the eastern slopes of the mountains. Also the snowfields had far less area on which to accumulate, and the absence

Plate IX.

ETCH PLAN —
: the —
GE AREA OF MᵀFIELD EAST

Glacial Remains.

V.I. = 200 Feet
Contours & heights approx.
Scale: 1/20000
except where otherwise shown.

Yards 1000                              2000 Yds

of Miles                    1 mile.

J. N. Lewis May 1921

Mt. FIELD
EAST 4165 feet

- ROUGH SKETCH PLAN -
- of the -
SOUTHERN DRAINAGE AREA OF McFIELD EAST
Showing Glacial Remains

(Fig. 1). Lake Fenton (looking East).

(Fig. 2). Lake Fenton (looking N.W.),
National Park, Tasmania.

of long, gently sloping, valleys militated against extensive glaciation on the south and east of Mt. Field East. But in places short glaciers formed and pushed down to about the 3,000 feet level.

One of these glaciers flowed down the valley now filled by Lake Fenton. (See Plate X., Fig. 1.) This was a small flow, arising from the limited snowfield on Kangaroo Moor and the low hills immediately surrounding the lake, and flowing down an old valley, of which the Lady Barron Falls Creek Valley is now the lower portion. The snowfield was too limited to supply a long ice-flow, and the glacier was probably never more than a mile in length, and probably no wider than we now see Lake Fenton. The ice pushed about a quarter of a mile below the present shore of the lake. The bank over which the Lake Fenton pack-track rises just after the sixth mile peg represents the end of the moraine deposited by this glacier.

The valley of the Lady Barron Falls Creek is bounded by the precipitous sides of Seager's Look-Out to the east and Mt. Monash to the west, forming a very sharp V, the sides of which are strewn with a talus of enormous blocks of diabase torn from their seats largely by the action of frost, and tumbled down the slopes in a perfect wilderness of huge rocks. Over the top of this valley the glacier has deposited its moraine until now, looking from Kangaroo Moor through this gap, a distinct U-shaped valley is seen.

The ice appears to have retreated very slowly, but very regularly, covering the bottom of the valley with glacial till extending a quarter of a mile. The surface of this moraine is very level, a noticeable fact on the walk to Lake Fenton, and here and there boulders of all sizes protrude from the reddish soil and gravels. The moraine completely blocks the valley, and dams back Lake Fenton, stretching from a few yards across the overflow from the lake right along the southern shore of the lake, and a little distance on to a spur running down from Mt. Monash.

The outlet from the lake at one time flowed over the eastern end of the moraine, but in the course of time it has washed the earth and lighter materials away from the boulders, and now, except in flood time, runs out of sight below an accumulation of loose rocks of all sizes.

The eastern shore of Lake Fenton is strewn with a mass of huge boulders, which have the appearance of

a talus. Perhaps they are the frost-disintegrated remains
of a small cliff carved out by the glacier, but more probably are a continuation of the talus slopes on the side
of Seager's Look-Out, to be seen below the lake, the bottom
portion of which has been covered by glacial and lacustrine
deposits, now forming the floor of Lake Fenton. On the
western side of the lake there is a narrow shore, which
shows slight traces of glaciation, before the ground rises
sharply to the hill behind.

Kangaroo Moor, especially along the northern shore
of the lake, shows traces of glacial till, and Wombat Moor
is covered with erratics, many of tremendous size. Probably
a feeder flowed from the snowfields north of Mt. Monash
into the Lake Fenton glacier, and about 200 yards from
Quiet Corner along the Lake Dobson track there is a ridge
of boulders crossing the moor that seems to be a small
moraine. Evidently just prior to the vanishing of the
glaciers, a small ice flow found its way down from Mt. Monash, scattering debris over Wombat Moor, but melting before
it reached Lake Fenton.

(b) The Lake Nicholls Area.    (See Plates IX. and XI.).

The southern slope of Mt. Field East drops precipitous-
ly some 700 feet from the edge of the plateau. At an altitude of 3,200 feet lies a considerable ledge on the mountain side, on which lie Lake Nicholls and Beattie's Tarn.
Circling round the south and south-west of Lake Nicholls,
and separating that lake from Beattie's Tarn, is a very
considerable ridge of morainal material. This rises sharply
from the eastern end of Lake Nicholls to a height of 200
feet above the level of the lake, and forms a round hill
between this lake and Beattie's Tarn, from which hill the
ridge dips in a wide U northward until it rests on the
diabase buttress of Mt. Field East. This U can be distinguished with equal clearness from either Beattie's Tarn
or Lake Nicholls. It is extremely steep on both sides, and
has the appearance of a pressure ridge, consisting of boulder
clay, containing some huge rocks, and probably largely
caused by the glacier passing materials up from below
and piling them over this bank.

There were probably several small glaciers flowing
down the several creases in the otherwise abrupt escarpment of Mt. Field East, the largest of which, flowing down
the gully at the head of Lake Nicholls, on reaching the

P. & P. Roy. Soc. Tas., 1921.

Plate XI.

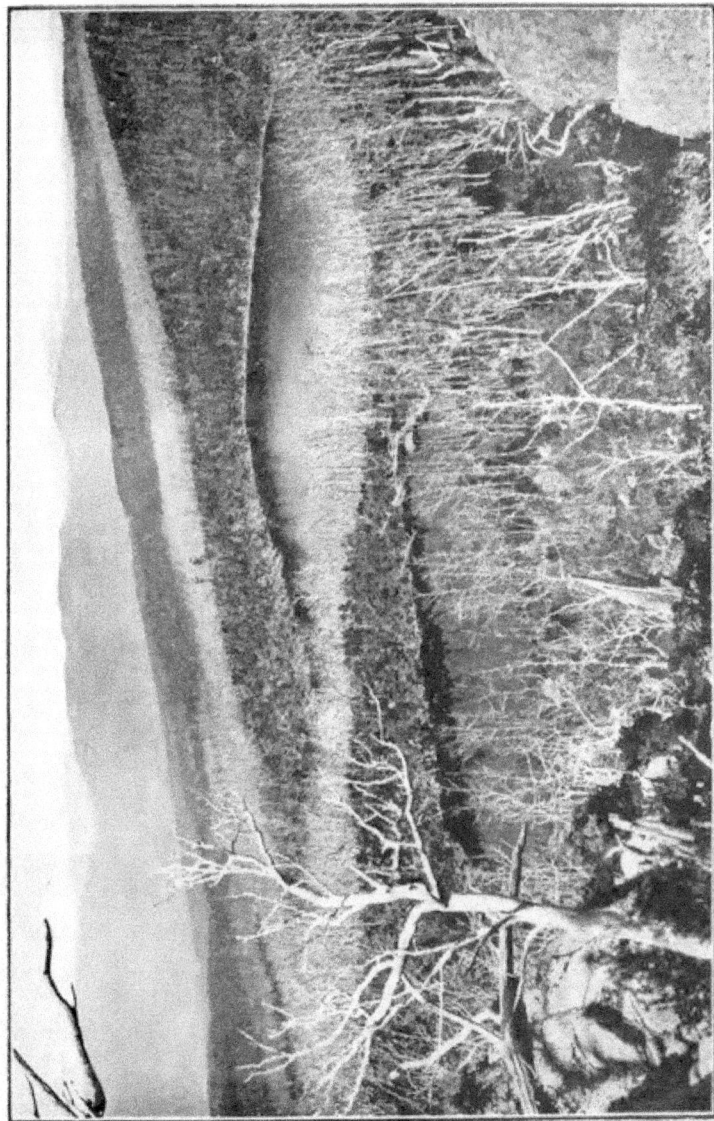

Lakes Rayner and Nicholls, National Park, Tasmania.

stretch of more level ground, gouged out a considerable portion of the bed of Lake Nicholls, which is of great depth, and shows us a good example of an over-deepened valley. This glacier flowed south-east for a few hundred yards down the branch of the Russell Falls Creek, and deposited a considerable quantity of boulder clay below the outlet from the lake. It is impossible to estimate the depth of this moraine, and difficult to determine how far the glacier descended the valley, but probably it did not flow many hundred yards beyond where we now see the shore of Lake Nicholls.

Another glacier flowing down a gully a little farther to the east was instrumental in forming Lake Rayner. This may have joined the larger Lake Nicholls glacier at a point below both lakes, but this is not certain. It had a smaller snowfield than the other, and probably melted somewhere below the present site of Lake Rayner. The hill below this lake is strewn with glacial debris. During one of its halts during the period of final retreat, it deposited the moraine that now encircles the lower side of Lake Rayner.

### (c) Beattie's Tarn Area.

The remaining glacier of this group had its origin immediately west of that of the Lake Nicholls glacier, but flowed west of the intervening ridge down towards the Lady Barron Falls Creek, instead of the Russell Falls Creek. This glacier has left several very prominent, if small, moraines, one of which banks back Beattie's Tarn. On the track to this lakelet one of these moraines is crossed. It stands out ten feet above the surrounding country fifty yards from the shore of the tarn, and consists of small boulders almost free from earth. To the left of the track, as you approach the tarn, another very distinct moraine, similarly constructed, stands out unmistakably. This marks the limit of this glacier, which melted at about the same altitude as the Lake Fenton glacier, a mile farther west.

These traces of past ice action are clearly discernible to even an untrained observer. They lie not six miles from the railway station, on an excellent track, and can be reached on horseback. An energetic person can here study the work of a glacier in the course of a day's trip from Hobart.

### III. THE WESTERN GLACIAL GROUP. (See Plate XII.).

The remaining area of glaciation lies west of the mountain mass running like a wall north from Mt. Mawson to the Derwent, and between that range and the Tyenna Peak-Mt. Field West system. It includes the Belcher-Belton Valley to the south, and the Hayes Valley farther north. Geographically, these lie end to end, separated only by the narrow ridge of K. Col. Before the glacial epoch these two valleys were probably in existence, but sloped in a broad, shallow hollow from K. Col, and the surrounding mountain peaks. Snowfields accumulated around K. Col, and probably precipitation in this part was heavier than farther east. Huge glaciers flowed north and south from K. Col, and their bases cut deep into the foot of that saddle, excavating the pair of enormous cirques we now see, and making K. Col a wonderful example of a Razorback ridge, with sides that stand a thousand feet perpendicularly from the lakes below. Both sides of the ridge are very much alike, and present an excellent example of glacial symmetry, a very uncommon feature.

### (a) The Belcher-Belton Valley. (See Plates XIII. and XIV.).

The glacier that filled this valley grew from the enormous snow-covered areas from Mt. Mawson past K. Col, and the Florentine Peaks to Tyenna Peak. It has cut into the mountain, forming an enormous cirque, over two miles long and a mile across, and 1,100 feet deep at the lowest point. It is really a composite cirque, consisting of at least three smaller curves. Down each of these flowed a tributary glacier, one from K. Col (see Plate XIV., Fig 4), a second from the saddle north of the rugged Florentine Peaks, and the third from the plateau between those crags and Tyenna Peak.

This glacier must have pushed over two miles down the valley to an altitude of about 2,700 feet, stopping near the spot where now the button-grass ceases. The floor of the valley is remarkably U-shaped, with a pair of ledges half-way up the sides, on the western of which reposes Lake Belton. The floor of this U is strewn for the whole two miles with a deposit of boulder clay, in which lies Lake Belcher. It is impossible to guess the depth of these deposits, which are remarkably evenly distributed, although piled here and there into the small ridges running at all angles typical of terminal moraine country. In one place,

Florentine Peak (also Lakes Belton and Belcher), National Park, Tasmania.

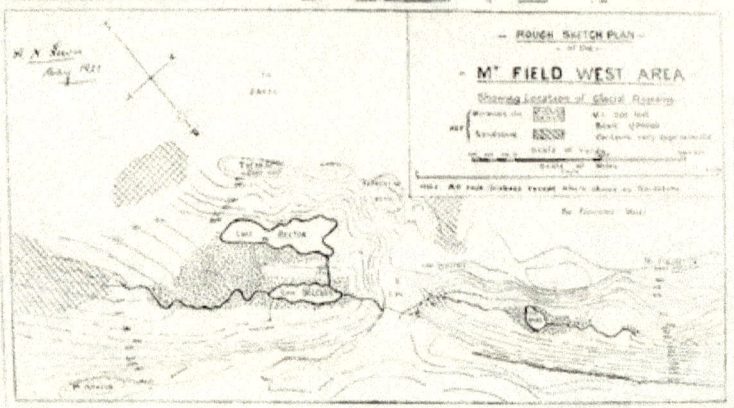

- ROUGH SKETCH PLAN -
- of the -
M<sup>T</sup> FIELD WEST AREA

*Showing Location of Glacial Features*

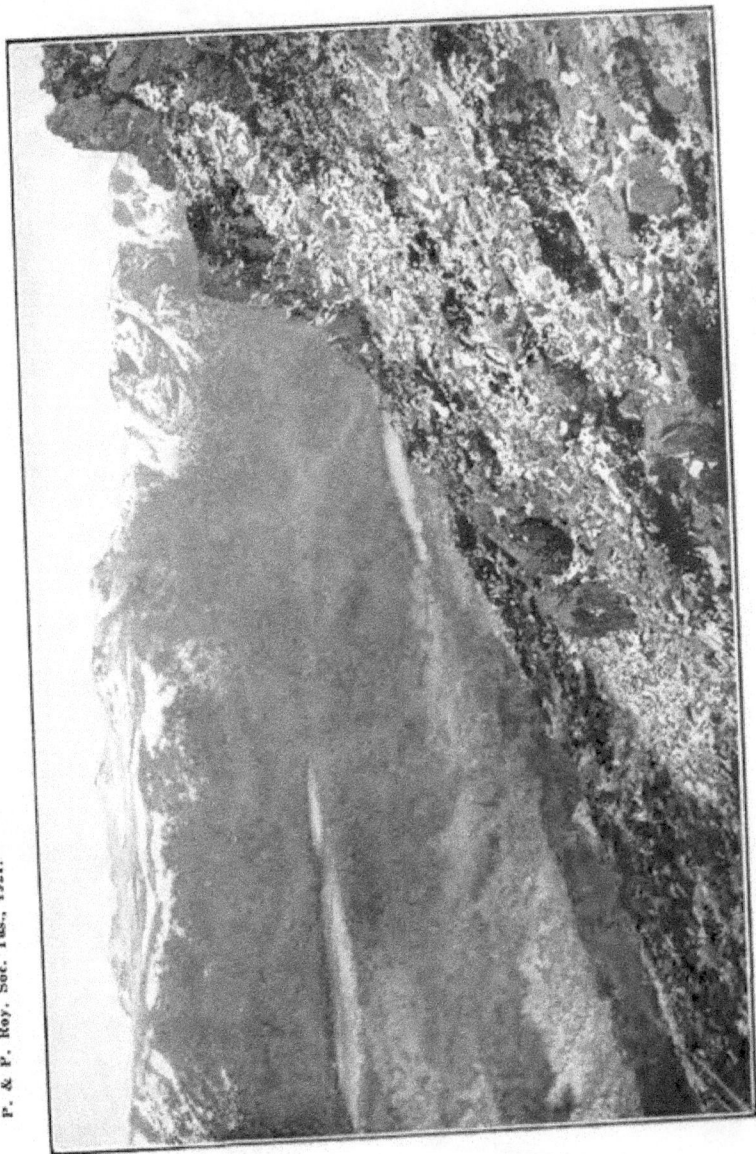

Florentine Peak (also Lakes Belton and Belcher), National Park, Tasmania.

(Fig. 3). Erratics in the Broad River Valley.

(Fig. 4). Lake Belcher and K. Col.

(Fig. 5). Lake Belton and Florentine Peak, National Park, Tasmania.

near the spot where the old Dobson-Belcher track crossed the Humboldt Creek, the water has cut about six feet into the glacial till, and falls in a cascade a few feet high over a layer of this boulder clay that has solidified sufficiently to cause the waterfall, and is almost conglomerate. The matrix is of sand, requiring a hammer to break it, and lying embedded in it are pebbles and cobbles of all sizes. They are absolutely unsorted, and have been worn by the glacier. One was found in the shape of a pyramid, but striæ, if they were ever developed on the diabase, have since rusted away. Perhaps this spot would be a likely place to search for ice-marked pebbles.

Lake Belton presents rather a problem. It appears to have been the work of two glaciers. The inner, or north-west, end is certainly a rock basin, scooped out by the glacier descending the gully that stands at its head, while the lower end is certainly impounded by a moraine that looks to be the work of the southern glacier. This moraine also extends the whole length of the eastern shore, and appears to have been formed either from a line of small glaciers or on the end of an extremely wide ice flow dropping down from Tyenna Peak and the Florentine Peaks. Perhaps this represents the melting point of several glaciers during their later stage, while a main glacier passed down the bottom of the valley, deepening that, and leaving Lake Belton as a hanging valley 300 feet above.

The moraine on the eastern shore of Lake Belton stands 20 or 30 feet above the slope of the hill, and is 100 yards in width, containing many charming pools and tarns. Below Lake Belton the slope of the hill is strewn with morainal material, as if the melting glacier tipped its load down the hillside. The configuration suggests that at a period of maximum glaciation a large glacier filled the valley to a point level with Lake Belton and its corresponding ridge on the eastern slope, scooping out a U-shaped floor in this large valley. Then, as the ice flows shrank, a small glacier cut out a second U within the larger one, at the bottom of the valley, while tributaries melting on the side of the hill were responsible for Lake Belton, making this latter lake an example, if a poor one, of a hanging valley.

### (b) The Lake Hayes Valley.

North of K. Col, a shorter glacier, growing from more limited snowfields, was responsible for the tremendous gulch east of Mt. Field West. It stretched down the valley about a mile to a point just beyond Lake Hayes. It deposited a considerable pile of morainal material that now stretches in a bank a quarter of a mile north of Lake Hayes, and through which the Bunyip Creek has cut to a depth of 50 feet. The glacier must have been melting in this vicinity throughout its existence, withdrawing very slowly and evenly. It deposited this considerable bed of glacial till behind which Lake Hayes now lies, and, gradually shrinking, covered the floor of the valley above the lake with debris.

The moraine is of interest from one point. Unfortunately, throughout the National Park the uniform diabase gives little variety in the textures of these moraines, but here, right in the centre of the cirque at the head of Lake Hayes Valley, is still to be found a tiny pocket of sandstone. This is only about 200 feet in depth, and below it, as above and all round the rock, is diabase. But there are several large blocks of this sandstone visible in the moraine beyond Lake Hayes, over a mile from where its parent bed is now to be seen. Some of these can be seen behind a large clump of King William Pines on the north-west side of the lake. This valley is not as extensive as most of the other areas, but shows the wonderful sculpturing action of an ice-river.

In conclusion, our National Park can afford a student of nature a comprehensive series of examples of the eroding and constructing work of glaciers, enabling him to study at his own back-door these mighty forces, and provides an insight into the geological history of our island, all obtainable with the expenditure of an insignificant expenditure of energy and time. It is doubtful if any other 40,000 acres of the surface of the globe can supply the variety of interests that the public of Tasmania is striving to save from destruction in its National Park.

LIST OF WORKS REFERRED TO IN TEXT.

Reid, A. McIntosh. 1918, "The North Pieman, Huskisson, and Stirling Valley Mining Fields," Geol. Surv. Tas. Bull. No. 28.

Waterhouse, L. L., 1916, "The South Heemskirk Tinfield," Geol. Surv. Tas. Bull., No. 21.

# DESCRIPTION OF A NEW SPECIES OF FOSSIL
## *LORICELLA* (ORDER *POLYPLACOPHORA*).
### WITH REMARKS ON SOME UNDESCRIBED CHARACTERS PRESENT IN *LORICELLA ANGASI*, AD. AND ANG., AND *L. TORRI*, ASHBY.

By EDWIN ASHBY, F.L.S., M.B.O.U.

(Communicated by C. E. Lord.)

Plate XV.

(Read 11th July, 1921.)

Mr. E. D. Atkinson, who for many years was resident at Sulphur Creek, North-West Tasmania, early in September last, sent me a very beautiful valve of a Chiton which he had obtained at Table Cape, a locality that has yielded to him and his son many fine forms of fossil mollusca. Three species of *Loricella* from the same locality, and the result of the joint work of the two, were described by Mr. A. F. Basset Hull (in Proc. Lin. Soc. of New South Wales, 1914, Vol. XXXIX., Pt. 4). Since receiving the specimen herein described from Mr. Atkinson, he has passed away. He was an assiduous collector, and many fine forms have been discovered as a result of his earnest labours, and we all owe a debt to his memory.

Mr. Hull, in the paper before mentioned, comments on the large number of species belonging to the genera *Loricella* and *Lorica* represented in the Table Cape deposits, and the apparent dwindling of species in recent times. He states that the genus *Loricella* "is represented by a single living "species," and, speaking of the genus *Lorica*, which also is well represented in the same beds, he says "one only *Lorica* "*volvox*, Reeve, is still extant."

Since Mr. Hull wrote thus, three living forms of this latter genus have been recognised, two of which are Australian, and one from New Zealand, also a second species of *Loricella* has been described by the writer, who, in addition, foreshadows the probability of yet another species being recognised. While it is evident that these southern seas were exceptionally rich in species belonging to these two genera at the time the Table Cape Beds were laid down, recent research indicates that both genera are better represented by living forms than was thought to be the case when Mr. Hull's paper was written.

### Loricella sculpta, n.sp.

Up to the present one median valve only has been discovered in the Table Cape Beds, but it is in an excellent state of preservation; its beautiful sculpture, which suggests the name I am giving it, is as perfect as it was during life. The shell is remarkably flat, although carinated.

*Pleural and Dorsal Areas.*—These are evenly decorated with narrow, strongly raised, wavy ribs; these in places are bridged by transverse ribs following the growth lines. These are particularly marked towards the anterior margin, where the transverse ribs resemble a string of small beads. Towards the posterior portion of the valve this feature of the sculpture is somewhat modified, and might be more correctly described as a series of irregularly and widely spaced grooves, following the growth lines and breaking to some extent the longitudinal ribs where they cross. These longitudinal ribs are more or less confluent on the jugum, and to a limited extent in the pleural area.

*Lateral Area.*—This area is much raised and strongly decorated with coarse, radiating, wavy ribs; these are broken at irregular intervals by deep grooves, which are a continuation of the growth lines which cross the pleural area, and turn abruptly at less than a right-angle across the lateral areas.

*Inside.*—Eaves well developed, insertion plates 1 slit, evidences of not very pronounced serrations. The sutural laminæ are well developed, and appear to be much less produced forward than is the case with *L. angasi*, Ad. and Ang., the anterior margin throughout being almost straight, but in places it is a little broken; therefore, in a perfect shell, this feature may be less pronounced. The suture is broad, and the slits on either side thereof are absent. The anterior margin of the callus portion is almost straight, and the thickening very pronounced. The tegmentum is folded over the posterior margin in a similar manner to both *L. angasi*, Ad. and Ang., and *L. torri*, Ashby, with this

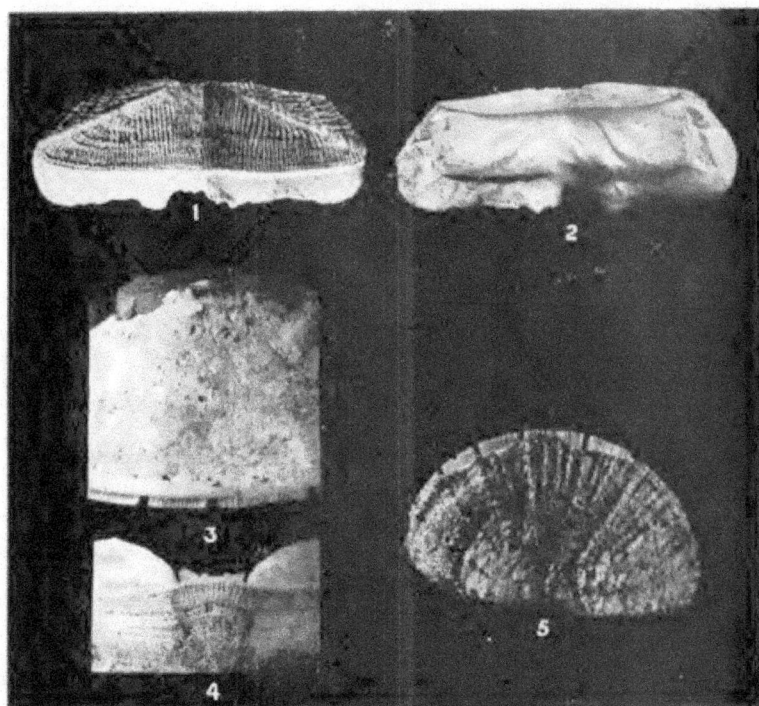

Plate XV.

Fig. 1. *Loricella sculpta*, Ashby.    Median valve, upper side.

Fig. 2. *Loricella sculpta*, Ashby.    Inside of median valve, showing callus portion and infolded tegmentum.

Fig. 3. *Loricella angasi*, Ad. and Ang.    Portion of anterior valve, upper side, showing serrated teeth.

Fig. 4. *Loricella angasi*, Ad. and Ang.    Portion of median valve, upper side, showing spade-like process between the sutural laminæ.

Fig. 5. *Loricella torri*, Ashby.    Anterior valve, upper side, showing serrated teeth.

difference, that in the fossil the margin is almost straight, whereas in the two species referred to, it curves outwards under the jugum, in a semi-circle.

*Note.*—The strength and character of the sculpture easily separate this species from any other of the known fossil *Loricella*.

### *Loricella angasi*, Ad. and Ang., and *L. torri*, Ashby.

In my paper on the genus *Loricella* (Trans. Roy. Soc. of S. Austr., Vol. XLIII., p. 61, 1919) reference is made to the lobed suture of the inside of the median valve of *L. angasi*, but only the superficial features distinguishing *L. torri*, Ashby, from that species were dealt with, as the valves were not disarticulated. It has now been possible to examine disarticulated specimens of both species. The sinus or space separating the sutural laminæ in the median valves is very broad, with a deep slit at each side, this slit penetrating to the tegmentum, having a spade-like process, with a denticulate margin, between the two slits. This feature is present in both the two living species, but in the fossil one under review these slits are either entirely absent or rudimentary. It suggests that this feature may have been developed in recent times, in which case the fossil *Loricella* might very properly receive sub-generic distinction.

The examination of separated valves for the purposes of this paper has revealed a further difference between *L. angasi* and *L. torri*.

While the latter has, especially in the anterior valve, sharply serrated and deeply propped and cut teeth, the teeth in the former *L. angasi*, as compared with it, are comparatively blunt, and the propping much less finely cut. The fossil species under review seems more closely to approach *L. angasi* in this respect.

*Note.*—Carpenter MS. is quoted by Pilsbry (Man. Con. Vol. XIV., 239) as follows, referring to *L. angasi*, Ad. and Ang.:—"The sutural plates separated, but having a lamina "between them, which is sometimes bilobate or denticulate," and again, "the sinus having a separate lamina, somewhat "lobed." The figure 11, pl. 51, in same volume, does not at all represent this character as it really is, I have therefore photographed a median valve of that species showing this spade-like process, which separates the sutural laminæ, and I also figure a photograph of the anterior valve of both species showing the serrated teeth, which are in both strongly propped outside, but only showing propping in the inside in the case of *L. torri*, Ashby. This is the first time that a dissected valve of this latter has been figured. The type of *Loricella sculpta*, Ashby, has been presented to the Tasmanian Museum, Hobart. (Tas. Museum No. C. 1672.)

## EXPLANATION OF PLATE XV.

Fig. 1.  *Loricella sculpta*, Ashby.  Median valve, upper side.

Fig. 2.  *Loricella sculpta*, Ashby.  Inside of median valve, showing callus portion and infolded tegmentum.

Fig. 3.  *Loricella angasi*, Ad. and Ang.  Portion of anterior valve, upper side, showing serrated teeth.

Fig. 4.  *Loricella angasi*, Ad. and Ang.  Portion of median valve, upper side, showing spade-like process between the sutural laminæ.

Fig. 5.  *Loricella torri*, Ashby.  Anterior valve, upper side, showing serrated teeth.

# AUSTRALIAN BOMBYLIIDÆ AND CYRTIDÆ
## (DIPTERA).

### By G. H. HARDY.

### Plates XVI. and XVII.

#### (Read 11th July, 1921.)

This catalogue of the *Bombyliidæ* and *Cyrtidæ* of Australia contains a key to the genera, and the description of two new species belonging to genera in which no previous species have been described from Australia. Also, there are numerous synonyms suggested, and a number of species have been placed in the genera they more readily conform to than those in which they were originally placed.

## BOMBYLIIDÆ.

This study of the *Bombyliidæ* is based upon several important collections. One of these, the Macleay Museum collection, contains a large number of species, many of which appear to be new, and it forms the basis for the study of the species described from Australia. The writer's own collection contains species conforming to most of those described from Tasmania by White, and also contains specimens from Western Australia and New South Wales. A small, but very valuable, collection formed by Dr. E. W. Ferguson, contains some specimens identified by White by comparison with Walker's types in the British Museum, and has been valuable in establishing the identity of some of the species. Other specimens, including those in the Australian Museum, the Queensland Museum, and the Agricultural Department of Queensland, have also been examined.

Much of the material in the above collections is inferior in condition, and as many of the species are closely related, making the differences between them difficult to determine from old specimens, it is advisable to wait till sufficient new material has accumulated before revising the species within the various genera.

The Australian species have been described under nearly one hundred and fifty names, of which less than one hundred are distinct, and of these fifty-two are recognised in the collections under revision.

A study of the Australian species shows conclusively that the generic characters utilised by various authors are often of less than specific value, and this is especially the case in the *Anthracinæ* and *Lomatiinæ*, and the taxonomy of the *Bombyliinæ* is complicated by the existence of species that contain graduating characters between some of the genera.

For all practical purposes the key given below will serve to separate the described species into groups of more or less generic value.

*Key to the Genera of the Australian Bombyliidæ.*

1. The bifurcation of the radial and cubital veins takes place at right angles and near the median cross vein.     *ANTHRACINÆ.* **4.**

 The bifurcation of the radial and cubital veins takes place at an acute angle at a considerable distance from the median cross vein.     **2.**

2. The radial vein, curving upwards at its apex, often forms an open loop, and always runs into the costa at an obtuse or right angle. The antennæ short, with the basal joint very thick. The abdomen generally more or less long, parallel sided, and depressed.  *LOMATIINÆ.* **8.**

 The radial vein normal, and running into the costa at an acute angle.     **3.**

3. The abdomen elongate, more or less compressed and cylindrical.     *SYSTROPINÆ.* **11.**

 The abdomen short, conical or oval.  *BOMBYLIINÆ.* **14.**

### *ANTHRACINÆ.*

4. The proboscis projecting beyond the epistoma.

        *Cytheræ.*

 The proboscis not, or scarcely, projecting beyond the epistoma.     **5.**

5. The apex of the antennæ bearing a tuft of hairs.

        *Argyramœba.*

 The apex of the antennæ at most with a style, never with a tuft of hairs.     **6.**

6. The third joint of the antennæ prolonged to a style-like process, at most with a minute differentiated style.     *Anthrax.*

 The antennal style long and distinct, separated from the prolonged third antennal joint by a distinct suture.     **7.**

7. Three submarginal cells present. *Exoprosopa.*
   Four submarginal cells present. *Hyperalonia.*

### LOMATIINÆ.

8. The abdomen cylindrical or slightly compressed.
   *Docidomyia.*
   The abdomen depressed. 9.

9. The radial vein curved upwards, and forming at
   most a very small loop. The abdomen narrow,
   parallel-sided. *Lomatia.*
   The radial vein forming a loop at least as long as
   wide before running into the costa. 10.

10. The radial veing forming a loop about as long as
    wide. The abdomen always broad. *Oncodocera.*
    The radial vein forming a loop at least twice as long
    as wide; if, however, the loop is small the abdo-
    men is invariably long and narrow. *Comptosia.*

### SYSTROPINÆ.

11. The wings with only two veins issuing from the
    discal cell. *Systropus.*
    The wings with three veins issuing from the discal
    cell. 12.

12. The abdomen with only six segments.
    *Antoniaustralia.*
    The abdomen with more than six segments. 13.

13. The palpi short, scarcely one-third the length of the
    proboscis; the thorax considerably arched; the
    thorax and head with bristles; the legs with
    long spines. *Marmasoma.*
    The palpi long, three-quarters the length of the
    proboscis; the thorax not conspicuously arched;
    the head and thorax without bristles; the legs
    with small inconspicuous spines. *Eclimus.*

### BOMBYLIINÆ.

14. The discal cell wanting. *Cyrtomorpha.*
    The discal cell present. 15.

15. The wings with two veins issuing from the discal
    cell. *Geron.*
    The wings with three veins issuing from the discal
    cell. 16.

16. The anal cell closed. 17.
    The anal cell open. 18.

17. The third joint of the antennæ and the face with
    long hairs in both sexes. The cubital fork with
    an appendix. *Aercotrichus.*

    The third joint of the antennæ and the face bare in
    the female. The cubital fork without an appen-
    dix. *Phthiria.*

18. The first posterior cell open, at most closed at the
    wing border.                                     19.

    The first posterior cell closed considerably before
    the wing border.                                 20.

19. The first basal cell much longer than the second;
    *i.e.*, the intermediate cross vein is situated to-
    wards or beyond the middle of the  discal cell.
                                             *Dischistus.*

    The two basal cells of about equal length; *i.e.*, the
    intermediate cross vein is situated near the
    base of the discal cell.                *Sisyromyia.*

20. The two basal cells of about equal length.
                                           *Systœchus.*

    The first basal cell much longer than the second.
                                           *Bombylius.*

## ANTHRACINÆ.

Genus *Hyperalonia*, Rondani.  (Pl. XVI., fig. 1.)

*Hyperalonia*, Rondani, Archiv. per la Zool. iii., 1863, p. 58.

### *Hyperalonia satyrus*, Fabricius.

*Bibio satyrus*, Fabricius, Syst. Ent., 1775, p. 758; and Sp.
      Ins. ii., 1781, p. 415; and Mant. Ins., ii., 1787, p. 329.

*Musca satyrus*, Gmel. Syst. Nat. v., 1792, p. 2,831.

*Anthrax satyrus*, Fabricius. Ent. Syst. iv., 1794, p. 259; and
      Syst. Ant., 1805, p. 123.  *Id.*, Wiedemann, Dipt.
      Exot., 1821, p. 151; and Auss. zweifl. Ins., i., 1828,
      p. 322.  *Id.*, Walker, List Dipt. B.M., ii., 1849, p. 243;
      and Ins. Saund. Dipt., 1852, p. 166.

*Exoprosopa satyrus*, v. d. Wulp, Tijd. v. Ent. (2), iii. (xi.),
      1868, p. 106, Pl. iii., fig. 10.  *Id.*, Osten-Sacken, Cat.
      Dipt. N. Amer., ed. 2, 1878, p. 87, note.  *Id.*, v. d.
      Wulp. Cat. Dipt. S. Asia, 1896, p. 69.

*Anthrax funestra*, Walker, List Dipt., B.M., ii., 1849, p. 242.

*Exoprosopa funestra*, Walker, Ins. Saund., Dipt. i., 1852,
      p. 165.

*Exoprosopa insignis*, Macquart, Dipt. Exot., suppl. 5, 1855,
      p. 73, Pl. iii., fig. 7.  *Id.*, Bergroth, Stett. Ent. Zeit.,
      lv., 1894, p. 72.

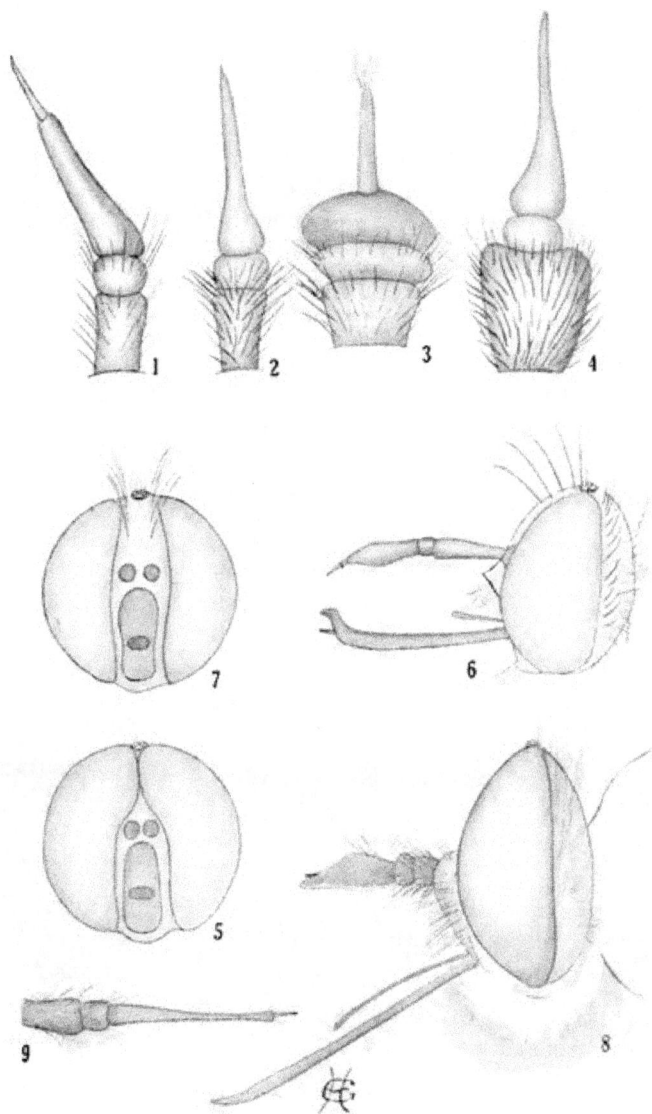

Australian Bombyliidæ.

*Synonymy.*—This species was described from Novæ Hollandiæ in 1775 from a specimen collected by Banks, and in 1778 Fabricius gives China as a locality; both these localities were repeated in 1794. Walker, in 1849, gives Georgia as the locality (perhaps King George's Sound was originally intended), and Osten Sacken in 1878 states that the species is not American.

In 1868 van der Wulp described and figured a specimen from Aru Island under the name, and this determination is accepted here as correct.

The identity of Fabricius' species has been fixed by description and figure on the authority of van der Wulp. Species in various collections conforming to van der Wulp's description are named by myself *Hyperalonia satyrus*, Fabricius. The same species has been named by Major E. E. Austen as *Hyperalonia funesta*, Walker, and is represented by a specimen so determined in the Queensland Museum; on this account Walker's name is placed here as a synonym. The description of *Exoprosopa insignis*, Macquart, also conforms to this species.

*Hab.*—There are twenty-four specimens in the Macleay Museum with labels bearing the following localities:— Northern Territory: Port Darwin. Queensland: Cape York, Rockhampton, Port Denison, Port Curtis, Endeavour River, and Lizard Island. New South Wales: Piper's Flats and Newcastle. South Australia. There are further specimens in other collections.

In the Agricultural Department of Queensland there is a specimen, bearing a label by Mr. Edmund Jarvis, and it conveys the information that the species is a hyperparasite on the scolid wasp *Dielis sp.* (now known as *Campsomeris radula*), which is a parasite on sugar-cane grubs.

Under the name *Hyperalonia funesta*, Walker, Mr. Jarvis also informs me that this species is a parasite of an Asilid, which is predaceous in the larval form upon the banana root weevil, *Calandra sordida*.

### *Hyperalonia sinuatifascia*, Macquart.

*Exoprosopa sinuatifascia*, Macquart, Dipt. Exot., suppl. 5, 1855, p. 72, Pl. iii., fig. 6.

*Exoprosopa macraspis*, Thomson, Eugenies Resa, Dipt., 1868, p. 479.

*Hyperalonia argenticincta*, Bigot, Ann. Soc. Ent. France (7), xli., 1892, p. 343.

*Synonymy.*—Specimens identified as belonging to Macquart's species were compared with the descriptions of Thomson and Bigot and found to agree.

*Hab.*—The three descriptions record the species from New South Wales, and two specimens, undoubtedly belonging here, were collected at Sydney during January, 1919, and at Blackheath, Blue Mountains, during November, 1919, respectively. In the Macleay Museum one specimen is labelled "South Australia."

## *Hyperalonia bombyliformis*, Macleay.

*Anthrax bombyliformis*, Macleay, in King's narrative Surv. S. Austr., ii., 1830, p. 468. *Id.*, Wiedemann, Auss. zweifl. Ins. ii., 1830, p. 648. *Id.*, Walker, List Dipt., B.M., ii., 1849, p. 241. *Id.*, Kirby, Ann. Mag. Nat. Hist. (5), xiii., 1884, p. 458.

*Ligyra bombyliformis*, Newman, Entom. i., 1841, p. 220. *Id.*, Walker, Ins. Saund. Dipt., 1852, p. 166.

*Exoprosopa punctipennis*, Macquart, Dipt. Exot., suppl. 4, 1849, p. 106, Pl. x., fig. 4.

*Exoprosopa albiventris*, Thomson, Eugenies Resa. Dipt., 1869, p. 480.

*Synonymy.*—The type of *Anthrax bombyliformis*, Macleay, is probably not traceable, and the description is confined to about four lines. It is described as having several discoidal spots on the wing, and from this character the known species to which it could be referred are limited to two species of *Lomatiinæ*, neither of which can in any way be associated with other described characters, and to a few species of *Anthracinæ*.

A comparison of the description with some specimens independently identified as *Exoprosopa punctipennis*, Macquart, shows that Macleay's description conforms satisfactorily to that species.

*Hab.*—This species, apparently, has a wide range. Twenty-one specimens in the Macleay Museum are labelled as follows:—One from King's Sound, North-West Australia; from Queensland there are six labelled Port Denison, five Cape York, and one Percy Island; eight are from New South Wales, two of which are labelled Piper's Flats. There are also specimens in the Australian Museum and in other collections.

*Hyperalonia cingulata*, v. d. Wulp.

*Exoprosopa cingulata*, v. d. Wulp, Notes Leyden Mus., vii., 1885, p. 62.

*Hab.*—The species was described from Adelaide. In the Macleay Museum there is one specimen from South Australia, one from Port Denison, and one from Darling River.

## Genus *Exoprosopa*, Macquart.

*Exoprosopa*, Macquart, Dipt. Exot., ii. (1), 1840, p. 35. *Id.*, White, Proc. Roy. Soc. Tasm., 1916, p. 205.

*Note.*—Four names are placed under this genus, and two of these belong to recognised species. The other two names apparently belong to distinct species which are not represented in the collections examined.

### *Exoprosopa laterimbata*, Bigot.

*Exoprosopa laterimbata*, Bigot, Ann. Ent. Soc. France (7), lxi., 1892, p. 346.

*Note.*—The third segment of the abdomen has a white lateral fascia, which reaches almost to the median line. The species was described from a specimen with incomplete antennæ and denuded abdomen.

*Hab.*—Five specimens in the Macleay Museum are identified as belonging to Bigot's species, and are labelled from:—Western Australia; Queensland, including Port Denison and Rockhampton; and New South Wales.

### *Exoprosopa stellifer*, Walker.

*Anthrax stellifer*, Walker, List Dipt. B.M., ii., 1849, p. 244.
*Litorhynchus stellifer*, Walker, Ins. Saund. Dipt., 1852, p. 166.

*Variations.*—Two specimens of a series agree with Walker's description too well to be mistaken, but the remainder have the hyaline area of the wings varying from a narrow strip to a triangular area which reaches from the hind border to a point slightly beyond half the length and nearly across the discal cell. The basal half of the abdomen is sometimes brown with a black median stripe, and the white abdominal fascia may form a band almost reaching across the abdomen or may be obsolete.

*Hab.*—Western Australia. In the Queensland Museum there is a specimen labelled "Cunderdin." South Australia: there are eight specimens in the Macleay Museum from this State.

### Exoprosopa adelaidica, Macquart.

Exoprosopa adelaidica, Macquart, Dipt. Exot., suppl. 5, 1855,
    p. 70, Pl. iii., fig. 4.

Note.—Several specimens are attributed to this species
in various collections, but they do not come from the type
locality, nor do they agree sufficiently closely with the description.

Hab.—Adelaide.

### Exoprosopa obliquifasciata, Macquart.

Exoprosopa obliquifasciata, Macquart, Dipt. Exot., suppl. 4,
    1850, p. 107, Pl. x., fig. 5. Id., White, Proc. Roy.
    Soc. Tasm., 1916, p. 205.

Hab.—This species was described from Tasmania, but
no recent specimen of the genus is known from the locality.
Many of the species of Diptera recorded from Tasmania by
Macquart are now found to be from the Northern portions
of Australia, and perhaps this is another instance of incor-
rect locality.

### Genus Anthrax, Scopoli.    (Pl. XVI., fig. 2.)

Anthrax, Scopoli, Ent. Carl., 1763, p. 358. Id., White, Proc.
    Roy. Soc. Tasm., 1916, p. 206.

Note.—Nine species described under the generic name
Anthrax appear to belong to that genus in its restricted
sense. The majority of these forms have been identified
from their descriptions in the various collections examined.

### Anthrax alterna, Walker.

Anthrax alterna, Walker, List Dipt. B.M., ii., 1849, p. 261.
Anthrax alternans, Macquart, Dipt. Exot., suppl. 4, 1850,
    p. 110. Id., White, Proc. Roy. Soc. Tasm., 1916,
    p. 208.

Synonymy.—It appears that Walker's species from Australia is the same as White's identification of A. alternans,
Macquart, from Tasmania.

### Anthrax argentipennis, White.

Anthrax argentipennis, White, Proc. Roy. Soc. Tasm., 1916,
    p. 212.

### Anthrax commista, Macquart.

Anthrax commista, Macquart, Dipt. Exot., suppl. 4, 1850,
    p. 109, Pl. x., fig. 10.

*Anthrax consimilis*, Thomson, Eugenies Resa, Dipt., 1868, p. 481.

*Synonymy.*—The above synonymy appears to be correct according to the descriptions, which agree with some specimens in the Macleay Museum.

### *Anthrax fuscicostata*, Macquart.

*Anthrax fuscicostata*, Macquart, Dipt. Exot., suppl. 1, 1846, p. 111. *Id.*, Schiner, Novara Reisa, 1868, p. 126.

*Anthrax marginata*, Walker, Ins. Saund. Dipt., 1850, p. 178. *Id.*, White, Proc. Roy. Soc. Tasm., 1916, p. 210.

*Anthrax albirufa*, Walker, Trans. Ent. Soc. Lond., iv., 1857, p. 143.

*Synonymy.*—White gives Macquart's name as a synonym of *A. marginata*, Walker, although Macquart described the species four years earlier than Walker. *A. albirufa*, Walker, appears from the description to be the same species.

### *Anthrax minor*, Macquart.

*Anthrax minor*, Macquart, Dipt. Exot., suppl. 4, 1850, p. 111. *Id.*, White, Proc. Roy. Soc. Tasm., 1916, p. 208.

*Anthrax vitrea*, Walker, Ins. Saund. Dipt., 1850, p. 181.

*Synonymy.*—The above synonymy is given on the authority of White, who makes no remarks concerning it. Macquart's species is from Tasmania, and Walker's from Western Australia.

### *Anthrax nigricosta*, Macquart.

*Anthrax nigricosta*, Macquart, Dipt. Exot., suppl. 4, 1850, p. 111. *Id.*, Froggatt, Austr. Ins., 1907, p. 296. *Id.*, White, Proc. Roy. Soc. Tasm., 1916, p. 209.

*Anthrax pellucida*, Walker, Ins. Saund. Dipt., 1854, p. 182.

*Synonymy.*—White overlooked Walker's description, which conforms to *A. nigricosta*, Macquart, and also was described from Tasmania.

*Hab.*—White records the species from New South Wales, South Australia, Victoria, and Tasmania. On Cradle Mountain, Tasmania, this species occurred in vast quantities, and was the only species of the genus taken there during January, 1917.

### *Anthrax resurgens*, Walker.

*Anthrax resurgens*, Walker, List Dipt. B.M., ii., 1849, p. 259.

D

### *Anthrax simplex*, Macquart.

*Anthrax simplex*, Macquart, Dipt. Exot., suppl. 2, 1847, p. 52, Pl. ii., fig. 4.    *Id.*, White, Proc. Roy. Soc. Tasm., 1916, p. 212.

*Note.*—Two specimens in Dr. Ferguson's collection were identified by White as this species. They are numbered 233 and 234, and were collected in Sydney by Gibbons.

### *Anthrax velox*, White.

*Anthrax velox*, White, Proc. Roy. Soc. Tasm., 1916, p. 211.

*Note.*—White compares this species with *A. albirufa*, Walker, which is here placed under *A. fuscicostata*, Macquart. He also compares it with *A. marginata*, Walker, also placed here under the same.

The species is not recognised in the collections under revision.

### Genus *Argyramœba*, Schiner.

*Argyramœba*, Schiner, Wien. Entom. Monatschr., iv., 1860, p. 51. *Id.*, White, Proc. Roy. Soc. Tasm., 1916, p. 213.

*Note.*—Four described species are placed here, and three of them have been recognised and labelled in the various collections.

### *Argyramœba concisa*, Macquart.

*Anthrax concisa*, Macquart, Dipt. Exot., suppl. 4, 1850, p. 111, Pl. x., fig. 11. *Id.*, Schiner, Reise Novara, Dipt., 1868, p. 125.

*Hab.*—New South Wales. One specimen in the Macleay Museum.

### *Argyramœba incompta*, Walker.

*Anthrax incompta*, Walker, List. Dipt. B.M., 1849, ii., p. 253.

*Hab.*—The species was originally described from Western Australia. In the Macleay Museum there are twenty-five specimens from South Australia, two from New South Wales, and four from Cape York, Queensland, all of which are referable to this species.

### *Argyramœba maculata*, Macquart.    (Pl. XVI., fig. 3.)

*Anthrax maculata*, Macquart, Dipt. Exot., suppl. 1, 1846, p. 112, Pl. ix., fig. 12.

*Argyramœba maculata*, White, Proc. Roy. Soc. Tasm., 1916, p. 213.

*Anthrax australis*, Walker, Ins. Saund. Dipt., 1850, p. 193.

*Anthrax diana*, Walker, List Dipt. B.M., 1849, p. 252.

*Synonymy.—Anthrax diana*, Walker, was described from a specimen without a locality and without a head. A series of specimens in the Queensland Museum, from which one was sent to and identified by Major E. E. Austen as *A. diana*, Walker, is identical with *Argyramœba maculata*, Macquart. Walker's description agrees with this species, and therefore the above information is accepted.

*Hab.*—Australia and Tasmania.

### *Argyramœba semimacula*, Walker.

*Anthrax semimacula*, Walker, List Dipt. B.M., ii., 1849, p. 254.

*Note.*—This species is undoubtedly placed here in its right genus, but it has not been recognised in the collections under revision.

### Genus *Cytherea*, Fabricius.

*Cytherea*, Fabricius, Ent. Syst., iv., 1794, p. 413.

*Note.*—There is one species belonging to this genus described from Australia. There are also three undescribed species, one in the Australian Museum, one in the Macleay Museum, and the third in Dr. Ferguson's collection.

### *Cytherea lipposa*, Bigot.

*Glossista lipposa*, Bigot, Ann. Ent. Soc. France (7), lxi., 1892, p. 353.

*Note.*—This species, described from a mutilated specimen from Sydney, has not been recognised in the collections under revision.

### *Species of uncertain generic position.*

Four of Macquart's species have not been recognised and their generic positions are uncertain.

*Exoprosopa bicellata*, Macquart, Dipt. Exot., suppl. 2, 1847, p. 51, Pl. ii., fig. 2. *Id.*, White, Proc. Roy. Soc. Tasm., 1916, p. 206. (Tasmania.)

*Anthrax flaveola*, Macquart, Dipt. Exot., suppl. 4, 1850, p. 109. (Eastern Australia.)

*Anthrax incisa*, Macquart, Dipt. Exot., suppl. 2, 1847, p. 52, Pl. ii., fig. 3. *Id.*, White, Proc. Roy. Soc. Tasm., 1916, p. 207. (Tasmania.) This species is said to have the abdomen with the apex silvery, and on this account the probable position would be under the genus *Argyromœba*, many species of which have this character.

*Anthrax obscura*, Macquart, Dipt. Exot., suppl. 1, 1846, p. 112.   (Australia.)

*Anthrax angularis*, Thomson, Eugenics Resa, Dipt., 1868, p. 482.   (New South Wales.)

## LOMATIINÆ.

Genus *Lomatia*, Meigen.   (Pl. XVII., fig. 10.)

*Lomatia*, Meigen. System. Beschreib., iii., 1822.

### *Lomatia sobicula*, Walker.

*Anthrax sobicula*, Walker, Trans. Ent. Soc. Lond., iv., 1857, p. 144.

*Lomatia australis*, Schiner. Novara Reise, Dipt., 1868. p. 129.

*Synonymy.*—Two specimens in Dr. Ferguson's collection, numbered 119 and 241, were identified by White as *Anthrax sobicula*, Walker, and were evidently compared with the type. Schiner's description appears to conform to the same species, which is represented by specimens from Sydney in most collections.

### *Lomatia* (?) *subsenex*, Walker.

*Anthrax subsenex*, Walker, Trans. Ent. Soc. Lond., iv., 1857, p. 144.

*Status.*—Judging from the comparison of descriptions between Walker's two species, it appears certain that they refer to the same genus, and, therefore, if *Anthrax sobicula* is referred to the genus *Lomatia*, it is probable that *Anthrax subsenex* belongs to the same group.

Genus *Oncodocera*, Osten-Sacken.   (Pl. XVII., fig. 11.)

*Ogcodocera*, Macquart, Dipt. Exot., ii. (1), 1840, p. 83.

*Oncodocera*, Osten-Sacken, Bull. U.S. Stat. Geol. Surv. of Territories (Heyden), iii., 1877, p. 247.

*Description.*—Six species of *Lomatiinæ* do not seem to conform to the characters of any genus better than those of *Oncodocera*, as illustrated by Williston in *North American Diptera*, 3rd edition, 1908, fig. 82. The following characters, taken from specimens of the group so far known, will help to isolate them from their nearest allies:—

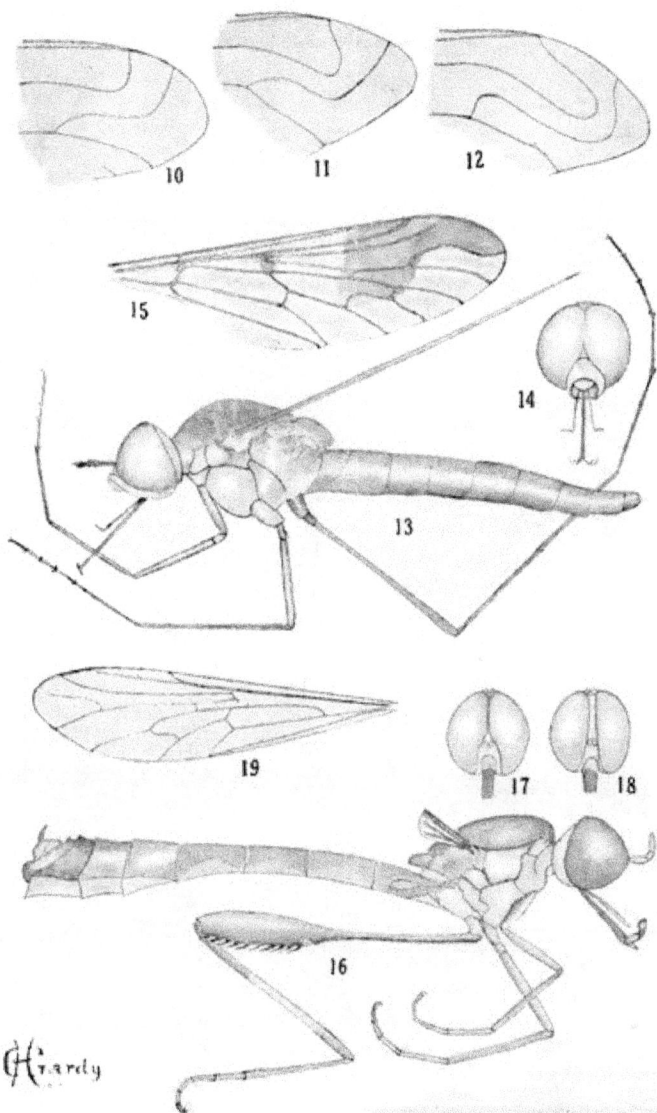

Australian Bombyliidæ.

Eyes contiguous in the male, separate in the female. Thorax a little broader than the head, broader posteriorly than anteriorly. Abdomen broader than the thorax. The abdomen of *Lomatia* is slender, rather elongate and parallel sided; that of *Oncodocera* is broad and not much longer than wide; the species of *Comptosia* have their abdomen generally like that of *Lomatia*, but vary to something approaching but not quite like that of *Oncodocera*. The latter case only occurs in a few large species, which can be readily separated by the difference in the loop of the radial vein.

### *Oncodocera ampla*, Walker. (Pl. XVII., fig. 11.)

*Anthrax ampla*, Walker, Ins. Saund. Dipt., 1850, pp. 167 and 185.

*Description.*—In the male the wing contains two recurrent veinlets situated on the vein between the discal and third posterior cells, one running into each of these cells; this character is not represented in the female nor in the other species placed under this genus.

*Hab.*—Described from Western Australia; there are two males and two females from this State in the Australian Museum. In the Macleay Museum there are two males and two females from South Australia.

### *Oncodocera anthracina*, Thomson.

*Comptosia anthracina*, Thomson, Eugenies Resa, 1868, p. 485.

*Lygira rubrifera*, Bigot. Ann. Soc. Ent. France (6), i.. 1881, p. 23.

*Synonymy.*—The above synonymy appears to be correct. The species must not be confused with various species of the genus *Comptosia*, which have a general similar appearance; the curvature of the radial vein will readily distinguish them.

*Hab.*—In the Macleay Museum there are seven specimens from South Australia and one from Piper's Flats, New South Wales. In Dr. Ferguson's collection there is one specimen from Victoria labelled "Mallee."

### *Oncodocera murina*, Newman.

*Neuria murina*, Newman, Entom., i., 1841, p. 221.

### *Oncodocera patula*, Walker.

*Anthrax patula*, Walker, List Dipt. B.M., ii., 1849, p. 273.
*Id.*, Walker, Ins. Saund. Dipt., 1852, p. 168.

*Oncodocera plana,* Walker.

*Anthrax plana,* Walker, List Dipt. B.M., ii.. 1849, p. 272.
*Id.,* Walker, Ins. Saund. Dipt., 1852, p. 168.

*Oncodocera tendens,* Walker.

*Anthrax tendens,* Walker, List Dipt. B.M., ii., 1849, p. 271.
*Id.,* Walker, Ins. Saund. Dipt., 1852, p. 168.

*Hab.*—Six specimens from Perth, Western Australia, were collected during or about December, 1911.

Genus *Comptosia,* Macquart. (Pl. XVI., fig. 4; Pl. XVII., fig. 12.)

*Comptosia,* Macquart, Dipt. Exot., ii. (1), 1840, p. 80. *Id.,* White, Proc. Roy. Soc. Tasm., 1916, p. 201.

*Neuria,* Newman, Entom., i., 1840, p. 220.

*Ligyra,* Newman, Entom.. i., 1840, p. 220. *Id.,* Becker, Ann. Mus. Zool. St. Petersb., xvii., 1912, p. 466, fig.

*Alyosia,* Rondani, Arch. per la Zool., iii.. 1863, p. 54. *Id.,* Becker, Ann. Mus. Zool. St. Petersb., xvii., 1912, p. 465.

*Synonymy.*—The type of genus *Comptosia* is *C. fascipennis,* Macquart, which is queried from Monte Video; and is supposed to have a white uniformly wide subapical band, three posterior cells, and an appendix. In Dr. Ferguson's collection, a specimen of *C. lateralis,* Newman, was identified by White as *C. fascipennis,* Macquart. and in accordance with the somewhat doubtful type locality this specimen must remain on record under the type specific name until the point of doubt concerning the locality can be settled.

The type of the genus *Neuria* is *N. lateralis,* Newman, from Sydney.

Newman placed *Anthrax bombyliformis,* Macleay, and *Anthrax silvanus,* Fabricius, under the genus *Ligyra,* and the former he gives as the representative. Macleay's species is placed here under the genus *Hyperalonia,* and Fabricius's species is apparently a large form of the species well known under the name *C. corculum;* Rondani gives the Chilian species. *L. lugubris,* Rondani, as the type species of *Ligyra,* and in this is followed by Becker.

The genus *Alyosia,* Rondani, is represented by the Tasmanian species *C. maculipennis,* Macquart, for the type.

For the purpose of this paper these genera cannot be accepted, and, indeed, considerable further study will be necessary before an adequate conclusion can be reached concerning the value of characters usually adopted for generic division in the subfamily.

### Comptosia ocellata, Newman.

*Neuria ocellata*, Newman, Entom., i., 1841, p. 221. *Id.*, Walker, Ins. Saund. Dipt., 1852, p. 167.

*Anthrax ocellata*, Walker, List Dipt. B.M., ii., 1849, p. 268

*Comptosia maculipennis*, Macquart, Dipt. Exot., suppl. 1, 1846, p. 116. *Id.*, White, Proc. Roy. Soc. Tasm., 1916, p. 201.

*Anthrax inclusa*, Walker, List Dipt. B.M., ii., 1849, p. 268.

*Anthrax cognata*, Walker, Ins. Saund. Dipt., 1852, p. 177.

*Synonymy.*—The above synonymy is given on the authority of White.

*Hab.*—*Anthrax cognata* was described from Western Australia, the others from Tasmania. One specimen from Piper's Flats, New South Wales, and two from Cape York, Queensland, are in the Macleay Museum. Other specimens represented in various collections are from Tasmania.

### Comptosia sylvana, Fabricius.

*Bibio sylvanus*, Fabricius, Syst. Ent., 1775, p. 758; and Sp. Ins., ii., 1781, p. 415; and Mant. Ins., ii., 1781, p. 329.

*Musca sylvanus*, Gmelin, Syst. Nat., v., 1792, p. 2,832.

*Anthrax sylvanus*, Fabricius, Ent. Syst. iv., 1794, p. 261; and Syst. Antl., 1805, p. 125. *Id.*, Wiedemann, Dipt. Exot., 1821, p. 151; and Auss. zweifl. Ins., i., 1838, p. 321. ?*Id.*, Walker, List Dipt. B.M., ii., 1849, p. 241; and Ins. Saund. Dipt., i., 1852, p. 166.

*Neuria atherix*, Newman, Entom., i., 1841, p. 222. *Id.*, Walker, Ins. Saund. Dipt., 1852, p. 167.

*Neuria corculum*, Newman, Entom., i., 1841, p. 221. *Id.*, Walker, Ins. Saund. Dipt., 1852, p. 167.

*Atherix corculum*, Walker, List Dipt. B.M., ii., 1849, p. 269.

*Comptosia corculum*, White, Proc. Roy. Soc. Tasm., 1916, p. 203. *Id.*, Hardy, Proc. Roy. Soc. Tasm., 1917, p. 66.

*Neuria maculosa*, Newman, Entom., i., 1841, p. 221.

*Neuria partita*, Newman, Entom., i., 1841, p. 221. *Id.*, Walker, Ins. Saund. Dipt., 1852, p. 167.

*Comptosia geometrica*, Macquart, Dipt. Exot., suppl. 2, 1847, p. 53. *Id.*, White, Proc. Roy. Soc. Tasm., 1916, p. 202.

*Neuria geometrica*, Walker, Ins. Saund. Dipt., 1852, p. 167.

*Alyosia geometrica*, Rondani, Archiv. per la Zool. iii., 1863, p. 54.

*Comptosia tricellata*, Macquart, Dipt. Exot., suppl. 2, 1847, p. 53, Pl. ii., fig. 6.

*Neuria tricellata*, Schiner, Reise Novara, 1868, p. 131.

*Neuria obscura*, Walker, Ins. Saund. Dipt., 1852, p. 167.

*Anthrax obscura*, Walker, Ins. Saund. Dipt., 1852, p. 176.

*Comptosia calophthalma*, Thomson, Eugenies Resa, 1868, p. 485.

*Neuria hemiteles*, Schiner, Reise Novara, 1868, p. 132.

*Comptosia fulvipes*, Bigot, Ann. Ent. Soc. France (7), lxi., 1892, p. 359.

*Synonymy.*—*Bibio sylvanus*, Fabricius, is described as a fuscous species with the scutellum and sides of the two first abdominal segments ferruginous; the wings have a sub-ferruginous anterior border and several fuscous spots; the legs are piceous.

This description could apply to a species of the genus *Hyperalonia*, and evidently Walker's reference refers to such, or to a species until recently generally known as *Comptosia coreulum*, some large specimens of which conform to this description far better than any known species of the genus *Hyperalonia*.

The type in the Banksian Collection was evidently collected at Botany Bay. The species here identified as *C. sylvanus*, Fabricius, is the commonest and most conspicuous Bombylid in that neighbourhood, and this fact, added to the comparatively good description, makes a plausible argument concerning the identity of Fabricius's species; on the other hand, specimens with the described ferruginous abdominal spots are rarely met with in this species.

Under the name *Comptosia sylvanus*, Fabricius, there are a number of specimens identified in various collections, and many of these have form names corresponding to special forms described, and are as follows:—

Form *coreulum*, Newman, from Western Australia, is small, and has three submarginal cells.

Form *tricellata*, Macquart, is rather large, and comes from Mt. Wellington, Tasmania; it corresponds to the *C. corculum* of White and Hardy, and not to the original of that name by Newman. This form also has three submarginal cells.

Form *geometrica*, Macquart, from Tasmania, invariably has two submarginal cells, and occurs in low localities, never on the mountains.

Form *hermeteles*, Schiner, from Sydney, has three submarginal cells, but differs from all the others by the absence of the usual fuscous spots in the hyaline area of the wing.

The usual form of *C. sylvanus* in collections has three or two submarginal cells, and occurs on the eastern side of Australia. It was referred to by Schiner as *N. tricellata*, which must not be confused with Macquart's name; *C. calophthalma*, Thomson, is the same.

There is insufficient material in collections to judge the values of *Neuria atherix*, *N. maculosa*, and *N. partita*, of Newman, or of *A. obscura*, Walker, and *C. fulvipes*, Bigot, but all these, from their descriptions, appear to be the same as the species here called *C. sylvanus*, Fabricius.

Much more material and information are required for the study of this species, but it seems certain that all the forms belong to one species, which varies somewhat under different conditions.

### *Comptosia plena*, Walker.

*Atherix plena*, Walker, List. Dipt. B.M., ii., 1849, p. 270.
*Neuria plena*, Walker, Ins. Saund. Dipt., 1852, p. 167.

*Note.*—This very distinctive species, from Perth, Western Australia, resembles the previous only in having fuscous spots on the wing, and differs by the whole wings being more or less uniformly suffused greyish and slightly darker along the anterior border. A further but apparently undescribed species from New South Wales agrees in these characters, and must not be confused with the Western Australian form.

### *Comptosia fasciata*, Fabricius.

*Anthrax fasciata*, Fabricius, Syst. Antl., 1805, p. 118.   *Id.*, Wiedemann, Dipt. Exot., 1821, p. 150; and Auss. zweifl. Ins., i., 1828, p. 321. *Id.*, Walker, List Dipt. B.M., ii., 1849, p. 267.

*Neuria fasciata*, Walker, Ins. Saund. Dipt., 1852, p. 167. *Id.*, Schiner, Reise Novara, 1868, p. 129.

*Comptosia fasciata*, Hutton, New Zealand Dipt., 1881, p. 24.
*Neuria nigricens*, Newman, Entom., i., 1841, p. 221.

*Synonymy.*—*Anthrax fasciatus*, Fabricius, is described from the Pacific Islands. Walker refers *N. nigricens*, Newman, to the same name, and gives New Holland for locality. Schiner uses the name for specimens from New Zealand.

*N. nigricens*, Newman, is from near Sydney, and undoubtedly is the same as specimens identified here as *C. fasciata*, Fabricius.

*Note.*—The species is similar to *C. lateralis*, Newman, *C. albofasciata*, Thomson, and *C. apicalis*, Macquart. It differs from the last of these by the white spot of the wing being subapical instead of apical, and from the other two by the abdomen being not red laterally.

### Comptosia lateralis, Newman

*Neuria lateralis*, Newman, Entom., i., 1841, p. 220. *Id.*, Walker, Ins. Saund. Dipt., 1852, p. 167. *Id.*, Schiner, Reise Novara, 1868, p. 131.

*Anthrax insignis*, Walker, List Dipt. B.M., ii., 1849, p. 266.

*Synonymy.*—Walker evidently changed the name of this species to *Anthrax insignis*, as *Anthrax lateralis* was preoccupied by Say in 1823; the species, however, belongs to the genus *Comptosia*, and in any case it cannot belong to the genus *Anthrax*.

White identified a specimen in Dr. Ferguson's collection as *C. fascipennis*, Macquart, which species is queried from Monte Video.

*Note.*—This species differs from the previous by the abdomen being bordered laterally with large separated, almost confluent reddish spots, and from the next species, *C. albofasciata*, Thomson, by the smaller size.

### Comptosia albofasciata, Thomson.

*Comptosia albofasciata*, Thomson, Eugenies Resa, 1868, p. 484. *Id.*, Froggatt, Austr. Ins., 1907, p. 296, Pl. xxviii., fig. 5.

*Note.*—It is possible that this species is only a large form of *C. lateralis*, Newman.

### Comptosia ducens, Walker.

*Anthrax ducens*, Walker, Ins. Saund. Dipt., 1850, p. 176.

*Neuria ducens*, Walker, *ibidem*, p. 167.

*Neuria grandis*, Schiner, Reise Novara, Dipt., 1868, p. 130.

*Synonymy.*—*A. ducens*, Walker, and *N. grandis*, Schiner, evidently belong to the same species, which varies remarkably in size. It differs from *C. albofasciata*, Thomson, and *C. lateralis*, Newman, by the absence of the white fascia on the wings.

## Comptosia aurifrons, Macquart.

*Comptosia aurifrons*, Macquart, Dipt. Exot., suppl. 4, 1850, p. 113, Pl. x., fig. 16.

*Note.*—This is a very common species, which is easily recognised by the golden pubescence on the front. It is represented in most collections.

*Hab.*—New South Wales and Victoria.

## Comptosia dorsalis, Walker.

*Anthrax dorsalis*, Walker, List Dipt. B.M., ii., 1849, p. 269.

*Neuria dorsalis*, Walker, Ins. Saund. Dipt., 1852, p. 167.

## Comptosia quadripennis, Walker.

*Anthrax quadripennis*, Walker, List Dipt. B.M., ii., 1849, p. 268.

*Neuria quadripennis*, Walker, Ins. Saund. Dipt., 1852, p. 167.
Id., Froggatt, Austr. Ins., 1907, p. 297.

*Note.*—This species is similar to *C. apicalis*, Macquart, but has three instead of two submarginal cells.

## Comptosia apicalis, Macquart.

*Comptosia apicalis*, Macquart, Dipt. Exot., suppl. 3, 1846, p. 35, Pl. iii., fig. 13.

*Alyosia apicalis*, Rondani, Arch. per la Zool., iii., 1863, p. 54.

*Neuria apicalis*, Schiner, Reise Novara, 1868, p. 132.

*Note.*—This species has the white fascia of the wings entirely covering the tip.

## Comptosia sobria, Walker.

*Anthrax sobria*, Walker, List Dipt. B.M., ii., 1849, p. 269.

*Neuria sobria*, Walker, Ins. Saund. Dipt., 1852, p. 167.

*Note.*—In Dr. Ferguson's collection there are three specimens numbered respectively 62, 257, and 258, all from Sydney, which were identified by White as Walker's species. In general appearance they resemble *C. ducens*, Walker, but differ structurally by having an appendix in the form of a recurrent vein on the upper branch of the cubital fork, and also the intermediate cross vein is situated rather close to the apex of the discal cell.

There are five further specimens in the Macleay Museum from New South Wales, and one of these is labelled "Wheeny "Creek, Jan. 8; Skuse."

### Genus *Docidomyia*, White.

*Docidomyia*, White, Proc. Roy. Soc. Tasm., 1916, p. 203.

### *Docidomyia pueralis*, White.

*Docidomyia pueralis*, White. Proc. Roy. Soc. Tasm., 1916, p. 204.

*Hab.*—Tasmania and New South Wales. This species is common on the sand-dunes of La Perouse, Botany Bay; specimens from this locality are, however, smaller than those examined from Tasmania.

### *Species Undetermined.*

*Comptosia moretonii*, Dipt. Exot., suppl. 5, 1854, p. 77, Pl. iii., fig. 15.

*Anthrax præargentata*, Macleay, in King's Narr. Surv. Austr., ii., 1832, p. 468. *Id.*, Wiedemann. Auss. Zweifl. Ins., ii., 1830, p. 648. *Id.*, Walker, List Dipt. B.M., 1849, p. 268.

*Neuria præargentata*, Newman, Entom.. i., 1841, p. 221. *Id.*, Walker, Ins. Saund. Dipt., 1852, p. 167.

(This species is possibly a true *Comptosia*, but no specimens in the collection under revision agree with the description.)

*Anthrax basilis*, Walker, List Dipt. B.M., ii., 1849, p. 267.

*Neuria basilis*, Walker, Ins. Saund. Dipt., 1852, p. 167.

*Anthrax decedens*, Walker, List Dipt. B.M., ii., 1849, p. 271.

*Neuria decedens*, Walker, Ins. Saund. Dipt., 1852, p. 167.

*Anthrax stria*, Walker, List Dipt. B.M., ii., 1849, p. 267.

*Neuria stria*, Walker, Ins. Saund. Dipt., 1852, p. 167.

*Anthrax extensa*, Walker, Ent. Mag., ii., 1835, p. 473. *Id.*, Walker. List Dipt. B.M. ii., 1849, p. 269.

*Neuria extensa*, Newman, Entom.. i., 1841, p. 221. *Id.*, Walker, Ins. Saund. Dipt., 1852, p. 167.

*Anthrax serpentiger*, Walker, List Dipt. B.M., ii., 1849, p. 270.

*Comptosia bicolor*, Macquart, Dipt. Exot., suppl. 4, 1850, p. 114, Pl. x., fig. 17.

*Neuria bicolor*, Schiner, Reise Novara, 1868, p. 131. (New Zealand.)

*Neuria rufoscutellata*, Jænnicke, Abhand. der Senkenb. naturf. G. vi., 1867, p. 345, Pl. xliii., fig. 9 (= ? *Comptosia ducens*, Walker.)

## SYSTROPINÆ.

*Note.*—Four genera are placed in this subfamily, and each is represented by one species. The genus *Systropus* belongs here, and the other three genera are provisionally placed here, and have been placed and suggested in subfamilies as follows:—Genus *Antoniaustralia* in the subfamily *Tomoyzinæ*, *Marmasoma* in the *Toxophorinæ*, and *Eclimus* in the *Cylleniinæ*. Becker included the *Toxophorinæ* under the *Cylleniinæ*, and the two Australian species known are too closely related for them to be separated into different subfamilies.

### Genus *Systropus*, Wiedemann.

*Systropus*, Wiedemann, Nov. Dipt. Gen., 1820, p. 18.

*Status.*—Under the subfamily *Systropinæ* Becker gives two genera which are characterised as follows:—*Systropus*, with contiguous eyes in both sexes and the abdomen clubform. *Dolichomyia*, with the eyes not contiguous in both sexes and the abdomen not club-form.

In the species described below the eyes are not contiguous in both sexes, and the abdomen is club-form in the male.

*Systropus clavifemoratus*, sp. nov. (Pl. XVII., figs. 16, 17, 18, and 19.)

*Description.*—A black and grey species with brownish yellow anterior and intermediate legs; the posterior legs are mostly black with partly yellow tibiæ, and the femora are swollen apically, and each has two rows of about ten ventral spines on the swollen part.

Male.—The head is dark grey with black eyes and vertex. The antennæ are black and short, about half the length of the head, and they contain a cylindrical first joint with short black hairs; the second joint is about half the length of the first; the third joint is compressed, apically pointed, and about as long as the first. The proboscis is black, about as long as the head, and the palpi are black, long, erect, and reach about as far as the upturned portion of the proboscis. The eyes are approximate near the black ocellar triangle and contiguous near the greyish antennal triangle. The face between the antennæ and the oral margin is very small, and extends as a thin strip to the cheeks. The occiput is slightly concave above and very convex below; it contains a row of minute marginal bristles and sparse white pubescence.

The thorax is black dorsally and greyish laterally with a black lateral ridge, and is covered with sparse short whitish hairs. Ventrally the thorax is greyish with black on the sutures between the sclerites, and contains some very sparse whitish hairs, the most perceptible of which consist of two rows of minute whitish bristly hairs on the mesonotum, one of which is under the lateral ridge and the other on that portion adjacent to the roots of the wings.

The compressed abdomen is black, with tracings of greyish lateral markings and a grey venter; the abdomen widens apically, as is usual in the genus, and terminates in a rather complex genitalia.

All the legs have their coxæ greyish, and the remainder of the anterior and intermediate legs are brownish yellow, and are stained with fuscous at the base and on the tarsi; the pulvilli are yellow. The hind femora are black with the apical third swollen, and they contain a ventral yellowish brown mark at the base of the swollen part, and beyond this each has two parallel rows of about ten ventral spines. The hind tibiæ are yellow with the base and apex broadly black; the tarsi are black with the pulvilli yellowish.

The wings are hyaline, and the halteres obscure brownish.

Female.—The female is similar to the male, but differs by the eyes being separated and the front greyish, and also the abdomen is not perceptibly clubbed.

Length.—Male and female, 8 mm.

Hab.—New South Wales, Blue Mountains, Blackheath; two males and one female were taken on flowering shrubs on the 25th November, 1919.

Type.—The male holotype and the female allotype are in the Australian Museum.

### Genus *Antoniaustralia*, Becker.

*Antoniaustralia*, Becker, Ann. Mus. Zool., St. Petersburg, xvii., 1912, p. 459.

### *Antoniaustralia hermanni*, Becker.

*Antoniaustralia hermanni*, Becker, Ann. Mus. Zool., St. Petersb., xvii., 1912, p. 459, fig.

Note.—This species is not represented in the collections under revision.

## Genus *Marmasoma*, White.

*Marmasoma*, White, Proc. Roy. Soc. Tasm., 1916, p. 188.

*Marmasoma sumptuosa*, White. (Pl. XVI., figs. 5, 6, and 7.)

*Marmasoma sumptuosa*, White, Proc. Roy. Soc. Tasm., 1916, p. 190.

*Description.*—Female. Similar to the male, eyes widely separated; the front is similar to the rest of the head in colour and vestiture, and contains about twelve black bristles; the abdomen is more conspicuously clothed with scales, and the apex contains a protruding lamella above.

*Hab.*—Tasmania, Brown's Cave Valley, off the Bagdad Valley. One male and one female allotype, taken on the 25th October, 1914.

*Type.*—The female allotype is in the Australian Museum.

## Genus *Eclimus*, Loew.

*Eclimus*, Loew, Stett. Ent. Zeit., v., 1844, p. 154.

*Note.*—The Australian species placed in this genus is represented by a single specimen which has the antennæ apparently mutilated; it is possible that this character is the result of an abortion due to an agency acting during the pupal, or less likely the emerging from the pupal, stage. The insect was captured in this condition by the writer, and the extremely short third joint of the antennæ was noted at the time whilst the insect was still alive. Probably the normal form of the antennæ is similar to that of other species placed under the genus *Eclimus*.

*Eclimus longipalpis*, sp. nov. (Pl. XVII., figs. 13, 14, and 15.)

*Description.*—The male is a black insect with short black pile; the thorax and scutellum have a little depressed yellow pile, and the whole insect ventrally is greyish. The wings are hyaline with a small fuscous spot at the base of the cubital vein, and a large black area beyond the apical half of the wing reaching from the costa to the discal cell.

Male.—The head is black with a greyish tomentum covering the face reaching to the cheeks, and is traceable on the antennæ. The antennæ consist of a rather long first joint, the second joint is a quarter the length of the first, and the third joint is scarcely longer than the second, and the apex is truncate, receding from the dorsal to the ventral surface, and the edge appears to be crowned with minute spines; the character of the third joint is unlike that of a Bombylid, and may be due to an abortion as explained under the genus. The black proboscis is about twice the length of the head, and the palpi, also black, reach to three-quarters the length of the proboscis.  The eyes are contiguous near the ocellar triangle and slightly separated near the antennæ.  In the oral aperture there is a pronouncedly rounded tubercle which contains a moustache of hairs which are white and predominantly black in colour. The face protrudes beyond the eyes, is free from hairs except on the cheeks, which contain a beard of long white hairs which merge into the long black hairs situated on the convex occiput and on the vertex.

The thorax dorsally contains a black  vestiture  of a velvety appearance and some black hairs; also there are some short depressed yellow hairs mostly confined to the median line.  Ventrally some long white hairs are present, and are more abundant on the mesopleura.  The scutellum is black and margined greyish, which colour extends to the humeral callus; depressed yellow pubescence is uniformly distributed and the lateral hairs are whitish.

The abdomen, containing  nine  segments, is  velvety black, and the incisions mostly have white pile.  From the third segment the depressed black pile becomes bristle-like, and on the last three segments these bristles are longer and more erect.  Ventrally the abdomen is grey as far as the seventh segment and has long whitish hairs.

The legs are very long and black, sparsely covered with white tomentum; there are very long white hairs on the coxæ and femora, and very short black spines on the other segments.

The wings are hyaline, and have a large fuscous blotch, which is bounded by the costal vein, the upper cubital fork, the base of the second submarginal cell, half the length of the first posterior cell, the base of the second and third posterior cells, and from thence by a more or less direct line to the costa.  There is a small spot at the base of the cubital vein.  The halteres are obscure yellowish brown.

*Length.*—7 mm.

*Hab.*—New South Wales, Botany Bay, La Perouse.  One male taken on a flowering shrub on the 8th December, 1918.

*Type.*—The unique male holotype is in the  Australian Museum.

## BOMBYLIINÆ.

### Genus *Cyrtomorpha*, White.

*Cyrtomorpha*, White, Proc. Roy. Soc. Tasm., 1916, p. 185.

### *Cyrtomorpha paganica*, White.

*Cyrtomorpha paganica*, White, Proc. Roy. Soc. Tasm., 1916, p. 186, fig. 30.

*Hab.*—Tasmania, Bellerive, near Hobart. Three specimens were collected on a coastal sand-dune on the 25th January, 1918; they were hovering over and settling on bare spaces amongst foliage, but owing to their small size they were extremely difficult to see even when settled on the bare patches.

*Note.*—White described the species from a single specimen which he considered to be a male; one of the three specimens examined has the male genitalia slightly exserted, and this determines the sex; the eyes are uniformly separated in all three specimens, and therefore probably all three specimens are males.

### Genus *Geron*, Meigen.

*Geron*, Meigen, System. Beschreib., ii., 1920, p. 223. *Id.*, White, Proc. Roy. Soc. Tasm., 1916, p. 186.

### *Geron australis*, Macquart.

*Geron australis*, Macquart, Dipt. Exot., ii. (1), 1840, p. 118, Pl. xiii., fig. 2.

*Geron dispar*, Macquart, Dipt. Exot., suppl. 4, 1850, p. 122, Pl. xi., fig 13. *Id.*, White, Proc. Roy. Soc. Tasm., 1916, p. 187.

*Geron cothurnatus*, Bigot, Ann. Soc. Ent. France (7), xli., 1892, p. 374.

*Geron hilaris*, White, Proc. Roy. Soc. Tasm., 1916, p. 188, text fig. 31.

*Synonymy.*—*Geron australis* is described from Port Jackson, and specimens from the locality and from New South Wales generally show a wide range of variation in size and characters, and there are no satisfactory characters whereby they can be divided into more than one species. Tasmanian specimens of *Geron dispar*, Macquart, are of a larger average size, but again show the same range of size, and cannot be divided from those of New South Wales. Specimens agreeing with the description of *Geron hilaris*, White, are represented in the collection under revision from New South Wales, but not from Tasmania, the type locality; nevertheless, there can be little doubt but that *G. hilaris*, White, does not represent a distinct species. *Geron cothurnatus*, Bigot, was placed as a synonym of *G. dispar*, Macquart, by White, and this is undoubtedly the correct position.

E

*Hab.*—New South Wales, Victoria, and Tasmania. This is one of the commonest species of the *Bombyliidæ*, is represented in most collections, and the dates range from November to April.

### Genus *Acreotrichus*, Macquart.

*Acreotrichus*, Macquart, Dipt. Exot., suppl. 4, 1849, p. 121.
  *Id.*, Becker, Ann. Mus., St. Petersb., xvii., 1912, p. 488.

#### *Acreotrichus gibbicornis*, Macquart.

*Acreotrichus gibbicornis*, Macquart, Dipt. Exot., suppl. 4, 1849, p. 121, Pl. xi., fig. 11.  *Id.*, Schiner, Reise Novara, 1868, p. 138. *Id.*, Froggatt, Austr. Ins., 1907, p. 297. *Id.*, Becker, Ann. Mus. Zool. St. Petersb., xvii., 1912, p. 488.

*Acreotrichus fusicornis*, Macquart, Dipt. Exot., suppl. 4, 1849, p. 122, Pl. xi., fig. 12.  *Id.*, Froggatt, Austr. Ins., 1907, p. 207.

*Acreotrichus inappendiculatus*, Bigot, Ann. Soc. Ent. France (7), lxi., 1892, p. 366.

*Synonymy.*—*A. fusicornis*, Macquart, is the female of *A. gibbicornis*, Macquart; specimens have been taken in copula on many occasions, and thus the sex relationship has been established. Specimens in the Macleay Museum were labelled with their sexes denoted, and the label conveying the synonymy was probably written by Skuse or Masters.

The description of *A. inappendiculatus*, Bigot, was probably taken from a female—not a male as stated in the description—of this species.

*Hab.*—New South Wales; Sydney.   This is the first species of Bombylid to appear in the spring, and it continues on the wing through the summer; it occurs everywhere where wild flowers are abundant, and at times twenty or thirty specimens can be taken with one sweep of the net, and indeed sometimes they are so abundant that they continuously divert one's attention from other insects.

### Genus *Phthiria*, Meigen.

*Phthiria*, Meigen, Ill. Mag. Ins., ii., 1803, p. 268.

#### *Phthiria hilaris*, Walker.   (Pl. XVI., fig. 8.)

*Phthiria hilaris*, Walker, Ins. Saund. Dipt., 1856, p. 194.

*Phthiria lineifera*, Walker, Trans. Ent. Soc. Lond., iv., 1857, p. 146.

*Phthiria pallipes*, Bigot, Ann. Soc. Ent. France (7), xli., 1892, p. 367.

*Synonymy.*—Apparently all the descriptions were taken from one variable species.

*Description.*—Female. A yellow and black species of very variable colour pattern; the eyes are widely separated.

Male.—This sex has not hitherto been described; it is of small size, and obscure black in colour with yellow markings restricted to the apex of the abdominal segments.

The head is black, the eyes are contiguous, the ocellar triangle is very small, and contains a little black pubescence; the antennal triangle and the face seen laterally stand prominently forward in front of the eyes. The antennæ are about as long as the head; the first joint is nearly twice the length of the second; the third joint is twice the length of the basal joints united and contains a minute subapical dorsal arista. The face, front, and antennæ as far as the middle of the third segment are covered with long black pubescence. The black pubescence on the cheeks extends into the black and yellow pubescence on the upper half of the occiput.

The thorax and scutellum are covered with a velvety black vestiture, and with long pubescence reflecting a whitish or reddish colour according to the angle at which it is viewed.

Dorsally the abdomen contains a velvety black vestiture, and the apices of the segments are margined yellow laterally; ventrally the abdomen is mostly yellow, but the bases of the last three segments and a pair of spots at the base of the two prior segments are black. The whole abdomen is covered with a similar pubescence to that of the thorax.

The legs are black; a pubescence similar to that on the thorax extends to the coxæ and femora, and merges into the fuscous pubescence on the tibiæ and tarsi.

The wings are hyaline, but there is a deep yellow tinge in the mediastinal cell.

*Length.*—Male, 5 mm.

*Hab.*—New South Wales; the allotype male, described above, was taken at Blackheath on the 25th November, 1919; there are three paratype males and six females from the same locality taken between the 16th and 25th November, 1919. Further specimens are represented in various collections under revision.

Victoria; Timboon, one female in the collection of Dr. Ferguson was collected by H. W. Davey.

*Type.*—The allotype male is in the Australian Museum.

*Note.*—The head characters read similar to those of *Acreotrichus gibbicornis*, Macquart, which differs, however, by the pubescence of the face being exceptionally long, and the third joint of the antennæ containing some long hairs on the apical half and little, if any, on the basal half. *Acreotrichus inappendiculatus*, Bigot. described from a specimen said to be a male cannot belong here, as the description conforms almost entirely to that of a female *A. gibbicornis.*

There are several apparently distinct species in the genera *Acreotrichus* and *Phthiria* in the collections under revision, and they show that their respective genera cannot be separated by the usual characters adopted. Those characters given by Bigot and Becker in their respective keys do not hold good for Australian species. The appendix of the upper branch of the cubital fork can be used as a somewhat imperfect guide, as it is rarely absent in *Acreotrichus* and never present on *Phthiria*. The females can be readily distinguished by the presence or absence, respectively, in these genera, of long thick pubescence on the front and face.

## Genus *Dischistus*, Loew.

*Dischistus*, Loew, Neue Beitr., iii., 1855, p. 45.  *Id.*, White, Proc. Roy. Soc. Tasm., 1916, p. 192 (in key).

*Note.*—It appears that the characters of *Sparnopolius limbatus*, Bigot, belong to those given to the genus *Dischistus* in the key, and on this account Bigot's species is placed under this genus.

Schiner states that a new genus will be required for *Dischistus crassilabris*, Macquart.

There are several undescribed species in various collections that come within the characters strictly attributed to the genus *Dischistus*, but until the positions of those already described can be ascertained it is inadvisable to add new descriptions that ultimately may cause further hindrance without benefiting the taxonomy of the group.

### *Dischistus crassilabris*, Macquart.

*Bombylius crassilabris*, Macquart, Dipt. Exot., suppl. 5, 1854, p. 77, Pl. iv., fig. 1.

*Dischistus crassilabris*, Schiner, Novara Reise, 1868, p. 138.

*Note.*—This species is represented in various collections.

? *Dischistus limbatus*, Bigot.

*Sparnopolius limbatus*, Bigot, Ann. Soc. Ent. France (7), lxi., 1892, p. 369.

*Note.*—This species has not been recognised in the various collections under revision.

## Genus *Systœchus*, Loew.

*Systœchus*, Loew, Neue Beitr., iii., 1855, p. 45. *Id.*, White. Proc. Roy. Soc. Tasm., 1916, p. 196.

*Choristus*, Walker, Ins. Saund. Dipt., 1852, p. 197.

*Note.*—There are fourteen names belonging to species that undoubtedly conform to the characters of the genus *Systœchus*, and of these only one has hitherto been placed in synonymy.

In the collections under revision three species are recognised as distinct, and conform in their characters to described species. A number of undoubtedly distinct species do not conform to the descriptions.

### *Systœchus platyurus*, Walker. (Pl. XVI., fig. 9.)

*Bombylius platyurus*, Walker, List Dipt. B.M., ii., 1849, p. 286.

*Bombylius crassus*, Walker, *ibidem*, p. 287.

*Systœchus crassus*, White, Proc. Roy. Soc. Tasm., 1916, p. 196, text fig. 34.

*Bombylius notatipennis*, Macquart, Dipt. Exot., suppl. 5, 1854, p. 78, Pl. iv., fig. 2.

*Bombylius punctipennis*, Thomson, Eug. Resa, Dipt., 1868, p. 487.

*Synonymy.*—There appear to be three distinctive forms of this species; one, *B. platyurus*, Walker, from Western Australia, was placed by White as a synonym of the East Australian form, *B. crassus*, Walker. The Tasmanian form was described by White as *S. crassus*. The names given by Macquart and Thomson evidently belong to the same species.

### *Systœchus retustus*, Walker.

*Bombylius retustus*, Walker, List Dipt., B.M., ii., 1849, p. 286.

*Bombylius sericans*, Macquart, Dipt. Exot., suppl. 4, 1850, p. 116, Pl. xi., fig. 3.

*Bombylius penicillatus*, Macquart, *ibidem*, p. 118, Pl. xi., fig. 7.

*Systœchus pausarius*, Jænnicke, Abhand. der Senck nat. G., vi., 1867, p. 348.

*Systœchus callynthrophorus*, Schiner, Reise Novara, 1868, p. 137.

*Bombylius spinipes*, Thomson, Eug. Resa, Dipt., 1868, p. 488.

*Synonymy.*—The above synonymy appears to be correct. The species is very common and very variable in size. In Dr. Ferguson's collection a female is labelled by White as *S. vetustus*, Walker, and a second female with fuscous spots traceable on the wings and with the front slightly wider is named *S. pencillatus*, Macquart. Macquart's description does not appear to agree with White's determination, as these characters are not mentioned; the length of the proboscis is too variable to be used for identification purposes, and therefore it seems advisable to consider Macquart's two names as belonging to probable variations of the same species.

### *Systœchus distinctus*, Walker.

*Bombylius distinctus*, Walker, Ins. Saund. Dipt., 1850, p. 201.

*Note.*—Three males and one female from Sydney, in the Macleay Museum, probably belong here; the female has an exceptionally wide head, and both sexes are uniformly light brown in colour.

### *Systœchus albiceps*, Macquart.

*Bombylius albiceps*, Macquart, Dipt. Exot., suppl. 3, 1848, p. 36.

### *Systœchus bifrons*, Walker.

*Choristus bifrons*, Walker, Ins. Saund. Dipt., 1850, p. 198, Pl. v., fig. 5.

### *Systœchus leucopygus*, v. d. Wulp.

*Systœchus leucopygus*, v. d. Wulp, Notes Leyden Mus., vii., 1883, p. 86.

### Genus *Sisyromyia*, White.

*Sisyromyia*, White, Proc. Roy. Soc. Tasm., 1916, p. 197.

*Note.*—Under this genus seventeen descriptions are placed. Two of these White placed to synonymy, and five further synonyms are suggested here. Three species are definitely recognised in the collections under revision as belonging to described species, a fourth species is temporarily retained under a fourth name, and six descriptions by Walker have not been recognised.

*Sisyromyia auratus*, Walker.

*Bombylius auratus*, Walker, List Dipt. B.M., ii., 1849, p. 289.

*Sisyromyia aurata*, White, Proc. Roy. Soc. Tasm., 1916, p. 198.

*Bombylius crassirostris*, Macquart, Dipt. Exot., suppl. 4., 1850, p. 117, Pl. xi., fig. 5.

*Bombylius albavitta*, Macquart, Dipt. Exot., suppl. 4, 1850, p. 117, Pl. xi., fig. 4.

*Bombylius loewii*, Jænnicke, Abh. der Senck nat. G., vi., 1867, p. 345.

*Bombylius pycnorhynchus*, Thomson, Eug. Resa, Dipt., 1868, p. 486.

*Bombylius lobalis*, Thomson, *ibid.*, p. 487.

*Bombylius scutellaris*, Thomson, *ibid.*, p. 488.

*Synonymy.*—A very variable group of Bombylids, including a variety with sulphur-coloured hair, and another with deep red hair, appears to form a species to which the above descriptions agree; it is possible, however, that some of these descriptions will ultimately be found to belong to *Sisyromyia decoratus*, Walker, or an allied species.

*Sisyromyia decoratus*, Walker.

*Bombylius decoratus*, Walker, List Dipt., B.M., ii., 1849, p. 291.

*Note.*—This species was described from Western Australia, but a specimen identified by White is in Dr. Ferguson's collection, and was taken in New South Wales. The specimen does not agree very well with Walker's description, but nevertheless it is retained in this position until it can be compared with the Western Australian form. The anterior border of the wing is fuscous, and is sharply defined from the hyaline area of the wing, whilst in *S. auratus*, Walker, the darker area on the anterior border of the wing is suffused.

*Sisyromyia brevirostris*, Macquart.

*Bombylius brevirostris*, Macquart, Dipt. Exot., suppl 4. 1850, p. 119, Pl. xi., fig. 9. *Id.* (?), Walker, Ins. Saund. Dipt., 1850, p. 202.

*Sisyromyia brevirostris*, White, Proc. Roy. Soc. Tasm., 1916, p. 199.

*Systæchus culabiatus*, Bigot, Ann. Soc. Ent. France (7), lxi., 1892, p. 366.

*Synonymy.*—The above synonymy is given on the authority of White.

### Sisyromyia pinguis, Walker.

Bombylius pinguis, Walker, List Dipt. B.M., ii., 1849, p. 290.

*Hab.*—Western Australia; King George's Sound; one female in the Macleay Museum conforms to the description.

### Sisyromyia altus, Walker.

Bombylius altus, Walker, List Dipt. B.M., ii., 1849, p. 288.

### Sisyromyia antecedens, Walker.

Bombylius antecedens, Walker, ibidem, p. 293.

### Sisyromyia immutatus, Walker.

Bombylius immutatus, Walker, ibidem, p. 292.

### Sisyromyia primogenitus, Walker.

Bombylius primogenitus, Walker, ibidem, p. 292.

### Sisyromyia rutilus, Walker.

Bombylius rutilus, Walker, ibidem, p. 289.

### Sisyromyia tetratrichus, Walker.

Bombylius tetratrichus, Walker, ibidem, p. 291.

### Genus Bombylius, Linnæus.

Bombylius, Linnæus, Syst. Nat. Edit., x., 1758, p. 606.  *Id.*,
      White. Proc. Roy. Soc. Tasm., 1916, p. 192.

*Note.*—There are fourteen descriptions that apparently belong to the genus *Bombylius* in its restricted sense; of these seven are recognisable in the collections under revision, three probably belong to synonyms, and five have not been recognised.

### Bombylius fuscanus, Macquart.

Bombylius fuscanus, Macquart, Dipt. Exot., suppl. 4, 1850,
      p. 119.  *Id.*, White, Proc. Roy. Soc. Tasm., 1916,
      p. 193.

*Note.*—Under this species White suggests that Walker's *B. matutinus* is a synonym, but no species of the genus *Bombylius* is definitely known to occur both in Australia and Tasmania. although some species from these localities are very closely allied, and therefore the suggested synonymy is not accepted here.  *B. fuscanus* is a dull uniformly coloured species.

### Bombylius tenuicornis, Macquart.

Bombylius tennicornis, Macquart, Dipt. Exct., suppl. 1, 1846, p. 116. *Id.*, White, Proc. Roy. Sec. Tasm., 1916, p. 192.

Bombylius matutinus, Walker, List Dipt. B.M., ii., 1849, p. 281.

Bombylius australianus, Bigot, Ann. Ent. Soc. France (7), lxi., 1892, p. 364.

*Synonymy.*—For the species allied to *B. fuscanus,* Macquart, the name *B. tenuicornis,* Macquart, is utilised. Macquart's localities are Australia and Tasmania, but the second locality was evidently taken from a species he described from Tasmania as *B. fuscanus,* four years later. *B. matutinus,* Walker, and probably *B. australianus,* Bigot, also belong here.

*Note.*—This species is of a uniform colour containing dense black and rather bright reddish pubescence; the descriptions by the various authors were taken from denuded specimens. The general appearance of the species is like that of *B. fuscanus,* but brighter in tone.

### Bombylius viduus, Walker.

Bombylius viduus, Walker, Ins. Saund. Dipt., 1850, p. 199.

Bombylius palliolatus, White, Proc. Roy. Soc. Tasm., 1916, p. 194.

*Synonymy.*—White overlooked the description of *B. viduus,* Walker, which agrees with *B. palliolatus,* White, and is also from Tasmania.

### Bombylius aureolatus, Walker.

Bombylius aureolatus, Walker, Trans. Ent. Soc. Lond., iv., 1857, p. 145.

*Note.*—This beautiful species is rather common round Sydney; it has three longitudinal silvery stripes on the abdomen and a pair of similar lateral stripes on the thorax.

### Bombylius hilaris, Walker.

Bombylius hilaris, Walker, List Dipt. B.M., ii., 1849, p. 274.

*Note.*—This beautiful Western Australian species has a colour pattern which is well described by Walker.

*Bombylius rubriventris*, Bigot.

*Bombylius rubriventris*, Bigot, Ann. Ent. Soc. France (7), lxi., 1892, p. 365.

*Note.*—This species was described from Sydney, but two specimens from King George's Sound agree rather well with Bigot's description and belong to or near this species. There are six specimens in the Macleay Museum which belong to or near here, and these are labelled from Cape York, Queensland; another specimen is from South Australia. These specimens range from 10 mm. long, and have a yellowish pubescence on a reddish ground colour and a black stripe on the abdomen. The thorax is black on the specimens in the Macleay Museum.

*Bombylius pictipennis*, Macquart.

*Bombylius pictipennis*, Macquart, Dipt. Exot., suppl. 4, 1850, p. 118.

*Hab.*—New South Wales; Sydney, August, 1915, and Newcastle.

*Note.*—This species is represented by two male specimens, numbered 234 and 235, in Dr. Ferguson's collection, and they were named by White as *B. hilaris*, Walker, but they differ from Walker's species in the wing markings. Three further specimens are in the Macleay Museum.

*Bombylius chrysendetus*, White.

*Bombylius chrysendetus*, White, Proc. Roy. Soc. Tasm., 1916, p. 195.

*Note.*—This species is not represented in the collections under revision.

*Bombylius nanus*, Walker.

*Bombylius nanus*, Walker, List Dipt. B.M., ii., 1849, p. 278.

*Note.*—This species is not represented in the collections under revision. White compared his *B. chrysendetus* with it.

*Bombylius albicinctus*, Macquart.

*Bombylius albicinctus*, Macquart, Dipt. Exot., suppl. 2, 1847, p. 54.

*Note.*—This species, described from Tasmania, is not represented in the collections under revision.

## Bombylius consobrinus, Macquart.

Bombylius consobrinus, Macquart, Dipt. Exot., suppl. 2, 1847, p. 54.

*Note.*—The description of this species is very inferior and short. It may be a small specimen of *B. tenuicornis*, Macquart, and moreover it is significant to note that the localities given by Macquart in both cases are "Australia and "Tasmania." It is probable that two species were mixed under one name, as a species of the genus is not definitely known from both localities.

### Species of uncertain generic position.

Bombylius australis, Guerin, Voy. Coq. (2), ii., 1830, p. 294, Pl. xx., fig. 4.

### Species erroneously recorded as Australian.

*Exoprosopa collaris*, Wiedemann. Kertesz (Cat. Dipt., v., 1909) gives "India or Australia" as localities for this species, but the latter locality was evidently intended for Africa. The species is placed as a synonym of *E. lar*, Fabricius, by Brunetti in the Fauna Brit. Ind., Dipt.-Brachycera, i., 1920.

*Anthrax semiatra* (Hoffmann), Macquart, Dipt. Exot., suppl. 4, 1850, p. 113. Hoffmann's species is referable to *Anthrax morio*, Linnæus, which is known from Europe and North America; Macquart recorded it from Australia.

## CYRTIDÆ.

*Characters.*—The family contains a group of abnormal flies of diverse shapes. The head is composed almost entirely of eyes, and is situated well down on the thorax. The antennæ are minute or very large, and may be placed close to the mouth or as far up as near the summit of the head, and the eyes may be contiguous on either side or on both sides of the antennæ. The thorax and abdomen are usually inflated, the squama large, covering the halteres, and the wing venation may be rudimentary or complex.

*Note.*—The family contains at least seven described Australian species, which have been given twenty-four specific names. There are six genera recognised, and one of these, *Epicerina*, may be identical with the genus *Panops*. The species are generally rare, usually variable in colour, and the sexes so far ascertained are dimorphic.

In the present paper new species are not described, but an attempt is made to complete the synonymy of those already known, and to collect together a complete catalogue of references. The species have been well illustrated by various authors, and therefore figures are not given with this catalogue.

### Key to the Genera of the family Cyrtidæ.

1. The antennæ very small and inconspicuous, and with a terminal style.         ·      2.

     The antennæ large and conspicuous and without a terminal style; eyes bare.      4.

2. The costa of the wing curved forward and angulate; the eyes pubescent.      *Pterodontia.*

     The costa of the wing normal.      3.

3. The venation more or less complete; the eyes pubescent.      *Nothra.*

     The venation obscure and vestigial; the eyes bare.

                             *Oncodes.*

4. The abdomen elongate and with the basal half strongly constricted.      *Leucopsina.*

     The abdomen oval, or if elongate then constricted between each segment.      5.

5. The proboscis short.      *Epicerina.*

     The proboscis long.      *Panops.*

### Genus *Pterodontia*, Gray.

*Pterodontia*, Gray, in Griff. Animal Kingd., xv., 1882, part 34. p. 779, Pl. cxxviii., fig. 3. *Id.*, White, Proc. Roy. Soc. Tasm., 1914, p. 68.

*Characters.*—The eyes are densely pubescent; the antennæ are very small and have a terminal style; the abdomen is bladder-form, *i.e.*, inflated, in appearance. The costa is curved forward and angulate at about four-fifths the length of the wing; the venation is complete, and the veins are comparatively few in number.

*Type.*—*P. flavipes*, Gray .. .. .. .. .. .. .. America.

### *Pterodontia mellii*, Erichson.

*Pterodontia flavipes*, Macquart (*nec* Grey), Dipt. Exot., i. (2), 1838, p. 175; and ii. (1), 1840, Pl. i., fig. 2; and ii. (3), 1843, Pl. xxxiv., fig. 3 (preoccupied).

*Pterodontia mellii*, Erichson, Entomog., i., 1840, p. 163. *Id.*, Walker, List Dipt. B.M., vi., suppl. 2, 1854, p. 348. *Id.*, Westwood, Trans. Ent. Soc. Lond., 1876, p. 513. *Id.*, Froggatt, Austra. Ins., 1897, p. 297.

*Pterodontia macquarti*, Westwood, Trans. Ent. Soc. Lond.,
1848, p. 97. *Id.*, Walker, List Dipt. B.M., vi., suppl.
2, p. 348. *Id.*, Westwood, Trans. Ent. Soc. Lond.,
1876, p. 513.

*Synonymy.*—It seems certain that only one species of
this genus has been described from Australia, and probably
the species described by White as *P. variegata* is identical,
but as specimens are not available for comparison the Tasmanian species is retained as distinct.

The name *P. macquarti*, Westwood, was created to take
the place of the preoccupied *P. flavipes*, Macquart, but *P.
mellii*, Erichson, takes priority.

### *Pterodontia variegata*, Walker.

*Pterodontia variegata*, White, Proc. Roy. Soc. Tasm., 1914,
p. 68, text fig. 10.

*Status.*—The holotype of this species is unique, and is
in the collection of Mr. F. M. Littler. When a series of
specimens is available for comparison this species will undoubtedly be found to be identical with *P. mellii*, Erichson.

### Genus *Nothra*, Westwood.

*Nothra*, Westwood, Trans. Ent. Soc. Lond., 1876, p. 514.

*Characters.*—The eyes contain long conspicuous pubescence; the antennæ are situated near the mouth, are very
small, and have a terminal style; the abdomen is bladder-
form. The wings are normal in shape, and the veins are
comparatively few in number and complete; the venation is
similar to that of the genus *Pterodontia*.

Type.—*N. bicolor*, Westwood .. .. .. Australia.

### *Nothra bicolor*, Westwood.

*Nothra bicolor*, Westwood, Trans. Ent. Soc. Lond., 1876,
p. 515, Pl. vi., fig. 4.

*Hab.*—There are two specimens from South Australia
in the Australian Museum.

### Genus *Oncodes*, Latrielle.

*Ogcodes*, Latrielle, Precis caract. gen. d'Ins., 1796, p. 154.

*Henops*, Meigen, Ill. Mag. f. Ins., ii., 1803, p. 266.

*Acrodes*, Froggatt, Austr. Ins., 1897, p. 298.

*Oncodes*, White, Proc. Roy. Soc. Tasm., 1914, p. 69.

*Characters.*—The eyes are bare; the antennæ are situated near the mouth, which is vestigial, and are very small,

inconspicuous, and terminate in a style. The venation is very incomplete and rudimentary.

Type.—*O. gibbosus*, Linnæus .. .. .. ..    Europe.

## *Oncodes basilis*, Walker.

*Henops basilis*, Walker, Ins. Saund. Dipt., 1852, p. 203.

*Oncodes basilis*, Hardy, Proc. Roy. Soc. Tasm., 1917, p. 60.

*Ogcodes darwinii*, Westwood, Trans. Ent. Soc. Lond., 1867, p. 516.

*Ogcodes fortumni*, Westwood, *ibidem*.

*Ogcodes ignava*, Westwood, *ibidem*.

*Ogcodes tasmanica*, Westwood, *ibidem*.

*Acrodes fumatus*, Froggatt, Austr. Ins., 1897, p. 298. ·

*Ogcodes doddi*, Wandolleck, Trans. Ent. Soc. Lond., 1906, p. 131, figs.

*Oncodes flavescens*, White, Proc. Roy. Soc. Tasm., 1914, p. 70, text fig. 11. *Id.*, Hardy, Proc. Roy. Soc. Tasm., 1916, p. 267.

*Oncodes nigrinervis*, White, *ibidem*, 1914, p. 71.

*Oncodes ater*, White, *ibidem*, 1914, p. 72.

*Oncodes pygmæus*, White, *ibidem*, 1914, p. 72.

*Synonymy.*—The above synonymy has already been published (see Hardy, 1917), with the exception of *Acrodes fumatus*, Froggatt. Mr. Froggatt informs me that *Acrodes* is a misprint for *Oncodes; Oncodes fumatus* was used by Erichson for a European species, and it is unlikely that the Australian species is identical with it. Mr. Froggatt's description conforms to that of a male, and specimens in the Agricultural Department under his name are females.

## Genus *Leucopsina*, Westwood.

*Leucopsina*, Westwood, Trans. Ent. Soc. Lond., 1876, p. 510.

*Characters.*—The eyes are bare; the antennæ are long, three jointed and without a terminal style, they are situated high up on the head, but are separated from the ocelli by the contiguous eyes. The face is linear, and the proboscis long. The wings are normal in shape, and have a rather complex and complete venation. The abdomen is elongate and club-form.

Type.—*L. odyneroides*, Westwood .. ..    Australia.

*Leucopsina odyneroides,* Westwood.

*Leucopsina odyneroides,* Westwood, Trans. Ent. Soc. Lond., 1876, p. 510, Pl. v., fig. 3.

## Genus *Epicerina,* Macquart.

*Epicerina,* Macquart, Dipt. Exct., suppl. 4, 1849, p. 97.

*Characters.*—The eyes are bare; the antennæ are long and without a style, they are situated near the ocelli; the proboscis is short; the abdomen is bladder-form. The wings have a rather complex venation similar to that of the genus *Panops,* Lamarck.

Type.—*E. nigricornis,* Macquart .. .. Tasmania.

*Status.*—The genus *Epicerina* differs from the genus *Panops* by the proboscis being short, and in other respects the generic characters agree. The genus is unknown in recent collections, but it is certain that it will not maintain its position as a separate genus when more is known concerning it.

### *Epicerina nigricornis,* Macquart.

*Epicerina nigricornis,* Macquart, Dipt. Exot., suppl. 4, 1849, p. 98, Pl. ix., fig. 8. *Id.,* Hardy, Proc. Roy. Sec. Tasm., 1917, p. 61.

## Genus *Panops,* Lamarck.

*Panops,* Lamarck, Ann. Mus. d'Hist. Nat., iii., 1804, p. 266, Pl. xxii., fig. 3.

*Mesophysa,* Macquart, Dipt. Exot., i. (2), 1838, p. 166.

*Characters.*—The eyes are bare; the antennæ are situated close to the ocelli, are long and without a terminal style; the proboscis is very long. The wings have the venation rather complex and complete. The abdomen in one species is bladder-form, in the other elongate and constricted between the segments.

Type.—*P. baudini,* Lamarck .. .. .. .. Australia.

### *Panops baudini,* Lamarck.

*Panops baudini,* Lamarck, Ann. Mus. d'Hist. Nat., iii., 1804, p. 226, Pl. xxii., fig. 3. *Id.,* Lamarck, Hist. Nat. sans Vert., iii., 1806, p. 316. *Id.,* Latrielle, Ency. Meth., viii., 1811, p. 710. *Id.,* Latrielle, Dict. d' Hist. Nat., xxiv., p. 467. *Id.,* Wiedemann, Auss. Zweifl. Ins., ii., 1803, p. 19. *Id.,* Macquart, Hist. Nat. Dipt., i., 1834, p. 356. *Id.,* Erichson, Entomogr., i., 1840, p. 141. *Id.,* Walker, List. Dipt. B.M., vi., suppl. 2, 1854, p. 333.

*Mesophysa marginatus*, Macquart, Dipt. Exot., i. (2), 1838,
p. 168.

*Mesophysa australasiæ*, Thomson, Eug. Resa, Dipt., 1868,
p. 475.

*Panops lamarckanus*, Westwood, Trans. Ent. Soc. Lond.,
1876, p. 508, Pl. v., fig. 1.

*Synonymy.*—According to the descriptions *Panops baudini*, Lamarck, and *Mesophysa marginatis*, Macquart, were described from male specimens, and *Mesophysa australasiæ*, Thomson, and *Panops lamarckianus*, Westwood, were described from female specimens; all belonging to the same species.

*Hab.*—New South Wales, Sydney.    A pair of specimens in the Macleay Museum bear a label conveying the information that they were taken on Sydney Swamp, and that they are the two sexes of the same species, which is identified as *Panops baudini*, Lamarck.    The identification appears to be correct.    There are two further specimens in the Macleay Museum, and two in the Australian Museum.

### *Panops flavipes*, Latrielle.

*Panops flavipes*, Latrielle, Ency. Meth., viii., 1811, p. 710.
*Id.*, Lamarck, Hist. Nat. sans Vert., iii., 1816, p. 412.
*Id.*, Wiedemann, Auss. Zweifl. Ins., ii., 1830, pp. 20
and 649.    *Id.*, Erichson, Entom., i., 1840, p. 141.
*Id.*, Walker, List Dipt. B.M., vi., suppl. 2, 1854,
p. 333.    *Id.*, Froggatt, Austr. Ins., 1897, p. 297.

*Mesophysa scapularis*, Macquart, Dipt. Exot., i. (2), 1838,
p. 167.

*Hab.*—New South Wales and Victoria.

*Note.*—The specimens examined are invariably males, which suggests that only the distinctive males have been recognised, and the females may be normal to the genus in shape, and either confused with *Panops baudini*, Lamarck, or may have been placed under another genus such as *Epicerina nigricornis*, Macquart.

### LIST OF WORKS.

This list only contains taxonomic works; it includes works containing the original generic descriptions and all those dealing with genera and species described from Australia.

Becker.   St. Petersburg.—Academie imperiale des Sciences.
Musee Zoologique.   Annals xvii., 1912.

Bergroth. Stettiner Entomologische Zeitung, lv., 1894.

**Bigot.** Paris.—Societe Entomologique de France. **Annales:**
      series 6, i., 1881: and series 7, xii., 1892.

Erichson. Entomographien. 1840.

Fabricius. Systema Entomologiæ. 1775.
      Species insectorum, ii., 1781.
      Mantissa Insectorum, ii., 1787.
      Entomologia systematica, 1792-4.
      Systema Antliorum. 1805.

Froggatt. Australian Insects. 1907.

Gray. In Griffith's Animal Kingdom, xv., **1832.**

Gmelin. Linnæus.—Systema naturæ; edit. x., 1790.

Hardy. Royal Society of Tasmania; Papers and Proceed-
      ings for the years 1916 and 1917.

**Hutton.** Catalogues of New Zealand Diptera, Orthoptera,
      Hymenoptera. 1881.

**Jænnicke.** Frankfort on the Main.—Senckenbergische
      Naturforschende Gesellschaft. Abhandlungen.
      vi., 1867.

Kertesz. Catalogus Dipterorum, v., 1909.

Kirby. Annals and Magazine of Natural History, series 5,
      xiii., 1884.

Lamarck. Historie naturelle des Animaux sans vertebres.
      1815-22.
      Paris.—Museum d'Historie Naturelle; Annals, iii.,
      1804.

Latrielle. Precis des caracteres Generiques des Insectes.
      1796.
      Encyclopedie Methodique, viii., 1811.
      Nouveau Dictionnaire d'Historie Naturelle. 1803-5.

Linnæus. Systema Naturæ. Edit. x., 1758.

Loew. Stettiner Entomologische Zeitung, v., 1844.
      Neue Beitrage zur Kenntniss der Dipteren, iii.,
      1855.

**Macleay.** In King's Narrative of a survey of the inter-
      tropical and western coasts of Australia. 1827.

Macquart. Diptere exotique nouveau ou peu connus. (Re-
      published from the Memoires Societe Royale
      Sciences de l'Agriculture et Arts. Lille. 1838-
      54). 1838-54.
      Historie Naturelle **des** Insectes.—Dipteres. i., 1834.
      (Forming one of Roret's "Collection des Suites
      a Buffon.")

F

Meigen.   In Illiger's Magazine fuer Insectenkunde, ii., 1803.

Newman.   The Entomologist, i., 1841.

Osten-Sacken.   Bulletin of the United States Geological Survey (Heyden), iii., 1877.

Smithsonian Institute.—Smithsonian miscellaneous
collections, xvi. (Catalogue of the Described
Diptera of North America, Edit. ii.), 1878.

Rondani.   Archivio per la Zoologia l'anatomia e la fisiologia,
iii., 1863.

Schiner.   Weiner Entomologische Monatschrift, iv., 1860.

Austria-Hungary. — Reise der Oesterreichischen
Fregatte Novara um die Erde, etc. Zoologischer
Theil, ii., Diptera. 1868.

Scopoli.   Entomologia Carniolica. 1763.

Thomson.   Sweden.—Kongliga Svenska Fregatten Eugenies
Resa omkring jorden. Diptera, 1869.

v. d. Wulp.   Hague.—Nederlandsche Entomologische Veree-
niging. Tijdschrift voor Entomologie (2), iii.
(xi.), 1868.

Notes from the Leyden Museum, viii., 1885.

Catalogue of the described Diptera from South
Asia, 1896.

Wandollock.   Entomological Society of London; Transactions
for the year 1906.

Walker.   The Entomological Magazine. ii., 1835.

British Museum (Natural History), Zoology (Diptera). List of the Dipterous insects in the
Museum, ii., 1849; and vi., supplement 2, 1854.

Insecta Saundersiana, i., Diptera. (Part of Saun-
ders' Insecta Saundersiana, 1850-1859). 1850-
56.

The Entomological Society of London; Transactions; new series. iv., 1857.

Westwood.   The Entomological Society of London; Transactions, v., 1848; and for the year 1876.

White.   Royal Society of Tasmania; Papers and proceedings
for the years 1914 and 1916.

Wiedemann.   Nova Dipterorum genera. 1820.

Diptera Exotica. 1821.

Aussereuropaische zweiflugelige Insekten, 1828-30.

## ILLUSTRATIONS.

### PLATE XVI.

Fig. 1. Genus *Hyperalonia;* the antennæ showing a large and well-defined apical style.

Fig. 2. Genus *Anthrax;* the antennæ of a form with a small apical style.

Fig. 3. *Argyramœba maculata,* Macquart; the antennæ showing the typical pencil of hairs at the apex which is to be seen in all species of the genus.

Fig. 4. Genus *Comptosia;* the antennæ.

Fig. 5. *Marmasoma sumptuosa,* White; the head of the male seen from the front.

Fig. 6. *Marmasoma sumptuosa,* White; the head of the female seen laterally.

Fig. 7. *Marmasoma sumptuosa,* White; the head of the female seen from the front.

Fig. 8. *Phthiria hilaris,* Walker; the head of the male seen laterally.

Fig. 9. *Systœchus platyurus,* Walker; the antennæ drawn from a Tasmanian specimen.

### PLATE XVII.

Fig. 10. *Lomatia sobricula,* Walker; a portion of the wing showing the contortion of the radial vein.

Fig. 11. *Oncodocera ampla,* Walker; a portion of the wing showing the contortion of the radial vein.

Fig. 12. *Comptosia sylvana,* Fabricius; a portion of the wing showing the contortion of the radial vein.

Fig. 13. *Eclimus longipalpis, sp. nov.*

Fig. 14. *Eclimus longipalpis;* the head seen from the front.

Fig. 15. *Eclimus longipalpis;* the wing.

Fig. 16. *Systropus clavifemoratus, sp. nov.*

Fig. 17. *Systropus clavifemoratus;* the head of the male.

Fig. 18. *Systropus clavifemoratus;* the head of the female.

Fig. 19. *Systropus clavifemoratus;* the wing.

G

# THE COMPLETION OF THE GENERAL MAGNETIC SURVEY OF AUSTRALIA BY THE CARNEGIE INSTITUTION OF WASHINGTON.

By

CAPT. EDWARD KIDSON, O.B.E., M.Sc.

[Originally written for the Hobart-Melbourne Meeting of the Australasian Association for the Advancement of Science, January, 1921.]*

(Read before the Royal Society of Tasmania, 8th August, 1921.)

The plan of the General Magnetic Survey of Australia by the Department of Terrestrial Magnetism of the Carnegie Institution of Washington was explained in a paper read by the author before the Australasian Association at Melbourne in 1913. As there stated, the object was to secure approximately one station for every 10,000 square miles of territory, or about 300 stations in all, with a uniform distribution over the Continent. Lack of facilities for travelling over large areas of the interior, of course, prevented the execution of this plan in its entirety, but the number and distribution of the stations established by the close of the survey in November, 1914, may be considered very satisfactory under the circumstances.

The finally accepted results are given in the appended table, which is self explanatory. Some have already been published in the volumes of the Department of Terrestrial Magnetism, where descriptions of stations will also be found, but some have not yet appeared in print.

I was assisted at various times during the progress of the work by the following observers:—F. Brown, F. W. Cox, A. L. Kennedy, W. C. Parkinson, and E. N. Webb. In the last column of the Table of Results the observer respon-

---

*Owing to the Shipping Strike, the meeting of the A.A.A.S., which was to have been held in Hobart, had to be held in Melbourne. As a consequence, numerous difficulties had to be overcome. It was found impossible to bring out the ordinary Report of the A.A.A.S. meeting and print all papers. Arrangements were made for certain papers to be read before the Society, and printed in the Papers and Proceedings for 1921.

sible for the observations is shown by his initials. When observations were made jointly by two observers, this fact is shown by the combination of their last initials.

A number of the expeditions made by members of the party entailed a considerable amount of organisation, and work was carried on under conditions which were frequently arduous and occasionally dangerous. The more important of these expeditions were:—(a) One carried out by myself from Wiluna to Hall's Creek, in Western Australia, along the disused Canning Stock Route; (b) Expeditions by Mr. Brown down the Yorke Peninsula, and by launch along the north coast of the Coburg Peninsula (N.T.); (c) A journey by Mr. Parkinson by Ford motor along the No. 1 Rabbit Proof Fence in Western Australia; (d) Mr. Kennedy's camel trip along the line of the transcontinental railway from Port Augusta. Short accounts of these expeditions, as well as of the instrumental equipment, will be published in the works of the Department of Terrestrial Magnetism.

On my journey along the Canning Stock Route an earth inductor was used extensively in the field for the first time, and gave excellent results, without any mishaps, proving itself far superior to the dip-circle.

Towards the end of 1914 the party was concentrated at Perth, and outstanding computations were finished up and instruments compared. The writer then returned to Washington, and other members of the party were assigned to work in other countries. A comparison at Washington between the Department standard instruments and some of those used in Australia gave a final check on the Australian observations. The various comparisons with standard instruments in Washington before and after going to the field, and between instruments while in the field, gave very satisfactory results. With the exception of dip-circles, the needles of which are apt to become slightly rusted, and less accurate in consequence, the instrumental corrections for the various elements remained small, and almost constant.

Considerable assistance was received in the execution of the work by all members of my party from the Government officials in each State.

| Station. | Date. | Lat. S. | Long. E. | Declination | Dip. S. | Horizontal Intensity. | Obs'r. |
|---|---|---|---|---|---|---|---|
| | | | | | | C.G.S | |
| Thursday Island, B | Oct. 21, 1912 | 10 34.5 | 112 13 | 4 59.0E | .. | .. | FWC |
| Thursday Island, C | Oct. 21, 1912 | 10 34.5 | 142 13 | 4 59.4E | .. | .. | FWC |
| Thursday Island, A | Oct. 10, 1912 | 10 34.9 | 142 12 | 4 54.6E | 33 18.8 | .36892 | K&C |
| | Oct. 11, 1912 | .. | .. | 4 57.1E | .. | .. | K&C |
| | Nov. 7, 1913 | .. | .. | 4 56.4E | 33 25.7 | .36863 | FB |
| Albany Island.. .. | Oct. 18, 1912 | 10 43.9 | 142 36 | 5 05.2E | 33 28.2 | .36762 | EK |
| Mapoon Mission .. | Nov. 15, 1913 | 11 57.8 | 141 53 | 4 58.9E | 35 48.9 | .36528 | FB |
| | Nov. 22, 1913 | .. | .. | 4 57.8E | .. | .. | FB |
| | Nov. 23, 1913 | .. | .. | 4 56.8E | .. | .. | FB |
| Connell's Creek .. | Sep. 23, 1912 | 12 17.4 | 131 33 | 3 25.6E | 37 46.9 | .36210 | EK |
| Port Darwin .. .. | Sep. 27, 1912 | 12 26.7 | 130 50 | 3 23.4E | 38 10.5 | .36229 | K&C |
| | Sep. 30, 1912 | .. | .. | 3 28.8E | .. | .. | K&C |
| | Oct. 1, 1912 | .. | .. | 3 28.2E | .. | .. | K&C |
| Weipa Mission .. | Dec. 1, 1913 | 12 44.6 | 142 10 | 5 03.6E | 37 08.6 | .36328 | FB |
| Batchelor .. .. | Sep. 14, 1912 | 13 03.6 | 131 03 | 3 29.5E | 39 06.0 | .35910 | K&C |
| Mion .. .. .. .. | Dec. 8, 1913 | 13 12.8 | 112 49 | 5 13.0E | 37 47.2 | .36216 | FB |
| Pine Creek .. .. | Sep. 11, 1912 | 13 49.6 | 131 51 | 3 28.2E | 40 19.4 | .35655 | EK |
| Coen .. .. .. .. | Dec. 12, 1913 | 13 57.2 | 143 12 | 5 22.6E | 38 57.6 | .36005 | FB |
| Katherine River .. | Sep. 4, 1912 | 14 26.1 | 132 17 | 3 38.4E | 41 14.3 | .35585 | EK |
| Leech's Billabong.. | Aug. 31, 1912 | 14 44.4 | 132 52 | 3 42.7E | 41 29.7 | .35464 | EK |
| Musgrave .. .. .. | Dec. 17, 1913 | 14 47.4 | 143 31 | 5 26.2E | 40 14.6 | .37748 | FB |
| Elsey Creek .. .. | Aug. 26, 1912 | 15 06.2 | 133 08 | 3 41.9E | 42 00.9 | .35356 | EK |
| Cooktown .. .. .. | Nov. 26, 1912 | 15 28.6 | 145 17 | 5 49.4E | 41 00.2 | .35539 | K&C |
| | Dec. 23, 1913 | .. | .. | 5 51.6E | 41 05.3 | .35184 | FB |
| Laura .. .. .. .. | Nov. 21, 1912 | 15 33.2 | 144 30 | 5 40.8E | 41 19.8 | .35480 | K&C |
| | Nov. 22, 1912 | .. | .. | 5 44.6E | .. | .35463 | K&C |
| | Nov. 22, 1912 | .. | .. | .. | .. | .35406 | K&C |
| | Nov. 23, 1912 | .. | .. | .. | .. | .35446 | K&C |
| | Nov. 23, 1912 | .. | .. | .. | .. | .35424 | K&C |
| Laura, Secondary.. | Nov. 22, 1912 | 15 33.2 | 144 30 | 5 42.4E | .. | .. | FWC |
| No. 3 Well .. .. | Aug. 23, 1912 | 15 38.0 | 133 13 | 3 16.0E | 42 46.4 | .35188 | EK |
| Daly Waters .. .. | Aug. 14, 1912 | 16 19.8 | 133 25 | 3 53.4E | .. | .35032 | EK |
| | Aug. 15, 1912 | .. | .. | .. | 43 56.0 | .. | EK |
| Milner's Well.. .. | Aug. 13, 1912 | 16 41.5 | 133 26 | 3 56.7E | 44 39.4 | .34795 | EK |
| Cairns .. .. .. .. | Nov. 18, 1912 | 16 55.6 | 145 46 | 5 59.6E | 43 04.8 | .35206 | EK |
| Frew's Ponds.. .. | Aug. 11, 1912 | 16 58.8 | 133 27 | 4 05.6E | .. | .34609 | EK |
| | Aug. 12, 1912 | .. | .. | .. | 45 10.6 | .. | EK |
| Chillagoe .. .. .. | Nov. 14, 1912 | 17 10.0 | 144 34 | 5 47.0E | 43 47.6 | .34918 | EK |
| Newcastle Waters.. | Aug. 9, 1912 | 17 23.0 | 133 26 | 3 48.0E | 45 47.3 | .34214 | EK |
| Newcastle Waters, Secondary .. .. | Aug. 9, 1912 | 17 23.0 | 133 26 | 3 46.9E | .. | .. | EK |
| Normanton .. .. .. | Nov. 4, 1912 | 17 41.4 | 141 06 | 5 25.8E | 45 01.1 | .34558 | EK |
| Burketown .. .. .. | Oct. 28, 1912 | 17 45.1 | 139 28 | 5 12.8E | 45 20.4 | .34707 | K&C |
| | Nov. 1, 1912 | .. | .. | .. | 45 19.5 | .. | K&C |
| Anthony Lagoon .. | Oct. 4, 1913 | 17 58.9 | 135 31 | 4 23.6E | 46 17.6 | .34193 | FB |
| Powell's Creek.. .. | Aug. 3, 1912 | 18 04.8 | 133 41 | 3 54.8E | 46 29.9 | .34108 | EK |
| Powell's Creek, Secondary .. .. | Aug. 5, 1912 | 18 04.8 | 133 41 | 3 42.4E | .. | .. | EK |
| Croydon .. .. .. | Nov. 6, 1912 | 18 13.1 | 142 15 | 5 35.4E | 45 35.3 | .34464 | K&C |
| Croydon, Secondary | Nov. 7, 1912 | 18 13.1 | 142 15 | 5 31.5E | .. | .. | FWC |
| Cardwell.. .. .. .. | Dec. 3, 1912 | 18 15.8 | 146 02 | .. | 45 19.6 | .. | FWC |
| | Dec. 4, 1912 | .. | .. | 6 10.3E | .. | .34332 | FWC |
| Renner Spring .. | Aug. 1, 1912 | 18 19.2 | 133 48 | 4 00.8E | 46 54.2 | .34021 | EK |
| Forsayth .. .. .. | Nov. 11, 1912 | 18 35.1 | 143 38 | 5 43.9E | 45 59.8 | .34270 | K&C |
| Mooketa Rock Hole | July 30, 1912 | 18 38.0 | 133 54 | .. | 47 20.1 | .. | EK |
| | July 31, 1912 | .. | .. | 3 58.5E | .. | .33946 | EK |
| Brunette Downs .. | Oct. 6, 1913 | 18 38.7 | 133 55 | .. | 47 08.6 | .. | FB |
| | Oct. 7, 1913 | .. | .. | 4 08.0E | .. | .34028 | FB |
| Attack Creek .. .. | July 28, 1912 | 19 00.9 | 134 10 | 4 07.6E | .. | .33785 | EK |
| | July 29, 1912 | .. | .. | .. | 47 43.0 | .. | EK |
| Alexandria .. .. .. | Oct. 2, 1913 | 19 04.0 | 136 39 | 4 18.0E | 47 28.0 | .33870 | FB |
| | Oct. 2, 1913 | .. | .. | .. | .. | .33836 | FB |
| Townsville .. .. .. | Nov. 29, 1912 | 19 14.6 | 146 50 | .. | 46 31.3 | .. | FWC |
| | Nov. 30, 1912 | .. | .. | 6 35.4E | .. | .34142 | FWC |
| | Nov. 24, 1913 | .. | .. | 6 39.6E | 46 35.4 | .34059 | EK |
| Canobie .. .. .. | Nov. 20, 1913 | 19 28.3 | 140 57 | 5 58.0E | 47 28.8 | .33686 | EK |
| Tennant's Creek .. | July 26, 1912 | 19 33.4 | 134 15 | 4 00.0E | 48 25.6 | .33475 | EK |
| Mount Samuel.. .. | July 24, 1912 | 19 43.0 | 134 11 | .. | 49 40.2 | .. | EK |
| | July 25, 1912 | .. | .. | 3 48.8E | .. | .33286 | EK |

| Station. | Date. | Lat. S. | Long. E. | Declination. | Dip. S. | Horizontal Intensity. | Obs'r. |
|---|---|---|---|---|---|---|---|
| | | | | | | C.G.S | |
| Camooweal .. .. .. | Sep. 30, 1913 | 19 55.6 | 138 06 | 4 27.0E | 48 39.6 | .33608 | FB |
| | Oct. 1, 1913 | .. | .. | 4 24.4E | .. | .33655 | FB |
| Bowen .. .. .. .. | Nov. 10, 1913 | 20 00.8 | 148 15 | 6 44.0E | 47 32.8 | .31111 | EK |
| | Nov. 11, 1913 | .. | .. | .. | 47 36.9 | .. | EK |
| Charters Towers .. | Nov. 13, 1913 | 20 04.4 | 146 15 | 6 31.4E | 47 29.9 | .33887 | EK |
| Gilbert Creek.. .. | July 22, 1912 | 20 11.8 | 134 14 | .. | 49 25.8 | .. | EK |
| | July 23, 1912 | .. | .. | 3 54.8E | .. | .33212 | EK |
| Wycliffe Well .. .. | July 20, 1912 | 20 41.4 | 134 15 | 3 57.5E | 50 07.9 | .33009 | EK |
| Cloncurry .. .. .. | Oct. 13, 1913 | 20 42.4 | 110 30 | 4 50.6E | 49 32.5 | .33626 | FB |
| Richmond .. .. .. | Nov. 17, 1913 | 20 45.2 | 113 09 | 5 45.5E | 49 03.8 | .33396 | EK |
| Hughenden .. .. .. | Nov. 15, 1913 | 20 50.4 | 144 12 | 6 05.4E | 49 06.2 | .33282 | EK |
| Mackay .. .. .. .. | Nov. 7, 1913 | 21 08.8 | 119 11 | 7 13.2E | 48 54.9 | .33237 | EK |
| Taylor's Crossing.. | July 18, 1912 | 21 14.8 | 134 08 | 3 32.6E | 50 59.1 | .32446 | EK |
| Barrow Creek .. .. | July 15, 1912 | 21 32.0 | 133 53 | 3 33.4E | 51 21.1 | .32506 | EK |
| Mount Douglas.... | Oct. 30, 1913 | 21 32.2 | 116 51 | 6 50.2E | 49 32.0 | .33110 | EK |
| Kynuna .. .. .. | Oct. 15, 1913 | 21 31.6 | 141 56 | 5 46.8E | 50 33.5 | .32786 | FB |
| Urandangi .. .. .. | Sep. 27, 1913 | 21 36.9 | 138 20 | 4 48.6E | .. | .32642 | FB |
| | Sep. 28, 1913 | .. | .. | 4 44.7E | 50 49.2 | .32636 | FB |
| Hanson's Well... | July 10, 1912 | 21 47.8 | 133 39 | .. | 51 46.6 | .. | K&C |
| | July 11, 1912 | .. | .. | 3 38.6E | .. | .32294 | K&C |
| Teatree Well .. .. | July 9, 1912 | 22 08.3 | 133 23 | 3 39.7E | 52 10.8 | .32012 | K&C |
| St. Lawrence.. .. | Nov. 4, 1913 | 22 20.8 | 149 32 | 7 31.1E | 50 33.6 | .32704 | EK |
| Winton .. .. .. .. | Oct. 17, 1913 | 22 24.1 | 143 03 | 6 09.2E | 51 23.5 | .32288 | FB |
| | Oct. 18, 1913 | .. | .. | 6 04.7E | .. | .32197 | FB |
| Eastmere .. .. .. | Oct. 22, 1913 | 22 29.7 | 145 53 | 6 37.4E | 51 22.3 | .32435 | EK |
| Ryan's Well .. .. | July 6, 1912 | 22 43.4 | 133 21 | 4 03.3E | 53 03.2 | .32000 | EK |
| Clermont .. .. .. | Oct. 25, 1913 | 22 49.2 | 147 38 | 7 04.2E | 51 02.8 | .32532 | EK |
| Boulia .. .. .. .. | Sep. 24, 1913 | 22 54.7 | 139 56 | 5 38.0E | 52 19.6 | .31987 | FB |
| Burt Well .. .. .. | July 4, 1912 | 23 13.0 | 133 45 | 3 43.6E | 53 30.8 | .31406 | EK |
| Winnecke's.. .. .. | July 1, 1912 | 23 19.7 | 134 15 | .. | 53 12.4 | .. | EK |
| | July 2, 1912 | .. | .. | 4 12.3E | .. | .31974 | EK |
| Rockhampton .. .. | Sep. 6, 1913 | 23 22.0 | 150 30 | .. | 51 12.5 | .. | FB |
| | Sep. 8, 1913 | .. | .. | 8 00.6E | .. | .32542 | FB |
| Arltunga .. .. .. | June 29, 1912 | 23 26.2 | 134 41 | 3 47.7E | 53 35.8 | .31728 | K&C |
| Arltunga, Secondary | June 29, 1912 | 23 26.2 | 134 41 | 3 45.0E | .. | .. | K&C |
| Longreach .. .. .. | Sep. 11, 1913 | 23 26.4 | 144 15 | 6 22.6E | 52 33.6 | .31903 | K&B |
| Emerald .. .. .. | Sep. 9, 1913 | 23 30.8 | 148 10 | 7 18.9E | 52 26.0 | .31874 | FB |
| Vergemont.. .. .. | Sep. 17, 1913 | 23 31.5 | 143 02 | 6 03.6E | 52 56.4 | .31770 | FB |
| | Sep. 17, 1913 | .. | .. | 6 08.0E | .. | .31775 | FB |
| Mayne Jn. Hotel.. | Sep. 19, 1913 | 23 32.1 | 141 23 | 5 54.6E | 53 21.9 | .31431 | FB |
| Jericho .. .. .. .. | Oct. 15, 1913 | 23 35.7 | 116 08 | .. | 52 45.3 | .. | EK |
| | Oct. 16, 1913 | .. | .. | 6 39.8E | .. | .31780 | EK |
| Alice Springs .. .. | June 22, 1912 | 23 40.8 | 133 54 | 3 45.0E | 54 05.0 | .31286 | EK |
| Alice Springs, Secondary .. .. | June 22, 1912 | 23 40.8 | 133 54 | 3 41.8E | .. | .. | EK |
| Gladstone .. .. .. | Oct. 4, 1913 | 23 51.0 | 151 15 | 8 08.0E | .. | .31982 | EK |
| | Oct. 6, 1913 | .. | .. | .. | 52 05.7 | .. | EK |
| Temple Bar.. .. .. | June 19, 1912 | 23 56.4 | 133 57 | .. | 54 30.2 | .. | EK |
| | June 20, 1912 | .. | .. | 3 50.7E | .. | .31107 | EK |
| Ooraminna Well.. | June 18, 1912 | 24 21.2 | 134 04 | 3 55.4E | 54 55.8 | .30939 | EK |
| Stonehenge .. .. .. | Sep. 13, 1913 | 24 21.2 | 143 18 | 6 05.8E | 53 53.4 | .31382 | K&B |
| Bedourie .. .. .. | Sep. 22, 1913 | 24 21.6 | 139 29 | 5 24.0E | 54 37.1 | .30864 | FB |
| Rolleston .. .. .. | Oct. 13, 1913 | 24 27.8 | 148 37 | 7 13.2E | 53 50.8 | .31196 | EK |
| Malvern Bore.. .. | Oct. 17, 1913 | 24 30.8 | 144 59 | 6 41.0E | 53 51.2 | .31427 | EK |
| Alice Well .. .. .. | June 15, 1912 | 24 47.4 | 134 09 | .. | 55 39.8 | .. | EK |
| | June 16, 1912 | .. | .. | 4 01.9E | .. | .30504 | EK |
| Tambo .. .. .. .. | Aug. 8, 1913 | 24 53.3 | 116 16 | .. | 54 02.4 | .. | EK |
| | Aug. 9, 1913 | .. | .. | 6 53.7E | .. | .31305 | EK |
| Currawilla .. .. .. | Aug. 16, 1913 | 25 08.4 | 141 20 | 5 41.8E | 55 04.9 | .30848 | K&B |
| Horseshoe Bend .. | June 13, 1912 | 25 11.1 | 134 15 | 3 43.6E | .. | .30384 | EK |
| | June 14, 1912 | .. | .. | .. | 56 00.8 | .. | EK |
| Windorah .. .. .. | Aug. 14, 1913 | 25 25.4 | 142 39 | 6 07.7E | 55 14.8 | .30764 | K&B |
| Crown Point .. .. | June 12, 1912 | 25 30.2 | 134 24 | 4 02.4E | 56 15.9 | .30238 | EK |
| Maryborough .. .. | Sept. 3, 1913 | 25 32.0 | 152 42 | .. | 54 01.7 | .. | FB |
| | Sept. 4, 1913 | .. | .. | 8 35.8E | .. | .31210 | FB |
| Gayndah .. .. .. | Oct. 8, 1913 | 25 37.7 | 151 37 | 8 12.0E | 54 04.8 | .31050 | EK |
| Goyder Creek.. .. | June 10, 1912 | 25 38.4 | 134 30 | 3 49.2E | 56 35.8 | .30087 | EK |
| Taroom .. .. .. | Sep. 30, 1913 | 25 38.8 | 149 48 | 7 51.7E | 54 27.8 | .31024 | EK |
| Adavale .. .. .. | Aug. 12, 1913 | 25 54.8 | 144 35 | 6 29.2E | 55 36.8 | .30533 | K&B |

| Station. | Date. | Lat. S. | Long. E. | Declination. | Dip. S. | Horizontal Intensity. | Obs'r. |
|---|---|---|---|---|---|---|---|
| | | | | | | C.G.S | |
| Charlotte Waters.. | June 7, 1912 | 25 55.9 | 134 55 | .. | 56 57.5 | .. | EK |
| | June 8, 1912 | .. | .. | 3 57.0E | .. | .29916 | EK |
| Blood's Creek .. .. | June 5, 1912 | 26 18.8 | 135 06 | 4 23.8E | 57 23.6 | .29500 | EK |
| Charleville.. .. .. | Aug. 7, 1913 | 26 24.4 | 146 14 | 7 03.8E | 56 01.0 | .30459 | K&B |
| Roma .. .. .. .. | Aug. 5, 1913 | 26 34.0 | 148 48 | 7 40.2E | 55 40.7 | .30541 | K&B |
| Meekatharra .. .. | Apr. 20, 1912 | 26 35.2 | 118 30 | .. | 59 01.9 | .. | EK |
| | Apr. 21, 1912 | .. | .. | 1 05.5W | .. | .28162 | EK |
| Meekatharra, Secondary .. .. | Apr. 22, 1912 | 26 35.2 | 118 30 | 1 00.9W | .. | .. | EK |
| Eromanga .. .. .. | Aug. 19, 1913 | 26 40.1 | 143 16 | 6 21.6E | 56 40.2 | .30013 | K&B |
| Woodgate's Swamp | Jun. 2, 1912 | 26 40.6 | 135 29 | .. | 57 32.4 | .. | EK |
| | Jun. 3, 1912 | .. | .. | 4 06.6E | .. | .29678 | EK |
| Chinchilla .. .. .. | Aug. 2, 1913 | 26 44.6 | 150 38 | 8 19.4E | 55 45.1 | .30412 | EK |
| Box Tree Flat .. .. | May 31, 1912 | 27 10.4 | 135 30 | 4 29.5E | 58 14.2 | .29299 | EK |
| Brisbane .. .. .. | July 17, 1913 | 27 27.0 | 153 02 | 9 03.3E | 56 09.9 | .30154 | EK |
| Brisbane University .. ..* .. .. | Nov. 29, 1913 | 27 28.7 | 153 02 | 9 14.3E | .. | .30135 | EK |
| | Nov. 30, 1913 | .. | .. | 9 12.4E | .. | .. | EK |
| | Dec. 1, 1913 | .. | .. | .. | 56 15.1 | .. | EK |
| Toowoomba . .. .. | Jul. 23, 1913 | 27 32.8 | 151 57 | 8 30.4E | 56 20.4 | .30120 | EK |
| Oodnadatta . .. .. | Aug. 21, 1911 | 27 33.1 | 135 28 | 4 10.4E | 58 26.5 | .29177 | K&W |
| | May 26, 1912 | .. | .. | 4 11.2E | 58 32.5 | .29190 | EK |
| Southport .. .. .. | Jul. 19, 1913 | 27 58.7 | 153 26 | 9 02.8E | 56 39.2 | .29868 | EK |
| Sandstone .. .. .. | Apr. 27, 1912 | 27 59.0 | 119 15 | 1 02.8W | 60 27.0 | .27261 | EK |
| Thargomindah . .. | Aug. 21, 1913 | 27 59.7 | 143 49 | 6 38.0E | 58 10.5 | .29319 | K&B |
| Mount Magnet, B* | Apr. 24, 1912 | 28 02.3 | 117 49 | 44 24.3E | 64 16.2 | .. | EK |
| | Apr. 25, 1912 | .. | .. | 52 15.1E | .. | .28834 | EK |
| Mount Magnet, C* | Apr. 24, 1912 | 28 02.3 | 117 49 | 21 29.2E | 72 10.5 | .. | EK |
| Mount Magnet, D* | Apr. 24, 1912 | 28 02.4 | 117 49 | 9 41.9E | 64 32.3 | .. | EK |
| Mount Magnet, E* | Apr. 24, 1912 | 28 02.5 | 117 49 | 13 14.7E | 63 40.0 | .. | EK |
| Mount Magnet, E* | Apr. 25, 1912 | .. | .. | 13 11.2E | .. | .23764 | EK |
| Mount Magnet, F* | Apr. 25, 1912 | 28 02.5 | 117 49 | 4 28.0E | .. | .. | EK |
| Mount Magnet, A* | Apr. 23, 1912 | 28 04.3 | 117 51 | 1 28.0W | 60 44.6 | .27078 | EK |
| Cunnamulla .. .. | Aug. 23, 1913 | 28 04.3 | 145 42 | 6 57.1E | 58 02.5 | .29365 | K&B |
| Lawlers . .. .. .. | May 1, 1912 | 28 05.2 | 120 30 | 0 22.6W | 61 06.6 | .27288 | EK |
| Lawlers, Secondary .. .. .. | May 1, 1912 | 28 05.2 | 120 30 | 0 11.0E | .. | .. | EK |
| Yalgoo .. .. .. .. | Apr. 18, 1912 | 28 20.6 | 116 40 | .. | 60 48.6 | .. | EK |
| | Apr. 19, 1912 | .. | .. | 1 45.6W | .. | .27246 | EK |
| Goondiwindi .. .. | Jul. 26, 1913 | 28 32.0 | 150 18 | 9 10.2E | 57 57.5 | .29395 | EK |
| Dirranbandi .. .. | Jul. 25, 1913 | 28 34.0 | 148 13 | 7 49.6E | 58 11.9 | .29263 | EK |
| Laverton .. .. .. | Mar. 28, 1912 | 28 37.5 | 122 26 | 0 41.6W | 61 17.3 | .27534 | EK |
| Boorthanna .. .. | Aug. 17, 1911 | 28 37.7 | 135 53 | 3 33.2E | 59 37.3 | .28571 | K&W |
| Byron Bay .. .. .. | May 9, 1913 | 28 39.2 | 153 36 | 9 17.7E | 57 29.8 | .29444 | EK |
| Geraldton .. .. .. | Apr. 16, 1912 | 28 47.0 | 114 37 | .. | 61 57.5 | .. | EK |
| | Apr. 17, 1912 | .. | .. | 3 27.2W | .. | .26196 | EK |
| Tenterfield .. .. .. | Apr. 24, 1913 | 29 04.3 | 152 02 | 9 04.0E | 58 02.2 | .29304 | EK |
| Mingenew .. .. .. | Apr. 15, 1912 | 29 12.4 | 115 26 | 3 50.9W | 62 32.8 | .25848 | EK |
| Coward Springs .. | Aug. 18, 1911 | 29 24.2 | 136 49 | 4 01.0E | 60 24.7 | .28078 | K&W |
| Moree .. .. .. .. | Aug. 18, 1911 | .. | .. | .. | 60 25.2 | .. | K&W |
| Hergott Springs .. | May 27, 1913 | 29 28 | 149 50 | 8 30.1E | 59 06.3 | .28741 | EK |
| Menzies .. .. .. .. | Aug. 16, 1911 | 29 39.1 | 138 02 | 5 13.8E | 60 29.9 | .28010 | K&W |
| | Mar. 29, 1912 | 29 41.0 | 121 04 | 1 21.0W | .. | .26174 | EK |
| | Mar. 30, 1912 | .. | .. | .. | 62 32.0 | .. | EK |
| Menzies, Secondary* | Mar. 30, 1912 | 29 41.0 | 121 04 | 1 16. W | .. | .. | EK |
| Wanaaring .. .. .. | Jun. 14, 1913 | 29 42.3 | 144 08 | 7 01.3E | 59 51.8 | .28252 | EK |
| Milparinka .. .. .. | Jun. 21, 1913 | 29 45.0 | 141 54 | 6 24.8E | 60 13.4 | .28097 | EK |
| Walgett .. .. .. | May 29, 1913 | 30 01.2 | 148 08 | 8 11.9E | 59 46.9 | .28255 | EK |
| Farina, B. .. .. .. | Aug. 24, 1911 | 30 04.3 | 138 16 | 6 01.8E | .. | .. | ENW |
| Farina, A. .. .. .. | Aug. 23, 1911 | 30 04.5 | 138 17 | 5 50.8E | .. | .27752 | K&W |
| Farina, Secondary . | Aug. 23, 1911 | 30 04.5 | 138 17 | .. | 60 54.2 | .. | ENW |
| Bourke .. .. .. .. | Jun. 11, 1913 | 30 05.0 | 145 57 | 7 33.3E | .. | .28058 | EK |
| | Jun. 12, 1913 | .. | .. | .. | 60 10.5 | .. | EK |
| Bourke, 1 .. .. .. | Jun. 12, 1913 | 30 05.0 | 145 57 | 7 29.7E | .. | .. | EK |
| Woolgoolga .. .. | May 5, 1913 | 30 07.2 | 153 12 | 9 19.9E | 59 09.3 | .28592 | EK |

*Local disturbance. The two declinations at Station Mount Magnet B were obtained at points less than 1 foot apart, showing great disturbance.

| Station. | Date. | Lat. S. | Long. E. | Declina- tion. | Dip. S. | Hori- zontal Inten- sity. | Obs'r. |
|---|---|---|---|---|---|---|---|
| | | | | | | C.G.S | |
| Narrabri ... ... | May 28, 1913 | 30 16.6 | 149 48 | 8 47.0E | 59 58.4 | .28166 | EK |
| Armidale.. ... .. | Apr. 23, 1913 | 30 31.4 | 151 41 | 9 10.6E | 59 45.6 | .28218 | EK |
| Moora . ... ... | Apr. 12, 1912 | 30 38.0 | 115 59 | 4 39.0W | 63 48.2 | .25132 | EK |
| Beltana . ... ... | Aug. 25, 1911 | 30 48.3 | 138 24 | 5 32.4E | | .27217 | K&W |
| | Aug 26, 1911 | .. | .. | .. | 61 34.2 | .. | K&W |
| Beltana, Secondary | Aug. 25, 1911 | 30 48.3 | 138 24 | .. | 61 35.6 | .. | EK |
| Coonamble .... | Jun. 6, 1913 | 30 57.1 | 148 24 | 8 41.1E | .. | .27829 | EK |
| | Jun. 7, 1913 | .. | .. | .. | 60 45.8 | .. | EK |
| Coolgardie . . . | Mar. 26, 1912 | 30 57.2 | 121 11 | 1 30.6W | 63 28.9 | .25616 | EK |
| Boorabbin .... | Mar. 20, 1912 | 31 12.8 | 120 20 | 2 01.0W | 63 59.1 | .25316 | EK |
| Southern Cross . | Mar. 19, 1912 | 31 13.8 | 119 21 | 2 13.7W | 64 06.0 | .25142 | EK |
| Werris Creek .. | Apr. 22, 1913 | 31 21.0 | 150 39 | 8 53.0E | 61 04.2 | .27540 | EK |
| Nanwoora . . . | Sep. 26, 1911 | 31 22.5 | 131 34 | 2 04.1E | 62 29.5 | .26962 | EK |
| White Wells . . . | Sep. 27, 1911 | 31 26.1 | 130 59 | 2 29.5E | .. | .26826 | EK |
| | Sep. 28, 1911 | .. | .. | .. | 62 55.8 | .. | EK |
| Port Macquarie . | Apr. 16, 1913 | 31 26.3 | 152 55 | 8 55.6E | 60 46.6 | .27770 | EK |
| Diamond Drill Tank | Sep. 29, 1911 | 31 27.4 | 129 33 | .. | 63 12.3 | .. | EK |
| | Sep. 30, 1911 | .. | .. | 1 06.0E | .. | .26450 | EK |
| Cundalabbie Tanks | Oct. 4, 1911 | 31 27.5 | 130 20 | 2 35.2E | .. | .26109 | EK |
| | Oct. 5, 1911 | .. | .. | .. | 63 30.6 | .. | EK |
| Merredin . . . . | Mar. 17, 1912 | 31 28.3 | 118 19 | 3 23.0W | .. | .25024 | EK |
| | Mar. 18, 1912 | .. | .. | .. | 64 19.6 | .. | EK |
| Cobar . . . . . | Jun. 26, 1913 | 31 29.9 | 115 49 | 7 41.1E | .. | .27282 | EK |
| | Jun. 27, 1913 | ... | .. | .. | 61 36.2 | .. | EK |
| Wilcannia . . . . | Jun. 16, 1913 | 31 33.7 | 143 23 | 6 59.6E | 61 59.6 | .27005 | EK |
| Wilcannia, 1 . . | Jun. 23, 1913 | 31 33.7 | 143 23 | 6 59.3E | .. | .. | EK |
| Nyngan . . . . | Jun. 28, 1913 | 31 34.0 | 147 11 | 7 13.8E | 61 26.0 | .27260 | EK |
| Colona . . . . | Oct. 7, 1911 | 31 37.6 | 132 05 | 3 02.9E | 63 33.3 | .25977 | EK |
| Northam . . . . | Mar. 15, 1912 | 31 38.6 | 116 41 | 4 30.0W | 64 43.4 | .24453 | EK |
| Eucla . . . . . | Oct. 2, 1911 | 31 43.8 | 128 53 | 1 44.4E | 63 32.0 | .25951 | EK |
| Broken Hill Reservoir . . . | Sep. 7, 1911 | 31 53.2 | 141 37 | 5 48.2E | 62 35.5 | .26606 | ENW |
| Hawker . . . . | Aug. 29, 1911 | 31 53.2 | 138 26 | 5 50.4E | 63 05.2 | .26244 | ENW |
| Bayswater, A . . | Feb. 14, 1912 | 31 55.2 | 115 55 | 4 41.6W | 64 51.4 | .24422 | EK |
| Bayswater, B† . . | Feb. 14, 1912 | 31 55.2 | 115 55 | 6 02.8W | .. | .. | EK |
| Bayswater, C† . . | Feb. 14, 1912 | 31 55.2 | 115 55 | 4 45.8W | .. | .. | EK |
| Yalata Head Station . . . . | Oct. 9, 1911 | 31 56.3 | 132 20 | 2 50.8E | 63 55.7 | .25600 | EK |
| Broken Hill . . . | Sep. 10, 1911 | 31 57.8 | 141 27 | 6 18.1E | 62 30.2 | .26710 | ENW |
| Perth . . . . . | Feb. 16, 1912 | 31 58.0 | 115 50 | 4 45.0W | 64 55.1 | .24356 | EK |
| Rottnest Island . | Feb. 17, 1912 | 32 00.2 | 115 33 | 4 38.1W | .. | .24293 | EK |
| | Feb. 18, 1912 | .. | .. | .. | 65 01.6 | .. | EK |
| Cockburn . . . . | Sep. 4, 1911 | 32 05.1 | 141 00 | 6 14.3E | .. | .26446 | ENW |
| | Sep. 5, 1911 | .. | .. | .. | 62 32.0 | .. | ENW |
| Ceduna . . . . . | Sep. 21, 1911 | 32 08.2 | 133 36 | 3 50.6E | 63 47.4 | .25785 | EK |
| Norseman . . . . | Mar. 23, 1912 | 32 12.2 | 121 48 | 1 29.6W | 64 46.8 | .24743 | EK |
| Dubbo, A . . . | Jun. 9, 1913 | 32 14.3 | 148 35 | 7 08.4E | 61 38.0 | .27941 | EK |
| Dubbo, 1* . . . | Jun. 9, 1913 | 32 14.3 | 148 35 | 4 05.1E | .. | .. | EK |
| Dubbo, B* . . . | Jun. 30, 1913 | 32 14.9 | 148 37 | 8 47.5E | 62 09.9 | .26979 | EK |
| Olary . . . . . | Sep. 2, 1911 | 32 17.1 | 140 20 | 6 10.2E | 63 32.4 | .25706 | ENW |
| Menindie . . . . | Jun. 18, 1913 | 32 23.9 | 142 26 | 6 50.4E | 63 02.3 | .26412 | EK |
| Quorn . . . . . | Aug. 14, 1911 | 32 31.4 | 138 02 | 6 09.8E | 63 33.8 | .26034 | K&W |
| Yunta . . . . . | Sep. 1, 1911 | 32 35.2 | 139 33 | 6 01.8E | 63 23.6 | .26119 | ENW |
| | Sep. 11, 1911 | .. | .. | 6 01.6E | .. | .. | ENW |
| East Maitland . . | Apr. 21, 1913 | 32 44.9 | 151 34 | 9 34.1E | 62 04.3 | .26980 | EK |
| Flinders . . . . | Sep. 18, 1911 | 32 47.9 | 134 11 | 3 15.6E | 61 16.6 | .25712 | EK |
| Ivanhoe . . . . | May 22, 1913 | 32 54.2 | 144 19 | 7 17.5E | 63 17.5 | .26258 | EK |
| Narrogin . . . . | Mar. 5, 1912 | 32 55.8 | 117 10 | 5 21.5W | .. | .23530 | EK |
| | Mar. 6, 1912 | .. | .. | .. | 66 06.6 | .. | EK |
| Petersburg . . . . | Sep. 13, 1911 | 32 58.4 | 138 48 | 5 42.8E | 63 58.6 | .25708 | ENW |
| Condobolin . . . | Jun. 4, 1913 | 33 04.8 | 147 09 | .. | 63 02.2 | .. | EK |
| | Jun. 5, 1913 | .. | .. | 7 51.8E | .. | .26402 | EK |
| Port Pirie, A . . | Sep. 15, 1911 | 33 11.3 | 138 01 | 6 21.0E | .. | .25894 | ENW |
| | Sep. 16, 1911 | .. | .. | 6 18.5E | 64 01.4 | .. | ENW |
| Port Pirie, B . . | Sep. 16, 1911 | 33 11.3 | 138 01 | 6 24.0E | .. | .25833 | ENW |
| Orange . . . . . | Jun. 3, 1913 | 33 17.6 | 149 07 | 9 10.2E | 63 02.6 | .26304 | EK |

†Artificial local disturbance.

*Local disturbance.

| Station. | Date. | Lat. S. | Long. E. | Declination. | Dip. S. | Horizontal Intensity. | Obs'r. |
|---|---|---|---|---|---|---|---|
| | | | | | | C.G.S | |
| Talia . . . . . . | Sep. 15, 1911 | 33 19.2 | 134 50 | 4 15.2E | 64 59.8 | .25051 | EK |
| Bunbury . . . . . | Feb. 21, 1912 | 33 19.5 | 115 38 | .. | 66 08.0 | .. | EK |
| | Feb. 22, 1912 | .. | .. | 5 46.3W | .. | .23542 | EK |
| Hillston . . . . | May 23, 1913 | 33 30.0 | 145 33 | 7 47.8E | 63 40.6 | .25977 | EK |
| Burra . . . . . . | Aug. 11, 1911 | 33 40.7 | 138 55 | 6 00.6E | 64 26.6 | .25452 | K&W |
| Cowell . . . . . | Sep. 22, 1911 | 33 40.9 | 136 54 | 3 52.1E | 65 01.0 | .25108 | ENW |
| Katanning . . . . | Mar. 4, 1912 | 33 41.3 | 117 33 | 4 21.8W | 66 34.2 | .23369 | EK |
| Red Hill, A . . . | Mar. 4, 1913 | 33 44.5 | 151 04 | .. | 63 12.2 | .. | EK |
| | Mar. 6, 1913 | .. | .. | 9 21.0E | .. | .26249 | EK |
| Red Hill, B . . . | Mar. 3, 1913 | 33 44.5 | 151 04 | 9 22.1E | .. | .26234 | EK |
| | Mar. 4, 1913 | .. | .. | 9 20.0E | .. | .26220 | EK |
| Garden Island . . | Mar. 28, 1913 | 33 51.9 | 151 14 | 9 35.9E | 63 17.0 | .26200 | EK |
| Wallaroo . . . . | Sep. 19, 1911 | 33 56.3 | 137 36 | 5 49.2E | 65 00.1 | .26578 | ENW |
| Bridgetown . . . | Feb. 23, 1912 | 33 57.4 | 116 09 | 5 35.2W | 66 42.7 | .23097 | EK |
| Morgan . . . . . | Oct. 26, 1911 | 34 02.5 | 139 40 | 6 21.2E | 64 57.8 | .25077 | EK |
| Mount Hope . . . | Sep. 12, 1911 | 34 06.3 | 135 20 | 4 24.2E | .. | .24677 | EK |
| | Sep. 13, 1911 | .. | .. | .. | 65 23.9 | .. | EK |
| Renmark . . . . . | Oct. 28, 1911 | 34 10.1 | 140 45 | 6 31.3E | 65 00.7 | .25074 | EK |
| Port Wakefield . . | Oct. 11, 1911 | 34 10.6 | 138 10 | .. | 65 48.9 | .. | ENW |
| | Oct. 12, 1911 | .. | .. | 5 46.1E | .. | .24690 | ENW |
| Mildura . . . . . | Nov. 1, 1911 | 34 11.8 | 142 11 | 6 43.4E | 64 48.0 | .25280 | EK |
| Hay . . . . . . . | May 20, 1913 | 34 30.5 | 144 51 | 7 41.0E | 64 45.2 | .25189 | EK |
| Harden . . . . . | Feb. 24, 1913 | 34 33.7 | 148 22 | 8 53.6E | 64 15.4 | .25498 | EK |
| Port Lincoln . . . | Sep. 9, 1911 | 34 42.6 | 135 48 | 3 26.0E | 66 00.0 | .24406 | EK |
| Narrandera . . . | May 17, 1913 | 34 44.3 | 146 34 | 8 23.3E | 64 41.4 | .25224 | EK |
| Goulburn . . . . | Feb. 26, 1913 | 34 45.8 | 149 44 | 9 08.2E | 64 19.7 | .25440 | EK |
| Adelaide (Botanical Park) | Oct. 18, 1911 | 34 55.3 | 138 37 | 5 35.2E | 66 04.8 | .24280 | ENW |
| Adelaide (South Park) . | Aug. 8, 1911 | 34 56.2 | 138 36 | 5 37.0E | 66 05.4 | .24319 | K&W |
| Albany . . . . . | Mar. 1, 1912 | 35 01.3 | 117 55 | .. | 67 16.8 | .. | EK |
| | Mar. 2, 1912 | .. | .. | 5 11.8W | .. | .22910 | EK |
| Edithburgh . . . . | Oct. 1, 1911 | 35 05.9 | 137 46 | 5 10.1E | 66 24.8 | .23940 | ENW |
| | Oct. 2, 1911 | .. | .. | 5 05.6E | .. | .. | ENW |
| Wagga Wagga . . | Feb. 22, 1913 | 35 06.2 | 147 23 | 8 13.2E | 64 57.3 | .25027 | EK |
| Murray Bridge . . | Aug. 4, 1911 | 35 07.2 | 139 16 | 5 36.3E | .. | .24091 | K&W |
| Murray Bridge, Secondary . . | Aug. 4, 1911 | 35 07.2 | 139 16 | .. | 66 17.3 | .. | K&W |
| Pinnaroo . . . . | Oct. 26, 1911 | 35 15.8 | 140 55 | 6 04.1E | 65 50.8 | .24421 | ENW |
| Mt. Pleasant . . . | Apr. 29, 1913 | 35 18.0 | 149 10 | 9 18.2E | 64 48.3 | .25150 | EK |
| Mt. Stromlo* . . . | Apr. 28, 1913 | 35 19.5 | 149 00 | 8 47.1E | 64 54.2 | .25092 | EK |
| Mt. Stromlo (1)* . | Apr. 28, 1913 | 35 19.5 | 149 00 | 9 26.7E | .. | .. | EK |
| Mt. Stromlo (2)* . | Apr. 28, 1913 | 35 19.5 | 149 00 | 9 41.3E | .. | .. | EK |
| Swan Hill . . . . | Jan. 21, 1913 | 35 20.2 | 143 34 | 7 19.7E | 65 43.1 | .24570 | FWC |
| Port Victor . . . | Sep. 29, 1911 | 35 31.8 | 138 37 | 5 46.8E | 66 36.6 | .23753 | ENW |
| Deniliquin . . . . | Jan. 27, 1913 | 35 32.0 | 144 58 | 8 02.4E | 65 42.9 | .24586 | FWC |
| Woomelang . . . | Nov. 2, 1911 | 35 41.0 | 142 41 | 7 03.8E | 66 11.5 | .24292 | EK |
| Coonalpyn . . . . | Aug. 3, 1911 | 35 41.9 | 139 53 | 5 46.6E | 66 21.7 | .24044 | K&W |
| Hog Bay . . . . | Oct. 8, 1911 | 35 43.2 | 137 56 | 5 12.8E | 67 01.4 | .23459 | ENW |
| Harvey's Return . | Oct. 6, 1911 | 35 43.7 | 136 39 | 4 32.8E | 66 59.8 | .23406 | ENW |
| Moruya . . . . . | Mar. 17, 1913 | 35 55.1 | 150 05 | 8 10.8E | 65 04.5 | .25200 | EK |
| Albury . . . . . | Dec. 15, 1911 | 36 05.1 | 146 55 | 8 30.5E | 65 58.4 | .24359 | EK |
| Echuca . . . . . | Jan. 24, 1913 | 36 06.4 | 144 44 | 7 50.7E | 66 17.2 | .24182 | FWC |
| Cooma . . . . . | Mar. 12, 1913 | 36 14.0 | 149 08 | 9 24.2E | 65 47.2 | .24476 | EK |
| Charlton . . . . | Jan. 17, 1913 | 36 16.6 | 143 22 | 6 59.0E | 66 36.0 | .23959 | FWC |
| Border Town . . | Aug. 2, 1911 | 36 18.5 | 140 46 | 6 26.4E | 67 02.9 | .23616 | K&W |
| Shepparton . . . | Jan. 30, 1913 | 36 22.6 | 145 24 | 8 15.7E | 66 23.9 | .24096 | FWC |
| Horsham . . . . | Aug. 1, 1911 | 36 43.0 | 142 12 | 7 21.2E | 67 08.4 | .23555 | K&W |
| Bendigo . . . . | Jan. 15, 1913 | 36 44.4 | 144 19 | 7 50.0E | 66 52.0 | .23699 | FWC |
| Mansfield . . . . | Feb. 11, 1913 | 37 02.9 | 146 07 | 8 28.7E | 66 55.9 | .23658 | FWC |
| Eden . . . . . . | Mar. 14, 1913 | 37 04.6 | 149 56 | 9 57.4E | 66 21.3 | .24044 | EK |
| Omeo . . . . . | Feb. 5, 1913 | 37 06.3 | 147 36 | 8 50.9E | 66 45.5 | .23748 | FWC |
| Ararat . . . . . | Jul. 31, 1911 | 37 17.0 | 142 57 | 7 26.8E | 67 22.2 | .23343 | K&W |
| Ballarat . . . . | Jan. 2, 1913 | 37 34.0 | 143 50 | .. | 67 57.5 | .. | FWC |
| | Jan. 3, 1913 | .. | .. | 6 50.0E | .. | .22998 | FWC |
| Casterton . . . . | Dec. 28, 1912 | 37 35.0 | 141 25 | 7 16.0E | .. | .22758 | FWC |
| | Dec. 29, 1912 | .. | .. | 7 15.9E | 68 06.8 | .22792 | FWC |

*Local disturbance.

| Station. | Date. | Lat. S. | Long. E. | Declination. | Dip. S. | Horizontal Intensity. | Obs'r. |
|---|---|---|---|---|---|---|---|
| | | | | | | C.G.S | |
| Casterton, | | | | | | | |
| Secondary . . . | Dec. 30, 1912 | 37 35.0 | 141 25 | 7 15.9E | | | FWC |
| Water's Homestead | Feb. 15, 1913 | 37 40.0 | 146 07 | 8 38.0E | 67 28.9 | .23268 | K&C |
| Bairnsdale . . . . | Feb. 3, 1913 | 37 49.5 | 147 39 | 9 07.6E | 67 28.9 | .23312 | FWC |
| Melbourne, A . . | Jul. 19, 1911 | 37 49.9 | 144 58 | 8 05.4E | .. | .23094 | K&W |
| | Jul. 21, 1911 | .. | .. | 8 04.6E | .. | .23108 | K&W |
| | Jul. 21, 1911 | .. | .. | 8 07.6E | .. | .23087 | K&W |
| | Jul. 22, 1911 | .. | .. | 8 07.3E | .. | .23101 | K&W |
| | Apr. 4, 1913 | .. | .. | 8 03.9E | .. | .23099 | EK |
| | Apr. 5, 1913 | .. | .. | 8 04.7E | .. | .23100 | EK |
| | Apr. 6, 1913 | .. | .. | 8 02.3E | .. | .23072 | EK |
| | Apr. 6, 1913 | .. | .. | 8 05.6E | .. | .23090 | EK |
| | Apr. 7, 1913 | .. | .. | 8 01.7E | .. | .23083 | EK |
| | Apr. 9, 1913 | .. | .. | .. | .. | .23104 | EK |
| | Apr. 9, 1913 | .. | .. | .. | .. | .23084 | EK |
| Melbourne, B . . . | Jul. 18, 1911 | 37 49.9 | 144 58 | 8 06.0E | .. | .23111 | K&W |
| | Jul. 19, 1911 | .. | .. | 8 05.6E | .. | .23085 | K&W |
| | Jul. 20, 1911 | .. | .. | 8 04.4E | .. | .23099 | K&W |
| | Jul. 21, 1911 | .. | .. | 8 04.2E | .. | .23096 | K&W |
| | Jul. 24, 1911 | .. | .. | 8 07.6E | .. | .23103 | K&W |
| | Jul. 25, 1911 | .. | .. | 8 04.1E | .. | .23123 | K&W |
| | Feb. 1, 1912 | .. | .. | .. | 67 42.7 | .. | EK |
| | Feb. 2, 1912 | .. | .. | .. | 67 43.1 | .. | EK |
| | Apr. 4, 1913 | .. | .. | 8 05.0E | .. | .23096 | EK |
| | Apr. 5, 1913 | .. | .. | 8 04.5E | .. | .23102 | EK |
| | Apr. 6, 1913 | .. | .. | 8 02.5E | .. | .23082 | EK |
| | Apr. 6, 1913 | .. | .. | 8 05.6E | .. | .23102 | EK |
| | Apr. 7, 1913 | .. | .. | 8 01.2E | .. | .23095 | EK |
| | Apr. 8, 1913 | .. | .. | .. | 67 42.5 | .. | EK |
| Melbourne, Dip | | | | | | | |
| Pier . . . . . | Dec. 11, 1911 | 37 49.9 | 144 58 | | 67 44.3 | | EK |
| | Dec. 11, 1911 | .. | .. | | 67 44.7 | | EK |
| | Dec. 11, 1911 | .. | .. | | 67 44.4 | | EK |
| | Feb. 1, 1912 | .. | .. | | 67 44.3 | | EK |
| | Feb. 2, 1912 | .. | .. | | 67 43.1 | | EK |
| | Apr. 7, 1913 | .. | .. | | 67 43.1 | | EK |
| | Apr. 8, 1913 | .. | .. | | 67 43.3 | | EK |
| Melbourne, Earth | | | | | | | |
| Inductor Pier . | Feb. 2, 1912 | 37 49.9 | 144 58 | .. | 67 42.1 | .. | EK |
| Geelong . . . . . | Dec. 17, 1912 | 38 09.0 | 144 23 | .. | 68 02.7 | .. | EK |
| | Dec. 18, 1912 | .. | .. | 7 52.0E | .. | .22771 | EK |
| Geelong, | | | | | | | |
| Secondary . . . | Dec. 17, 1912 | 38 09.0 | 144 23 | 7 58.2E | .. | .. | EK |
| Portland . . . . . | Dec. 24, 1912 | 38 20.6 | 141 37 | .. | 68 44.8 | .. | FWC |
| | Dec. 26, 1912 | .. | .. | 6 30.2E | .. | .22226 | FWC |
| | Dec. 26, 1912 | .. | .. | .. | .. | .22238 | FWC |
| Portland, | | | | | | | |
| Secondary . . . | Dec. 24, 1912 | 38 20.6 | 141 37 | 6 49.0E | .. | .. | FWC |
| Warrnambool . . . | Dec. 21, 1912 | 38 23.6 | 142 29 | 7 10.4E | 68 30.6 | .22378 | K&C |
| Warrnambool, | | | | | | | |
| Secondary . . . | Dec. 21, 1912 | 38 23.6 | 142 29 | 7 03.7E | .. | .. | FWC |
| Alberton . . . . | Jan. 11, 1913 | 38 37.4 | 146 40 | 9 00.7E | 68 08.5 | .22764 | FWC |
| Beech Forest . . . | Dec. 19, 1912 | 38 37.5 | 143 34 | .. | 68 31.4 | .. | EK |
| | Dec. 20, 1912 | .. | .. | 7 33.4E | .. | .22358 | EK |
| Longford . . . . | Dec. 22, 1913 | 41 35.9 | 147 08 | 9 22.4E | .. | .20610 | EK |
| | Dec. 23, 1913 | .. | .. | .. | 70 40.0 | .. | EK |
| Dee Bridge . . . | Dec. 26, 1913 | 42 17.8 | 146 40 | 8 47.2E | 71 21.8 | .20091 | EK |
| Sorell . . . . | Dec. 30, 1913 | 42 47.6 | 147 33 | 9 46.5E | 71 22.2 | .20090 | EK |
| Hobart, A* . . . . | Nov. 13, 1911 | 42 52.0 | 147 22 | 7 46.8E | .. | .19597 | JMB |
| | Nov. 14, 1911 | .. | .. | 7 38.8E | .. | .19576 | JMB |
| | Nov. 15, 1911 | .. | .. | .. | 71 53.1 | .. | EK |
| | Nov. 15, 1911 | .. | .. | .. | 71 53.1 | .. | EK |
| | Nov. 16, 1911 | .. | .. | .. | 71 53.9 | .. | EK |
| | Nov. 17, 1911 | .. | .. | 7 45.1E | 71 53.9 | .. | K&W |
| | Nov. 17, 1911 | .. | .. | 7 43.7E | 71 53.5 | .. | K&W |
| | Nov. 18, 1911 | .. | .. | 7 44.2E | .. | .19590 | JMB |
| | Nov. 20, 1911 | .. | .. | .. | .. | .19594 | EK |
| | Nov. 20, 1911 | .. | .. | .. | .. | .19594 | ENW |

*Local disturbance.

| Station. | Date. | Lat. S. | Long. E. | Declination. | Dip. S. | Horizontal Intensity. C.G.S | Obs'r. |
|---|---|---|---|---|---|---|---|
| Hobart, A* . . . . | Nov. 20, 1911 | .. | .. | .. | .. | .19606 | W&K |
| | Nov. 21, 1911 | .. | .. | .. | .. | .19590 | EK |
| | Nov. 21, 1911 | .. | .. | .. | .. | .19610 | W&K |
| Hobart, B* . . . | Nov. 13, 1911 | 42 52.0 | 147 22 | 6 45.7E | .. | .1926S | ENW |
| | Nov. 14, 1911 | .. | .. | 6 37.6E | .. | .19260 | ENW |
| | Nov. 15, 1911 | .. | .. | .. | 72 17.8 | .. | ENW |
| | Nov. 15, 1911 | .. | .. | .. | 72 17.4 | .. | ENW |
| | Nov. 16, 1911 | .. | .. | .. | 72 19.4 | .. | ENW |
| | Nov. 18, 1911 | .. | .. | 6 42.4E | .. | .19274 | ENW |
| Hobart, C* . . . . | Nov. 13, 1911 | 42 52.0 | 147 22 | 8 26.2E | .. | .19760 | EK |
| | Nov. 14, 1911 | .. | .. | 8 18.0E | .. | .19756 | EK |
| | Nov. 18, 1911 | .. | .. | 8 23.0E | .. | .19763 | EK |
| Thursday Island, A | Nov. 12 1915 | 10 34.9 | 142 12 | 4 56.9E | 33 27.7 | .36780 | WCP |
| Cape Croker . . . | Aug. 12, 1914 | 10 58.4 | 132 32 | .. | 35 23.3 | .. | FB |
| | Aug. 13, 1914 | .. | .. | 3 42.2E | .. | .36721 | FB |
| Cape Wessel . . . | Aug. 30, 1914 | 11 00.7 | 136 45 | 4 08.4E | 34 51.4 | .36698 | FB |
| Cape Wessel, Secondary . . . | Aug. 30, 1914 | 11 00.7 | 136 45 | 4 07.1E | .. | .. | FB |
| Piper Head . . . | May 6, 1914 | 11 16.3 | 130 23 | 3 10.1E | 36 08.3 | .36590 | FB |
| Brenton Bay . . . | Sep. 13, 1914 | 11 18.4 | 131 13 | .. | 36 06.3 | .. | FB |
| | Sep. 14, 1914 | .. | .. | 3 26.7E | .. | .36643 | FB |
| Cape Cockburn . . | Aug. 17, 1914 | 11 20.4 | 132 52 | 3 58.7E | 36 01.2 | .36540 | FB |
| Bowen Straits Aboriginal Stn. | Sep. 11, 1914 | 11 20.6 | 132 33 | 3 47.6E | 36 09.9 | .36592 | FB |
| | Sep. 11, 1914 | .. | .. | .. | .. | .36578 | FB |
| Victoria . . . . . | Aug. 10, 1914 | 11 22.5 | 132 08 | 3 27.0E | 36 23.7 | .36566 | FB |
| Bynoe . . . . . . | May 9, 1914 | 11 45.3 | 130 40 | .. | 37 02.2 | .. | FB |
| | May 10, 1914 | .. | .. | 3 24.8E | .. | .36341 | FB |
| Mission Station, Bathurst Island | May 1, 1914 | 11 45.5 | 130 39 | 3 27.4E | 37 01.5 | .36340 | FB |
| Bromby's Islands . | Sep. 2, 1914 | 11 51.9 | 136 34 | 4 10.1E | 36 24.2 | .36476 | FB |
| Bromby's Islands, Secondary . . . | Sep. 2, 1914 | 11 51.9 | 136 34 | 4 08.3E | .. | .. | FB |
| Alger Island . . . | Sep. 6, 1914 | 11 53.6 | 135 57 | 4 06.6E | 36 37.4 | .36472 | FB |
| | Sep. 6, 1914 | .. | .. | .. | .. | .36470 | FB |
| Twenty Mile Landing . . . . | Aug. 20, 1914 | 11 54.7 | 133 24 | 3 43.6E | 36 53.0 | .36444 | FB |
| Cape Hotham . . . | Jul. 16, 1914 | 12 04.0 | 131 16 | 3 22.4E | 37 24.5 | .36346 | FB |
| Cadell's Landing . | Aug. 22, 1914 | 12 06.3 | 134 11 | 3 52.0E | 37 07.5 | .36416 | FB |
| Cadell's Landing, Secondary . . . | Aug. 22, 1914 | 12 06.3 | 134 11 | 3 50.8E | .. | .. | FB |
| Connell's Creek . . | Jul. 31, 1914 | 12 17.4 | 131 32 | .. | 37 51.2 | .. | FB |
| | Aug. 1, 1914 | .. | .. | 3 28.4E | .. | .36180 | FB |
| Goyder River . . | Aug. 25, 1914 | 12 18.7 | 135 13 | 3 59.7E | 37 20.6 | .36308 | FB |
| | Aug. 25, 1914 | .. | .. | .. | .. | .36329 | FB |
| Goyder River, Secondary . . . | Aug. 25, 1914 | 12 18.7 | 135 13 | 4 02.0E | .. | .. | FB |
| Oenpelli . . . . | Jul. 25, 1914 | 12 19.8 | 133 02 | 3 49.6E | 37 31.6 | .36587 | FB |
| | Jul. 26, 1914 | .. | .. | 3 49.4E | .. | .36600 | FB |
| Oenpelli, Secondary . . | Jul. 26, 1914 | 12 19.8 | 133 02 | 3 44.9E | .. | .. | FB |
| Cahill's Landing . | Jul. 24, 1914 | 12 21.4 | 132 57 | .. | .. | .36246 | FB |
| | Jul. 27, 1914 | .. | .. | 3 51.4E | 37 34.9 | .36253 | FB |
| Point Charles Lighthouse . | Oct. 3, 1914 | 12 23.4 | 130 39 | .. | 38 05.2 | .. | FB |
| | Oct. 4, 1914 | .. | .. | 3 25.4E | .. | .36212 | FB |
| | Oct. 6, 1914 | .. | .. | .. | 38 03.3 | .. | FB |
| Point Charles Lighthouse, Secondary . . . | Oct. 3, 1914 | 12 23.4 | 130 39 | 3 27.1E | .. | .. | FB |
| Arnhem Bay . . . | Sep. 4, 1914 | 12 26.6 | 136 03 | 4 08.0E | 37 25.6 | .36300 | FB |
| Darwin . . . . . | May 19, 1914 | 12 26.7 | 130 50 | 3 25.2E | 38 11.4 | .36178 | FB |
| Batchelor . . . . | May 14, 1914 | 13 03.6 | 131 03 | 3 30.1E | .. | .35870 | FB |
| | May 15, 1914 | .. | .. | .. | 39 06.6 | .. | FB |
| Pine Creek (Playford) . . | Apr. 28, 1914 | 13 49.6 | 131 51 | 3 34.0E | 40 07.4 | .35757 | FB |
| Pine Creek, B . . | Apr. 29, 1914 | 13 49.6 | 131 51 | 3 33.6E | 40 10.2 | .35772 | FB |

*Local disturbance.

| Station. | Date. | Lat. S. | Long. E. | Declination | Dip. S. | Horizontal Intensity. | Obs'r. |
|---|---|---|---|---|---|---|---|
| | | | | | | C.G.S | |
| Katherine River . | Apr. 25, 1914 | 14 26.1 | 132 17 | 3 41.8E | 41 14.1 | .35508 | FB |
| Mission Station, Roper River . . | Jun. 8, 1914 | 14 44.9 | 134 50 | 4 02.5E | 41 21.0 | .35624 | FB |
| Port George IV. . | Sep. 24, 1914 | 15 21.1 | 124 43 | 2 18.8E | .. | .34792 | WCP |
| | Sep. 26, 1914 | .. | .. | .. | 43 34.4 | .. | WCP |
| Victoria River . . | Apr. 8, 1914 | 15 24.5 | 130 02 | 3 08.0E | 43 03.0 | .35099 | FB |
| Six Mile Hotel . . | Sep. 20, 1914 | 15 29.8 | 128 08 | 2 59.2E | .. | .34868 | EK |
| | Sep. 21, 1914 | .. | .. | .. | 43 29.5 | .. | EK |
| Sir Edward Pellew Islands . . . . | Jun. 23, 1914 | 15 35.1 | 136 43 | 4 20.7E | 42 21.7 | .35319 | FB |
| Depot, Victoria River . . . . | Apr. 13, 1914 | 15 37.0 | 130 27 | 3 18.0E | 43 25.2 | .34964 | FB |
| Timber Creek . . | Apr. 14, 1914 | 15 38.1 | 130 79 | 3 19.1E | 43 26.0 | .34929 | FB |
| Delamere . . . . | Apr. 19, 1914 | 15 44.1 | 131 32 | 3 30.9E | 43 18.8 | .35025 | FB |
| Cheese Tin . . . | Sep. 17, 1914 | 15 49.8 | 128 20 | 2 54.5E | 43 56.1 | .34800 | EK |
| Montgomery Islands | Sep. 29, 1914 | 15 53.7 | 124 18 | 2 14.4E | 44 39.0 | .34404 | WCP |
| Black Rocks . . | Jun. 22, 1914 | 15 56.4 | 136 31 | 4 16.4E | 43 04.6 | .35151 | FB |
| Five Mile Bar . . | Jun. 17, 1914 | 16 00.2 | 136 24 | 4 16.6E | 43 09.3 | .35107 | FB |
| Borroloola . . . . | Jun. 13, 1914 | 16 04.2 | 136 22 | 4 17.1E | .. | .35066 | FB |
| | Jun. 14, 1914 | .. | .. | .. | 43 17.1 | .. | FB |
| Ryan's Bend . . . | Jun. 15, 1914 | 16 08.2 | 136 08 | 4 13.0E | 43 29.6 | .34982 | FB |
| Wild Dog Spring . | Sep. 15, 1914 | 16 14.1 | 128 21 | 2 55.0E | 44 28.5 | .34598 | EK |
| Sunday Island . . | Oct. 4, 1914 | 16 24.5 | 123 12 | 2 05.6E | 45 28.7 | .34121 | WCP |
| Bow Creek . . . | Sep. 13, 1914 | 16 39.8 | 128 12 | 2 44.1E | 45 14.6 | .34452 | EK |
| Turkey Creek . . | Sep. 11, 1914 | 17 01.9 | 128 13 | 2 06.2E | 45 50.3 | .34481 | EK |
| Derby . . . . . | Sep. 9, 1914 | 17 17.8 | 123 38 | 2 08.5E | .. | .33787 | WCP |
| | Sep. 10, 1914 | .. | .. | .. | 46 43.4 | .. | WCP |
| Fourteen-mile Creek . . . . | Sep. 7, 1914 | 17 44.8 | 127 52 | 2 45.7E | 46 45.4 | .33897 | EK |
| Rosie's Creek . . | Sep. 5, 1914 | 17 47.3 | 127 48 | 2 41.7E | 46 56.3 | .33876 | EK |
| Broome, B . . . | Oct. 12, 1914 | 17 58.1 | 122 13 | 1 56.4E | .. | .. | WCP |
| Broome, A . . . | Sep. 7, 1914 | 17 58.4 | 122 13 | 1 49.7E | 47 59.0 | .33260 | WCP |
| Moola Bulla . . . | Sep. 2, 1914 | 18 11.8 | 127 28 | 2 31.2E | 47 42.4 | .33598 | EK |
| Hall's Creek . . | Aug. 25, 1914 | 18 15.3 | 127 46 | 2 24.1E | 47 37.9 | .33546 | EK |
| Flora Valley . . | Aug. 18, 1914 | 18 16.0 | 127 59 | 2 31.2E | 48 01.7 | .33580 | EK |
| Cow Creek . . . | Aug. 14, 1914 | 18 38.5 | 128 22 | .. | 48 15.3 | .. | EK |
| | Aug. 15, 1914 | .. | .. | 2 52.3E | .. | .33428 | EK |
| Sturt Creek . . . | Aug. 12, 1914 | 19 08.2 | 128 13 | 2 47.3E | 48 45.8 | .33220 | EK |
| Wolf Creek . . . | Aug. 10, 1914 | 19 22.3 | 127 48 | 2 35.4E | 49 12.1 | .33047 | EK |
| Cutharra Pool . . | Aug. 7, 1914 | 19 43.5 | 127 34 | 2 33.6E | 49 49.7 | .32730 | EK |
| Lungan Pool . . | Aug. 5, 1914 | 20 01.4 | 127 26 | 2 34.7E | 50 12.7 | .32614 | EK |
| Well No. 50 . . . | Aug. 3, 1914 | 20 12.8 | 127 01 | 2 36.6E | 50 31.5 | .32457 | EK |
| Well No. 48 . . . | Jul. 31, 1914 | 20 15.2 | 126 35 | 2 13.6E | 50 51.7 | .32106 | EK |
| Port Hedland . . | Aug. 31, 1914 | 20 18.7 | 118 35 | 0 22.6E | 51 40.8 | .31742 | WCP |
| Kuduarra . . . . | Jul. 29, 1914 | 20 38.4 | 126 20 | 2 16.8E | 51 07.1 | .32280 | EK |
| Ballaballa . . . | Sep. 3, 1914 | 20 41.4 | 117 49 | 0 17.8E | 52 21.0 | .31346 | WCP |
| Pijallinga Claypan | Jul. 27, 1914 | 20 54.5 | 126 10 | 2 11.8E | 51 26.5 | .32127 | EK |
| Marble Bar . . . | Aug. 27, 1914 | 21 11.4 | 119 44 | 1 33.4E | 52 40.5 | .31482 | WCP |
| Billowaggi . . . | Jul. 24, 1914 | 21 13.8 | 125 59 | .. | 51 52.0 | .. | EK |
| | Jul. 25, 1914 | .. | .. | 2 03.8E | .. | .32000 | EK |
| Guli . . . . . . | Jul. 23, 1914 | 21 19.5 | 125 53 | .. | 52 05.7 | .. | EK |
| | Jul. 24, 1914 | .. | .. | 2 02.7E | .. | .31938 | EK |
| Wadawalla . . . | Jul. 21, 1914 | 21 40.3 | 125 47 | 1 58.8E | 52 31.9 | .31702 | EK |
| Nullagine . . . . | Aug. 20, 1914 | 21 53.0 | 120 07 | 0 49.2E | 53 34.8 | .30823 | WCP |
| Wardabunna . . | Jul. 19, 1914 | 21 57.8 | 125 31 | 1 53.7E | 52 53.3 | .31538 | EK |
| Wanda . . . . . | Jul. 16, 1914 | 22 08.4 | 125 15 | .. | 53 09.0 | .. | EK |
| | Jul. 17, 1914 | .. | .. | 1 51.9E | .. | .31436 | EK |
| Spinifex Camp . . | Jul. 14, 1914 | 22 18.2 | 124 47 | 1 55.5E | 53 24.4 | .31320 | EK |
| Well No. 31 . . . | Jul. 11, 1914 | 22 31.7 | 124 21 | .. | 53 57.9 | .. | EK |
| | Jul. 12, 1914 | .. | .. | 1 32.4E | .. | .31088 | EK |
| Well No. 29 . . . | Jul. 9, 1914 | 22 33.4 | 123 48 | 1 27.6E | 53 51.3 | .31121 | EK |
| Well No. 27 . . . | Jul. 7, 1914 | 22 47.8 | 123 34 | .. | 54 17.6 | .. | EK |
| | Jul. 8, 1914 | .. | .. | 0 55.2E | .. | .31014 | EK |
| Ethel Creek . . . | Aug. 17, 1914 | 22 54.5 | 120 10 | 0 23.2E | 55 10.5 | .30188 | WCP |
| Karara Soaks . . | Jul. 5, 1914 | 23 06.8 | 123 18 | 0 52.3E | 55 10.6 | .30365 | EK |
| Well No. 21 . . . | Jul. 2, 1914 | 23 10.8 | 122 44 | 1 09.7E | 54 47.1 | .30535 | EK |
| Rockhampton . . | Mar. 25, 1914 | 23 22.0 | 150 30 | 8 03.4E | 51 12.2 | .32525 | FB |
| Well No. 19 . . . | Jun. 30, 1914 | 23 25.2 | 122 28 | .. | 55 12.3 | .. | EK |
| | Jul. 1, 1914 | .. | .. | 1 10.4E | .. | .30313 | EK |
| Water No. 17 . . | Jun. 28, 1914 | 23 43.5 | 122 27 | 0 50.0E | 55 34.5 | .30160 | EK |

| Station. | Date. | Lat. S. | Long. E. | Declination | Dip. S. | Horizontal Intensity. | Obs'r. |
|---|---|---|---|---|---|---|---|
|  |  |  |  |  |  | C.G.S |  |
| Mundawindi . . . | Aug. 16, 1914 | 23 53.4 | 120 10 | 0 07.6E | 56 10.2 | .29651 | WCP |
| Well No. 15 . . . | Jun. 25, 1914 | 24 08.4 | 122 10 | .. | 56 09.3 | .. | EK |
|  | Jun. 26, 1914 | .. | .. | 0 51.5E | .. | .30006 | EK |
| Well No. 13 . . . | Jun. 23, 1914 | 24 25.5 | 121 57 | .. | 56 43.5 | .. | EK |
|  | Jun. 24, 1914 | .. | .. | 0 39.6E | .. | .29585 | EK |
| Goodwin Soak . . | Jun. 21, 1914 | 24 44.6 | 121 43 | 0 33.6E | 57 13.6 | .29092 | EK |
| Bald Hill . . . . | Aug. 14, 1914 | 24 49.5 | 119 36 | 0 20.8W | 57 05.5 | .29617 | WCP |
| Carnarvon . . . . | Dec. 13, 1914 | 24 53.2 | 113 39 | 2 22.1W | 58 01.8 | .28275 | FB |
| Weld Spring . . . | Jun. 18, 1914 | 25 01.2 | 121 33 | 0 43.2E | 57 05.9 | .29511 | EK |
| Well No. 7 . . . | Jun. 16, 1914 | 25 09.7 | 121 17 | 0 11.4E | 57 09.7 | .29439 | EK |
| Well No. 6 . . . | Jun. 14, 1914 | 25 22.8 | 121 01 | .. | 51 46.2 | .. | EK |
|  | Jun. 15, 1914 | .. | .. | 0 22.1W | .. | .28916 | EK |
| Well No. 4 . . . | Jun. 11, 1914 | 25 37.2 | 120 33 | 0 21.0E | 57 24.3 | .29335 | EK |
| Peak Hill . . . . | Aug. 12, 1914 | 25 37.6 | 118 44 | .. | 58 02.1 | .. | WCP |
|  | Aug. 13, 1914 | .. | .. | 0 10.8W | .. | .28600 | WCP |
| Birdsville . . . . | Jun. 9, 1914 | 25 54.3 | 139 21 | 5 29.4E | .. | .30286 | ALK |
|  | Jun. 10, 1914 | .. | .. | .. | 56 09.5 | .. | ALK |
| Water No. 2A . . | Jun. 8, 1914 | 26 00.9 | 120 20 | 0 29.8W | 58 40.5 | .28489 | EK |
| Miranda . . . . | Jun. 6, 1914 | 26 03.9 | 139 52 | 5 28.0E | 56 20.7 | .30206 | ALK |
| Cadelga . . . . | Jun. 3, 1914 | 26 05.5 | 140 24 | 5 37.4E | 56 20.7 | .30148 | ALK |
| Cart Hole Water-hole . . . . | Jun. 12, 1914 | 26 20.9 | 139 15 | 5 17.2E | 56 49.7 | .29962 | ALK |
| Haddon Downs . | May 31, 1914 | 26 21.0 | 140 50 | 5 42.4E | 56 32.8 | .30092 | ALK |
| Kookabubba Well . | Jun. 6, 1914 | 26 21.2 | 120 18 | 0 34.4W | 58 54.3 | .28312 | EK |
| Wiluna . . . . | Jun. 3, 1914 | 26 34.7 | 120 14 | 0 25.6W | 59 01.0 | .28187 | EK |
| Meekatharra . . | Aug. 11, 1914 | 26 35.2 | 118 30 | 1 06.8W | 59 02.4 | .28058 | WCP |
| Cordillo Downs . | May 27, 1914 | 26 42.9 | 140 38 | 5 42.5E | .. | .29844 | ALK |
|  | May 28, 1914 | .. | .. | .. | 57 02.3 | .. | ALK |
| Abercromby Well . | May 31, 1914 | 26 51.6 | 120 20 | 0 32.7W | 59 31.1 | .28008 | EK |
| Moorilyanna . . . | Sep. 25, 1914 | 26 52.2 | 133 01 | 3 19.6E | .. | .29121 | GFD |
|  | Oct. 1, 1914 | .. | .. | .. | 58 22.4 | .. | GFD |
| Moorilyanna, Secondary . . . | Oct. 1, 1914 | 26 52.5 | 133 01 | 3 44.2E | .. | .28678 | GFD |
|  | Oct. 2, 1914 | .. | .. | .. | 58 51.0 | .. | GFD |
| Goyder's Lagoon . | Jun. 15, 1914 | 26 56.7 | 138 57 | 5 14.7E | .. | .29598 | ALK |
|  | Jun. 16, 1914 | .. | .. | .. | 57 27.1 | .. | ALK |
| Wantapella . . . | Sep. 17, 1914 | 27 00.9 | 133 28 | 3 31.4E | .. | .29184 | GFD |
|  | Oct. 10, 1914 | .. | .. | .. | 58 14.5 | .. | GFD |
| Todmorden . . . | Sep. 7, 1914 | 27 08.5 | 131 45 | 4 01.1E | .. | .29243 | GFD |
|  | Sep. 8, 1914 | .. | .. | .. | 58 09.4 | .. | GFD |
| Logan Well . . . | May 29, 1914 | 27 15.7 | 120 28 | .. | 59 52.3 | .. | EK |
|  | May 30, 1914 | .. | .. | 0 33.8W | .. | .27759 | EK |
| Musgrave Range . | Sep. 10, to Nov. 1, 1914 | 27 16 | 131 01 | 3 11 E | (Mean of 20 determinations with compass.) | .. | GFD |
| Mount Gason Bore | Jun. 18, 1914 | 27 20.2 | 138 45 | 5 15.8E | .. | .29342 | ALK |
|  | Jun. 19, 1914 | .. | .. | .. | 57 58.0 | .. | ALK |
| Patchawarra Well, 1 | May 16, 1914 | 27 20.9 | 140 41 | 5 51.7E | .. | .29336 | ALK |
| Patchawarra Well, 2 | May 20, 1914 | 27 20.9 | 140 41 | 5 52.6E | .. | .29366 | ALK |
|  | May 21, 1914 | .. | .. | .. | 57 50.5 | .. | ALK |
| Cue . . . . . | Aug. 8, 1914 | 27 25.6 | 117 53 | 1 38.2W | 60 22.9 | .27257 | WCP |
| Brisbane . . . . | Mar. 23, 1914 | 27 27.0 | 153 02 | 9 01.3E | 56 07.9 | .30146 | FB |
| Marble Well . . | Oct. 16, 1914 | 27 33.1 | 134 00 | 4 23.0E | .. | .. | GFD |
| Stanley's Well . . | Oct. 22, 1914 | 27 42.6 | 134 07 | .. | 58 44.5 | .. | GFD |
|  | Oct. 23, 1914 | .. | .. | 3 28.8E | .. | .28870 | GFD |
| Lake Miranda . . | May 27, 1914 | 27 43.2 | 120 33 | 0 52.0W | 60 03.5 | .27799 | EK |
| Mirra-mitta Bore . | Jun. 21, 1914 | 27 43.7 | 138 44 | 5 06.0E | 58 26.0 | .29048 | ALK |
| Innamincka, 1 . . | May 5, 1914 | 27 45.5 | 140 44 | 5 53.3E | 58 16.6 | .29180 | ALK |
|  | May 6, 1914 | .. | .. | .. | 58 13.5 | .. | ALK |
| Innamincka, 2 . . | May 12, 1914 | 27 45.7 | 140 44 | 5 53.5E | .. | .29194 | ALK |
| Christlieb Well . . | Oct. 27, 1914 | 27 57.2 | 134 46 | 1 17.4E | .. | .28700 | GFD |
| Lawlers . . . . | May 25, 1914 | 28 05.2 | 120 30 | 0 19.8W | 61 08.8 | .27185 | EK |
| Raspberry Creek Bore . . . . | Oct. 30, 1914 | 28 08.2 | 135 05 | 3 43.6E | 59 26.0 | .28546 | GFD |
| Nappacoongie Well | May 2, 1914 | 28 11.8 | 140 30 | 5 48.4E | 58 47.0 | .28920 | ALK |
| Nilpinna . . . . | Nov. 3, 1914 | 28 13.1 | 135 42 | 4 07.4E | .. | .28391 | GFD |
|  | Nov. 4, 1914 | .. | .. | .. | 59 47.6 | .. | GFD |
| Ooroowilanie Reservoir . . . | Jun. 24, 1914 | 28 17.0 | 138 40 | 5 08.5E | 59 03.6 | .28748 | ALK |
| Bunbenoo, A . . | Oct. 14, 1916 | 28 17.0 | 115 54 | 2 38.7W | 62 02.1 | .26202 | W&P |

| Station. | Date. | Lat. S. | Long. E. | Declination | Dip. S. | Horizontal Intensity. C.G.S | Obs'r. |
|---|---|---|---|---|---|---|---|
| Bunbenoo, A . . . | Oct. 16, 1916 | .. | .. | .. | 62 01.2 | .. | W&P |
| Bunbenoo, B . . | Oct. 16, 1916 | 28 17.1 | 115 54 | 2 55.9W | 61 51.0 | .. | W&P |
| Bunbenoo, C . . | Oct. 16, 1916 | 28 17.1 | 115 54 | 2 41.4W | 61 50.4 | .. | W&P |
| Tallering, A . . | Oct. 11, 1916 | 28 19.9 | 115 49 | 2 41.8W | 62 01.6 | .26258 | W&P |
| Tallering, B . . . | Oct. 12, 1916 | 28 20.0 | 115 49 | 2 50.9W | 61 50.0 | .26342 | W&P |
| Tallering, C . . | Oct. 13, 1916 | 28 20.0 | 115 49 | 2 34.3W | 61 42.8 | .26378 | W&P |
| Warren's Flat, A . | Oct. 17, 1916 | 28 20.0 | 115 47 | 2 27.2W | 61 50.1 | .26432 | W&P |
|  | Oct. 18, 1916 | .. | .. | .. | 61 50.9 | .. | W&P |
| Warren's Flat, B . | Oct. 18, 1916 | 28 20.1 | 115 47 | 2 36.7W | 61 53.9 | .. | W&P |
| Warren's Flat, C . | Oct. 18, 1916 | 28 20.1 | 115 47 | 2 32.5W | 61 58.2 | .. | W&P |
| Tallering (Sand-plain), A . . | Oct. 19, 1916 | 28 21.1 | 115 48 | 2 36.5W | 61 46.4 | .26538 | W&P |
|  | Oct. 20, 1916 | .. | .. | .. | 61 45.4 | .. | W&P |
| Tallering (Sand-plain), B . . | Oct. 20, 1916 | 28 21.2 | 115 48 | 2 23.4W | 62 08.1 | .. | W&P |
| Tallering (Sand-plain), C . . | Oct. 20, 1916 | 28 21.2 | 115 48 | 2 06.4W | 61 43.5 | .. | W&P |
| Woondenooka, A . | Oct. 23, 1916 | 28 24.5 | 115 29 | 3 49.3W | 61 43.8 | .26459 | W&P |
| Woondenooka, B . | Oct. 23, 1916 | 28 24.6 | 115 29 | 3 45.5W | 61 48.2 | .. | W&P |
| Woondenooka, C . | Oct. 23, 1916 | 28 24.6 | 115 29 | 3 44.2W | 61 48.2 | .. | W&P |
| Pindar, B . . . | Sep. 15, 1916 | 28 28.2 | 115 45 | 3 07.4W | 61 50.1 | .26408 | W&P |
| Pindar, D . . . . | Sep. 18, 1916 | 28 28.2 | 115 45 | 3 12.8W | 61 51.2 | .26452 | W&P |
|  | Sep. 18, 1916 | .. | .. | 3 09.8W | .. | .. | W&P |
| Pindar, A . . . | Sep. 14, 1916 | 28 28.3 | 115 45 | 3 07.4 | 61 49.8 | .26442 | W&P |
| Pindar, C . . . | Sep. 16, 1916 | 28 28.3 | 115 45 | 3 10.0W | 61 50.9 | .26450 | W&P |
| Pindar, E . . . | Sep. 19, 1916 | 28 29.6 | 115 48 | 3 04.0W | 61 54.6 | .26272 | W&P |
| Pindar, G . . . | Sep. 21, 1916 | 28 29.6 | 115 48 | 2 34.7W | 62 01.8 | .26232 | W&P |
| Pindar, F . . . | Sep. 20, 1916 | 28 29.7 | 115 48 | 2 56.5W | 61 56.2 | .26242 | W&P |
| Mullewa, A . . . | Oct. 24, 1916 | 28 32.0 | 115 30 | 3 29.5W | 62 00.5 | .. | W&P |
| Mullewa, B . . | Oct. 24, 1916 | 28 32.1 | 115 30 | 3 26.9W | 61 59.4 | .. | W&P |
| Mullewa, C . . | Oct. 24, 1916 | 28 32.1 | 115 30 | 3 31.2W | 62 04.8 | .. | W&P |
| Murta Murta Well | Apr. 29, 1914 | 28 36.7 | 140 17 | 5 42.8E | .. | .28667 | ALK |
|  | Apr. 30, 1914 | .. | .. | .. | 59 15.2 | .. | ALK |
| Etadunna . . . . | Jun. 27, 1914 | 28 43.1 | 138 38 | 5 23.2E | 59 28.9 | .28484 | ALK |
| Leonora . . . . . | May 20, 1914 | 28 52.0 | 121 18 | 0 30.0W | 61 32.9 | .26811 | EK |
| Dromedary Hill . | Aug. 6, 1914 | 29 02.1 | 118 27 | 1 40.9W | 62 11.2 | .25961 | WCP |
| Carraweena . . . | Apr. 26, 1914 | 29 11.0 | 139 59 | 5 43.2E | .. | .28336 | ALK |
|  | Apr. 27, 1914 | .. | .. | .. | 59 57.8 | .. | ALK |
| Clayton Bore . . | Jun. 30, 1914 | 29 16.8 | 138 23 | 5 16.8E | 60 02.7 | .28282 | ALK |
| Murnpeowie . . . | Apr. 19, 1914 | 29 35.3 | 139 03 | 5 31.8E | 60 20.2 | .28048 | ALK |
| Mount Hopeless Bore . . . | Apr. 23, 1914 | 29 36.4 | 139 45 | 5 26.2E | .. | .28050 | ALK |
|  | Apr. 24, 1914 | .. | .. | .. | 60 17.7 | .. | ALK |
| Hergott· Springs . | Jul. 5, 1914 | 29 39.4 | 138 03 | 5 11.5E | 60 33.2 | .27934 | ALK |
| Pinjarrega, B . . | Nov. 15, 1916 | 30 02.5 | 115 57 | 4 09.5W | 63 21.8 | .25356 | W&P |
| Pinjarrega, C . . | Nov. 17, 1916 | 30 02.5 | 115 57 | 4 03.2W | 63 20.9 | .25321 | W&P |
| Farina, A . . . . | Apr. 9, 1914 | 30 04.4 | 138 17 | 5 52.0E | 61 01.4 | .27632 | ALK |
|  | Apr. 10, 1914 | .. | .. | .. | 61 01.5 | .. | ALK |
| Marchagee, A . . | Nov. 9, 1916 | 30 05.1 | 115 56 | 4 20.8W | 63 24.8 | .25317 | W&P |
|  | Nov. 10, 1916 | .. | .. | .. | 63 23.0 | .. | W&P |
| Marchagee, D . . | Nov. 10, 1916 | 30 05.1 | 115 56 | 4 16.2W | 63 26.8 | .. | W&P |
|  | Nov. 11, 1916 | .. | .. | .. | .. | .25326 | W&P |
| Marchagee, B . . | Nov. 10, 1916 | 30 05.2 | 115 56 | 4 16.0W | 63 23.4 | .. | W&P |
|  | Nov. 11, 1916 | .. | .. | .. | .. | .25330 | W&P |
| Marchagee, C . . | Nov. 10, 1916 | 30 05.2 | 115 56 | 4 17.8W | 63 25.8 | .. | W&P |
|  | Nov. 11, 1916 | .. | .. | .. | .. | .25334 | W&P |
| Mount Lyndhurst . | Apr. 15, 1914 | 30 11.0 | 138 42 | 5 32.9E | 61 02.2 | .27534 | ALK |
| Watheroo, A . . | Dec. 20, 1916 | 30 17.8 | 116 03 | 4 10.1W | 64 01.3 | .25100 | W&P |
| Watheroo, Obser- tory Site, B . . | Feb. 10, 1917 | 30 18.9 | 115 53 | 4 23.8W | 63 43.2 | .25052 | W&P |
| Watheroo, Obser- vatory Site, C . | Feb. 12, 1917 | 30 19.0 | 115 53 | 4 21.7W | 63 42.2 | .25082 | W&P |
| Watheroo, Obser- vatory Site, D . | Feb. 13, 1917 | 30 19.0 | 115 53 | 4 25.7W | 63 42.0 | .25074 | W&P |
| Managum Well, A | Feb. 5, 1917 | 30 20.6 | 115 58 | 4 57.7W | 63 49.7 | .24998 | W&P |
|  | Feb. 9, 1917 | .. | .. | .. | 63 53.8 | .. | W&P |
| Managum Well, B | Feb. 9, 1917 | 30 20.6 | 115 58 | 4 51.2W | 63 52.2 | .. | W&P |
| Managum Well, C | Feb. 9, 1917 | 30 20.6 | 115 58 | 5 06.3W | 63 52.5 | .. | W&P |
| Rabbit-proof Fence No. 3 . . . . . | Aug. 4, 1914 | 30 23.4 | 118 32 | 2 34.6W | 63 21.4 | .25528 | WCP |

| Station. | Date. | Lat. S. | Long. E. | Declination. | Dip. S. | Horizontal Intensity. | Obs'r. |
|---|---|---|---|---|---|---|---|
| | | | | | | C.G.S | |
| Carnding Well . . | Sep. 12, 1914 | 30 27.4 | 134 13 | 4 07.6E | .. | .26680 | ALK |
| | Sep. 13, 1914 | .. | .. | .. | 62 10.8 | .. | ALK |
| Ooldea Bore . . . | Sep. 23, 1914 | 30 27.9 | 131 50 | 3 07.2E | .. | .26782 | ALK |
| | Sep. 24, 1914 | .. | .. | .. | 62 16.6 | .. | ALK |
| Yallalie Well . . . | Jan. 27, 1917 | 30 28.2 | 115 47 | 4 11.8W | 63 53.8 | .24928 | W&P |
| Bore A . . . . . | Sep. 25, 1914 | 30 30.2 | 131 25 | 2 56.0E | 62 04.9 | .26874 | ALK |
| Green's Well . . | Jan. 25, 1917 | 30 31.5 | 115 44 | 4 06.5W | 63 55.0 | .24886 | W&P |
| Bench Mark, 56½ | Sep. 19, 1914 | 30 32.8 | 132 46 | 3 00.4E | 61 44.6 | .27210 | ALK |
| Wynbring Rock Hole . . . . . | Sep. 16, 1914 | 30 33.7 | 133 39 | 3 45.8E | 63 04.7 | .26448 | ALK |
| Bore B . . . . . | Sep. 26, 1914 | 30 34.1 | 130 55 | 2 27.0E | 62 11.8 | .26850 | ALK |
| Karamara, 4N . . | Jul. 14, 1916 | 30 37.9 | 115 52 | .. | 63 57.7 | .. | P&R |
| Karamara, 6N . . | Jul. 14, 1916 | 30 37.9 | 115 52 | .. | 63 58.6 | .. | P&R |
| Moora . . . . . | Jul. 22, 1914 | 30 38.0 | 115 59 | 4 40.9W | 63 52.8 | .25016 | WCP |
| Karamara, A . . | Jul. 14, 1916 | 30 38.0 | 115 52 | .. | .. | .24875 | P&R |
| Karamara, 2N . . | Jul. 14, 1916 | 30 38.0 | 115 52 | .. | 63 58.9 | .. | P&R |
| Karamara, 2S . . | Jul. 14, 1916 | 30 38.0 | 115 52 | .. | 63 57.7 | .. | P&R |
| Karamara, 4S . . | Jul. 14, 1916 | 30 38.1 | 115 52 | .. | 63 59.7 | .. | P&R |
| Karamara, 6S . . | Jul. 14, 1916 | 30 38.1 | 115 52 | .. | 63 58.5 | .. | P&R |
| Tarcoola . . . . | Sep. 8, 1914 | 30 41.8 | 134 34 | 4 04.8E | 62 09.4 | .26544 | ALK |
| Gilbert's Well . . | Sep. 5, 1914 | 30 51.4 | 135 06 | .. | 62 08.8 | .. | ALK |
| | Sep. 6, 1914 | .. | .. | 3 36.2E | 62 09.5 | .26796 | ALK |
| Wongan Hills, A . | Jul. 29, 1916 | 30 53.6 | 116 43 | 3 40.0W | 64 12.8 | .24908 | WCP |
| | Sep. 9, 1916 | .. | .. | 3 37.8W | 64 14.4 | .24881 | W&P |
| Wongan Hills, A, Secondary . . | Jul. 29, 1916 | 30 53.6 | 116 43 | 3 35.7W | .. | .. | WCP |
| Wongan Hills, B . | Sep. 10, 1916 | 30 53.6 | 116 43 | 1 50.1W | 64 07.0 | .24897 | W&P |
| Wongan Hills, C . | Sep. 11, 1916 | 30 53.6 | 116 43 | 3 36.6W | 64 06.4 | .24990 | W&P |
| | Sep. 11, 1916 | .. | .. | 3 31.9W | .. | .. | W&P |
| Coolgardie . . . | May 9, 1914 | 30 57.2 | 121 11 | 1 33.6W | 63 32.5 | .25522 | EK |
| McArthur's Well . | Sep. 13, 1914 | 31 01.4 | 135 43 | 4 15.5E | 62 30.9 | .26732 | ALK |
| Nealyon's Rockhole | Oct. 1, 1914 | 31 07.0 | 131 17 | 3 15.0E | 62 50.0 | .26353 | ALK |
| Wirraminna . . . | Sep. 1, 1914 | 31 10.9 | 136 16 | 4 20.7E | 62 40.6 | .26560 | ALK |
| East-West Railway Siding . . . . | Aug. 27, 1914 | 31 16 | 136 47 | 4 28.1E | .. | .26729 | ALK |
| | Aug. 28, 1914 | .. | .. | 4 27.6E | 62 31.2 | .26716 | ALK |
| Burracoppin, D . | Aug. 31, 1916 | 31 21.0 | 118 33 | 2 05.2W | 64 25.1 | .24850 | WCP |
| Burracoppin, B . | Aug. 29, 1916 | 31 21.1 | 118 33 | 2 21.0W | 64 49.3 | .24483 | W&P |
| Burracoppin, C . | Aug. 30, 1916 | 31 21.2 | 118 33 | 2 36.4W | 64 43.2 | .24447 | W&P |
| Burracoppin, A . | Aug. 26, 1916 | 31 24.4 | 118 31 | 2 00.2W | 64 24.7 | .24876 | W&P |
| Mallabie Tanks . . | Oct. 4, 1914 | 31 27.8 | 130 39 | 2 04.2E | .. | .25917 | ALK |
| | Oct. 5, 1914 | .. | .. | .. | 63 38.1 | .. | ALK |
| Yangoonabie . . . | Oct. 6, 1914 | 31 28.5 | 130 05 | 2 02.8E | 63 46.8 | .25826 | ALK |
| Merredin, A . . . | Sep. 2, 1916 | 31 28.6 | 118 17 | 3 28.2W | 64 32.6 | .24810 | W&P |
| Merredin, B . . . | Sep. 4, 1916 | 31 28.6 | 118 17 | 3 05.4W | 64 58.0 | .24448 | W&P |
| Bunabie . . . . . | Oct. 8, 1914 | 31 31.2 | 129 22 | 1 48.7E | .. | .26018 | ALK |
| | Oct. 9, 1914 | .. | .. | .. | 63 17.7 | .. | ALK |
| Rabbit-proof Fence 2 . . . . . . | Aug. 2, 1914 | 31 39.0 | 118 42 | 2 56.2W | 64 58.5 | .24640 | WCP |
| Eucla . . . . . . | Jun. 12, 1914 | 31 43.3 | 128 53 | 1 43.7E | 63 37.6 | .25832 | WCP |
| | Jun. 14, 1914 | .. | .. | 1 41.4E | .. | .25840 | WCP |
| | Jun. 14, 1914 | .. | .. | 1 39.6E | .. | .. | WCP |
| | Oct. 31, 1914 | .. | .. | 1 48.6E | 63 35.2 | .25836 | ALK |
| Madura . . . . . | Jun. 17, 1914 | 31 54.2 | 127 02 | 2 01.0E | 64 00.6 | .25110 | WCP |
| Bookooloo . . . . | Aug 23, 1914 | 31 54.2 | 137 22 | 4 45.8E | 63 18.4 | .26101 | ALK |
| Perth . . . . . . | Apr. 6, 1914 | 31 58.0 | 115 50 | 4 43.0W | 65 06.8 | .. | WCP |
| | Apr. 8, 1914 | .. | .. | .. | .. | .24244 | WCP |
| | Apr. 13, 1914 | .. | .. | 4 41.6W | 65 03.1 | .24239 | EK |
| | Jun. 13, 1916 | .. | .. | 4 41.8W | .. | .24152 | WCP |
| | Jun. 15, 1916 | .. | .. | 4 45.1W | .. | .. | WCP |
| Cottesloe, A . . . | Nov. 18, to Nov. 25, 1914 | 31 59.0 | 115 45 | 4 43.8W | .. | .24230 | EK |
| | Nov. 26, to Dec. 5, 1914 | .. | .. | .. | 65 03.6 | .. | K&B |
| | Jun. 30, 1916 | .. | .. | 4 44.0W | .. | .24138 | WCP |
| | July 1, 1916 | .. | .. | 4 42.2W | .. | .. | WCP |
| | July 6, 1916 | .. | .. | .. | 65 11.1 | .. | WCP |
| | Aug. 16, 1916 | .. | .. | 4 45.6W | .. | .. | WCP |
| | Oct. 2, 1916 | .. | .. | 4 48.4W | .. | .. | WCP |
| | Nov. 16, 1916 | .. | .. | 4 46.5W | .. | .. | WCP |

| Station. | Date. | Lat. S. | Long. E. | Declination. | Dip. S. | Horizontal Intensity. C.G.S | Obs'r. |
|---|---|---|---|---|---|---|---|
| Cottesloe, B . . . | Nov. 18, to |  |  |  |  |  | WCP |
|  | Nov. 25, 1914 | 31 59.0 | 115 45 | 4 42.6W | .. | .24226 | WCP |
|  | Nov. 26, to |  |  |  |  |  |  |
|  | Dec. 5, 1914 | .. | .. |  | 65 03.4 | .. | WCP |
| Cottesloe, C . . . | Nov. 18, to |  |  |  |  |  |  |
|  | Nov. 25, 1914 | 31 59.0 | 115 45 | 4 42.6W | .. | .24227 | B&K |
| Rottnest Island . | Apr. 14, 1914 | 32 00.2 | 115 33 | 4 47.6W | 65 27.3 | .24164 | WCP |
| Norseman . . . . | Jun. 25, 1914 | 32 12.2 | 121 48 | 4 34.6W | 64 47.7 | .24692 | WCP |
| Cardanumbi . . | Jun. 8, 1914 | 32 16.3 | 125 38 | 0 12.5E | 64 36.2 | .25040 | WCP |
| Balladonia . . . | Jun. 6, 1914 | 32 28.4 | 123 53 | 0 22.7W | 65 08.6 | .24533 | WCP |
|  | Jun. 20, 1914 | .. | .. |  | 65 04.2 | .. | WCP |
| Port Augusta . . | Aug. 6, 1914 | 32 29.7 | 137 46 | 4 48.7E | .. | .25607 | ALK |
|  | Aug. 7, 1914 | .. | .. | 4 53.7E | 64 07.0 | .25605 | ALK |
| Wilmington . . . | Sep. 2, 1916 | 32 39.3 | 138 05 | .. | 64 08.6 | .. | GFD |
|  | Sep. 5, 1916 | .. | .. | 5 43.8E | .. | .25614 | GFD |
| Melrose . . . . . | Sep. 12, 1916 | 32 48.4 | 138 12 | .. | 64 03.2 | .. | GFD |
|  | Sep. 13, 1916 | .. | .. | 5 47.0E | .. | .25618 | GFD |
| Booleroo Centre . | Sep. 20, 1916 | 32 53.0 | 138 21 | .. | 63 58.4 | .. | GFD |
|  | Sep. 21, 1916 | .. | .. | 5 40.8E | .. | .25686 | GFD |
|  | Sep. 23, 1916 | .. | .. | 5 41.5E | .. | .25637 | GFD |
| Rabbit-proof Fence. 1 . . . | May 21, 1914 | 32 54.0 | 119 48 | .. | 65 48.4 | .. | WCP |
|  | May 22, 1914 | .. | .. | 2 25.4W | .. | .23978 | WCP |
| Bunbury . . . . | Apr. 25, 1914 | 33 19.5 | 115 38 | 5 41.8W | 66 11.5 | .23404 | WCP |
| Israelite Bay . . | May 30, 1914 | 33 36.4 | 123 48 | .. | 66 00.8 | .24066 | WCP |
| Red Hill, A . . | May 26, 1916 | 33 44.5 | 151 04 | .. | 63 17.8 | .. | WCP |
|  | May 27, 1916 | .. | .. | 9 18.8E | .. | .26117 | WCP |
| Red Hill, B . . . | Jan. 12, 1915 | 33 44.5 | 151 04 | 9 19.2E | 63 15.7 | .26170 | WCP |
| Esperance . . . . | May 27, 1914 | 33 51.4 | 121 53 | 2 23.2W | 66 34.6 | .23371 | WCP |
| Hopetoun . . . . | May 19, 1914 | 33 53.6 | 120 09 | 3 22.1W | 66 25.0 | .23354 | WCP |
| Eleven-mile Dam, A | July 23, 1916 | 34 16.8 | 117 45 | .. | 67 13.4 | .. | WCP |
| Eleven-mile Dam, B | July 23, 1916 | 34 16.8 | 117 45 | .. | 67 19.0 | .. | WCP |
| Kapunda . . . . | Dec. 23, 1915 | 34 20.4 | 138 55 | 6 30.2E | 65 11.4 | .24810 | GFD |
| Cape Leeuwin . . | Apr. 28, 1914 | 34 22.1 | 115 08 | 5 50.8W | 67 37.1 | .22404 | WCP |
| Marra . . . . . | May 16, 1914 | 34 25.4 | 118 47 | 6 24.8W | 68 47.3 | .21899 | WCP |
| Angaston . . . . | Dec. 21, 1915 | 34 30.5 | 139 03 | 6 43.6E | 65 43.0 | .24894 | GFD |
| Roseworthy . . . | Sep. 6, 1915 | 34 32.0 | 138 45 | 6 11.8E | .. | .24592 | GFD |
|  | Sep. 7, 1915 | .. | .. | .. | 65 40.2 | .. | GFD |
| Gawler . . . . . | Dec. 16, 1915 | 34 37.1 | 138 44 | .. | 65 52.6 | .. | GFD |
|  | Dec. 17, 1915 | .. | .. | 6 00.6E | .. | .24454 | GFD |
| Adelaide (South Park) . . . . . | Mar. 6, 1914 | 34 56.2 | 138 36 | 5 48.4E | 66 08.2 | .24273 | FB |
| Port Frankland . | May 5, 1914 | 34 59.8 | 116 49 | 5 56.3W | 67 37.8 | .22476 | WCP |
| Blackwood, A . . | Mar. 11, to |  |  |  |  |  |  |
|  | Mar. 14, 1914 | 35 00.6 | 138 36 | 5 17.1E | 66 08.2 | .24203 | WCP |
| Blackwood, B . . | Mar. 11, to |  |  |  |  |  |  |
|  | Mar. 14, 1914 | 35 00.6 | 138 36 | 5 18.3E |  | .24202 | EK |
| Blackwood, C . . | Mar. 11, to |  |  |  |  |  |  |
|  | Mar. 14, 1914 | 35 00.6 | 138 36 | 5 19.0E |  | .24204 | FB |
| Albany . . . . . | May 9, 1914 | 35 01.3 | 117 55 | 5 18.3W | 67 20.7 | .22822 | WCP |
|  | Jun. 18, 1916 | .. | .. | 5 12.2W | 67 26.9 | .22770 | WCP |
| Nairne . . . . . | Jan. 9, 1918 | 35 02.4 | 138 54 | 6 18.5E | .. | .24050 | D&G |
|  | Jan. 10, 1918 | .. | .. | 6 06.6E | 66 03.3 | .. | D&G |
| Murray Bridge . | Mar. 20, 1914 | 35 07.2 | 139 16 | 5 31.8E | 66 18.2 | .24051 | KPK |
| Goolwa . . . . . | Jan. 16, 1918 | 35 30.0 | 138 47 | .. | 66 33.3 | .. | G&D |
|  | Jan. 17, 1918 | .. | .. | 5 28.5E | .. | .23781 | D&G |
|  | Jan. 18, 1918 | .. | .. | .. | 66 38.8 | .. | D&G |
| Port Victor . . . | Mar. 17, 1914 | 35 31.8 | 138 37 | .. | 66 39.4 | .. | P&K |
|  | Mar. 18, 1914 | .. | .. | 5 43.6E | 66 39.2 | .23690 | P&K |
| Port Victor, Secondary . . . | Mar. 18, 1914 | 35 31.8 | 138 37 | .. | 66 39.8 | .. | EK |
| Border Town . . | Mar. 21, 1914 | 36 18.5 | 140 46 | 6 22.4E | 67 04.2 | .23600 | P&K |
|  | May 26, 1916 | .. | .. | .. | 67 07.7 | .. | GFD |
|  | May 27, 1916 | .. | .. | 6 14.6E | .. | .23520 | GFD |
| Kingston . . . . | Mar. 6, 1917 | 36 49.8 | 139 51 | 5 49.2E | 67 51.8 | .23182 | D&G |
| Kybybolite . . . . | May 16, 1917 | 36 53.2 | 140 55 | .. | 67 43.8 | .. | D&G |
|  | May 19, 1917 | .. | .. | 5 55.1E | .. | .22864 | D&G |
| Naracoorte . . . . | May 29, 1916 | 36 57.0 | 140 45 | 6 25.9E | .. | .23124 | G&B |
|  | May 30, 1916 | .. | .. | 6 21.8E | .. | .. | G&B |
| Robe . . . . . . | Feb. 26, 1917 | 37 09.8 | 139 45 | 5 31.8E | .. | .22771 | D&G |

| Station. | Date. | Lat. S. | Long. E. | Declination. | Dip. S. | Horizontal Intensity. C.G.S | Obs'r. |
|---|---|---|---|---|---|---|---|
| Robe . . . . . . | Feb. 27, 1917 | .. | .. | .. | 67 58.7 | .. | D&G |
| Long Gully . . . . | Feb. 28, 1917 | 37 18.2 | 139 50 | 5 36.9E | 68 09.8 | .22746 | D&G |
| Penola . . . . . | Dec. 20, 1916 | 37 22.6 | 140 50 | 6 32.6E | .. | .22838 | D&G |
|  | Dec. 21, 1916 | .. | .. | .. | 67 58.0 | .. | D&G |
| Beachport . . . . | Mar. 23, 1914 | 37 28.8 | 140 00 | 5 33.1E | .. | .22530 | P&K |
|  | Mar. 24, 1914 | .. | .. | .. | 68 25.8 | .. | P&K |
| Beachport, Secondary . . . | Mar. 23, 1914 | 37 28.8 | 140 00 | .. | 68 25.4 | .. | EK |
|  | Mar. 24, 1914 | .. | .. | 5 27.8E | .. | .. | EK |
| Mount Ruskin . . | Feb. 25, 1918 | 38 03.0 | 140 58 | .. | 68 35.2 | .. | D&G |
|  | Feb. 26, 1918 | .. | .. | 6 19.0E | .. | .22254 | D&G |
| Port MacDonnell . | Feb. 12, 1918 | 38 03.4 | 140 42 | 6 06.0E | .. | .22260 | D&G |
|  | Feb. 14, 1918 | .. | .. | .. | 68 37.8 | .. | D&G |
| Currie, B . . . . | Jan. 20, 1914 | 39 54.3 | 143 51 | 8 02.5E | 69 37.2 | .21543 | EK |
| Currie, A . . . . | Jan. 18, 1914 | 39 56.0 | 143 50 | .. | 69 39.6 | .. | EK |
|  | Jan. 19, 1914 | .. | .. | 8 09.1E | .. | .21513 | EK |
| Currie, A, Secondary . . . | Jan. 19, 1914 | 39 56.0 | 143 50* | 8 19 E | .. | .. | EK |
| White Mark . . . | Jan. 22, 1914 | 40 07.4 | 148 02 | 9 36.5E | 69 18.3 | .21786 | FB |
|  | Jan. 23, 1914 | .. | .. | 9 30.0E | .. | .. | FB |
|  | Jan. 23, 1914 | .. | .. | 9 35.4E | .. | .. | FB |
| White Mark, Secondary . . . | Jan. 23, 1914 | 40 07.4 | 148 02 | 9 31.2E | .. | .. | FB |
| Gladstone . . . . | Jan. 14, 1914 | 40 57.6 | 148 00 | 9 44.1E | 69 59.8 | .21180 | FB |
|  | Jan. 14, 1914 | .. | .. | 9 50.9E | .. | .. | FB |
| Latrobe . . . . . | Jan. 14, 1914 | 41 14.8 | 146 27 | 9 36.9E | .. | .20028 | EK |
|  | Jan. 15, 1914 | .. | .. | .. | 70 25.2 | .. | EK |
| Scamander, A . . | Jan. 12, 1914 | 41 26.7 | 148 18 | 9 55.6E | 70 21.6 | .20929 | EK |
| Scamander, B . . | Jan. 12, 1914 | 41 26.7 | 148 18 | 9 49.8E | .. | .. | EK |
| Strahan . . . . | Jan. 18, 1914 | 42 09.6 | 145 21 | 9 01.8E | 71 17.7 | .20183 | FB |
| Oatlands . . . . | Jan. 9, 1914 | 42 17.2 | 147 23 | 9 17.7E | 71 00.8 | .20268 | K&B |
| Hobart, D . . . . | Jan. 7, 1914 | 42 52.2 | 147 21 | 9 01.6E | 71 23.4 | .19932 | K&B |
|  | Jan. 7, 1914 | .. | .. | 9 02.4E | .. | .. | K&B |
| Hobart, D, Secondary . . . | Jan. 7, 1914 | 42 52.2 | 147 21 | 9 06.8E | .. | .. | EK |
| Southport, A . . | Jan. 2, 1914 | 43 25.9 | 147 01 | 10 56.6E | .. | .19003 | EK |
|  | Jan. 3, 1914 | .. | .. | .. | 72 24.2 | .. | EK |
| Southport, B . . | Jan. 3, 1914 | 43 25.9 | 147 01 | 10 21.8E | 72 15 | .. | EK |
| Southport, C . . | Jan. 4, 1914 | 43 26.2 | 147 00 | 10 04.9E | 72 12.5 | .19401 | EK |

Note: A number of stations were occupied in South Australia by Mr. G. F. Dodwell (GFD), Government Astronomer, with a magnetometer loaned by the Department of Terrestrial Magnetism. These observations have been included in the above. Mr. Dodwell was assisted during one period by Prof. Kerr Grant, of the Adelaide University (D&G).

# SKELETONS OF THE MONOTREMES IN THE COLLECTIONS OF THE ARMY MEDICAL MUSEUM AT WASHINGTON.

By Dr. R. W. Shufeldt, C.M.Z.S., Washington, D.C.

Plates XVIII.-XXII.

[Originally written for the Hobart-Melbourne meeting of the Australasian Association for the Advancement of Science, January, 1921]*

(Read before the Royal Society of Tasmania, 8th August, 1921.)

Attention was recently invited to the existence in the collections of the Army Medical Museum, of the Surgeon General's Office, at Washington, of the mounted skeletons of certain of the *Monotremata*; and as these curious mammals are now becoming extremely rare, a brief account of the specimens of them will probably prove of value to the comparative anatomists of the future, and of more or less interest to those of the present time. [1]

These skeletons consist of one of an Echidna, and two of the Duckbill *Platypus* or *Ornithorhynchus*. On the Echidna skeleton the label reads:—"2496 Comp. Anat. Ser.—Spiny "ant-eater; echidna aculeata or hystrix. From New South "Wales. The jaws are without teeth; roof of mouth and "tongue covered with horny spines." This is apparently an adult specimen, prepared and mounted by the Wards of Rochester, and in perfect condition. One of their labels is pasted on the under side of the stand and bears the number 3760 and the statement that the animal was obtained in New South Wales.

The better specimen of the two Duckbills was also prepared by the Wards; it is on a large, solid black-walnut stand without trimmings, and has their unnumbered label

*Owing to the Shipping Strike, the Meeting of the A.A.A.S., which was to have been held in Hobart in January, had to be held in Melbourne. It was found impossible to bring out the usual Report of the A.A.A.S. Meeting and to print all papers. Arrangements were, therefore, made for certain papers to be read before the Society and printed in the Papers and Proceedings for 1921.

(1) SHUFELDT, R. W.—"The Section of Comparative Anatomy of the "Army Medical Museum." *Medical Review of Reviews*, New York, Feb., 1919, Vol. XXV., No. 2, pp. 85-90, 4 figs. Presents a nearly complete list of the vertebrate skeletons in the Section at the time the article appeared.

on the under side, which simply states that it is an *"Ornitho-*
*"rhynchus anatinus; Ornithorhynchus, Australia."* This is
the larger of the Duckbills, and its Army Medical Museum
label reads:—"1304 Comp. Anat. Ser.—Duck bill platypus
"from Australia: ornithorhynchus anatinus." Finally we
have the smaller skeleton of the *Ornithorhynchus,* in which
the skull is broken. It is mounted on a pine board, painted
black, and varnished. (Figs. 1 and 2.) It is altogether too
long for the specimen, and has an amateurish appearance
generally. Its Army Medical Museum label is as follows:—
"2639 Comp. Anat. Ser.—Duck-bill male; or ornithorhynchus
"paradoxus. From Brazil. The young have functional molar
"teeth, but the adult has only transverse horny ridges to
"strain the food from the water." [2]         •

All of these species of monotremes are now being ex-
terminated in nature, especially in those sections of their
habitats where man has occupied the country in the greatest
numbers. This extermination is, in fact, being effected
almost entirely through man's agency, which will fully
account for the certainty and more or less rapid increase
of the same, and its very probable complete accomplishment
in time. As in the case of all other animals, the value of
their skeletal remains enhances the nearer their complete
extinction is approached; and we may be well assured that,
in due time, these three skeletons, should they be preserved,
will come to be extremely valuable material.

Not long after the first monotremes fell into the hands
of working morphologists, accounts of their anatomy, and
particularly their osteology, appeared in numerous places
and languages. With the passing of the years, this literature became almost voluminous; while later on the subject
was scarcely touched upon.

Pictorially, the bones of the skeleton in both the echidnas
and the Duckbill Platypus have been figured a good many
times, Sir Richard Owen being one of the heaviest contributors to this side of the subject. When Sir Richard wrote,
however, the idea dominated his mind that the vertebrate
skull was composed of four metamorphosed vertebræ, and

---

(2) Perhaps it will be just as well to note here the errors upon this
label, to eliminate any chance of the reader of the article gaining
the idea that they were made either by the author or the printer.
There is no necessity for the word "or" before "ornithorhynchus,"
which latter should begin with a capital O. The animal does not
come from "Brazil," and the horny ridges on its jaws are placed
longitudinally and not "transverse." It is not likely that they are
intended to "strain the food from the water," as any one will be
convinced of by a casual examination.

R.W.S.

Plate XVIII.

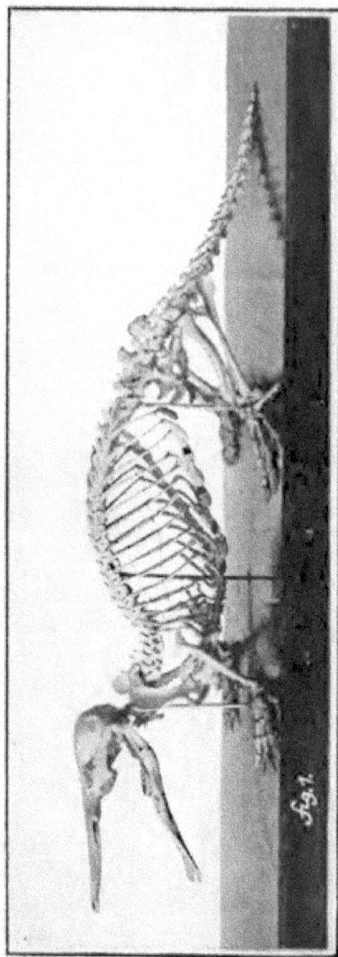

Fig. 1.

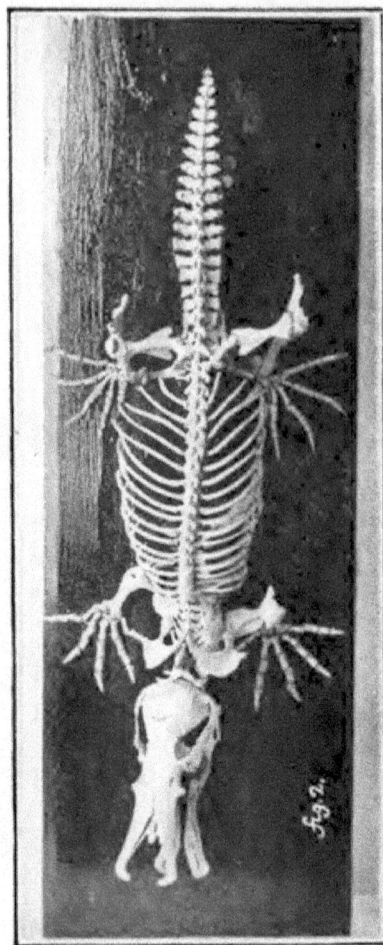

Fig. 2.

consequently ornithorhynchine osteology in his hands was
duly stamped thereby. Nearly all the illustrations of these
curious mammals were prepared by zoological draughtsmen,
who, in many instances, knew little or nothing of osteology;
the consequence was that this deficiency was reflected, to a
greater or less extent, in their work. So far as my knowledge
carries me, little or nothing has been done photographically
with monotreme osteology; so the illustrations to the present
paper should be especially acceptable to mammalian anatomists.

There is one prominent exception to this statement,
however, and it is to be found in the admirable memoir by
Dr. D. M. S. Watson on "The Monotreme Skull, a Contribu-
"tion to Mammalian Morphogenesis." (*Phil. Trans. Ser. B.*,
Vol. 207, March, 1916.)

Among the earliest works we have for consultation on
the skeletology of this order of mammals, is the famous
monograph by Dr. E. d'Alton, with its royal quarto plates
and text matter. [3] About seventeen years after the appearance of this work, there was published in the third
volume (1841) of *The Encyclopædia of Anatomy and Physiology* (1839-1847), pp. 366-407, Figs. 168-202, the extensive
article by Owen on the *Monotremata*, in which he brought
all the then known facts about the group up to date. In
1866, in his *Comparative Anatomy and Physiology of Vertebrates* (Vol. II., pp. 312-328), he included the revised account
of the osteology of the Monotremes. We meet with various
other contributions by the same author; but as they refer
to other systems of anatomy of these animals, as well as to
special organs and parts, and not to the skeleton they need
not be cited here.

Under the article *Mammalia, Platypus* and *Echidna* in
the Ninth Edition of the *Encyclopædia Britannica*, Sir William Henry Flower sums up a large part of our knowledge
of these animals (1883); while with respect to their skeletons, we find more detailed accounts in his *Osteology of the
Mammalia* (3d. Ed., 1885).

(3) D'ALTON, E., DR.—"Die Skelete der Zahnlosen Thiere," abge-
bildet und verglichen. Bonn, 1824 (In Commission bei Eduard
Weber). Pt. I., No. 8. *Vorrede and Einleitung* occupies 4 pp. of
text. *Allgemeine Verglrichungen des Skeletes der Zahnlosen Tiere.*
pp. 4-10; p. 11, Description of Plates. Plate I., Skeleton: side view
of Ornithorhynchus, nat. size. (Fairly good). II.: Bones of same
and an oblique view of the skeleton. Skull to front. Right side
shown. III.: Lateral view of skeleton of Echidna; IV.: Skull and
other bones of Echidna. 21 figs. Large lithographic plates, and
very good for the time. See also the celebrated work of

MECKEL.—*Ornithorhynchi paradoxi Descriptio Anatomica;* Fol. 1826.

Previous to studying these three skeletons of the monotremes in the Army Medical Museum collection—or in connection with their study—the works of Cuvier on the same subject were examined (Leçons d'Anat. Comp. 1837, II., p. 455), as well as the works of Mc. Eydoux and Lament, [4] Geoffrey (Mem. du Museum, tom. XV., p. 32); De Blainville on the Spur and Poison Gland (Bull. Soc. Philomatique, 1817); Blumenbach (Philos. Trans., 1800); Shaw (Naturalists' Miscellany, 1798, Gen. Zool., Vol. I., 1800); Voigt; Home (Philos. Trans., 1802, pp. 67, 356, 1819); Symington and Johnson, who wrote on the homology of the dumb-bell shaped bone in Ornithorhynchus (separate papers under the same title); and the various writings of Carl Gegenbaur. [5]

Of all the general manuals on the osteology of mammals, perhaps no two of them are in more constant use among the researchers of Great Britain, her Colonies, and the United States, than the second volume of Owen's *Comparative Anatomy and Physiology of Vertebrates*, and the last

---

(4) Voyage de la Favorite, 1839, tom. V., pl. 9, p. 161.

(5) The following are some of the works that appeared after the third edition of Flower's *Osteology of the Mammalia* in 1885; and through the kindness of Mr. Newton P. Scudder, the Librarian at the United States National Museum, these have all been carefully examined.

RUGE, GEORG, Prof. Dr. (Amsterdam)—"Das Knorpelskelet des aus"seren Ohres der Monotremen—ein Derivat des Hyoidbogens." Mit 6 Figuren im Text. *Morph. Jahrb.* Leipzig, 1898; pp. 202-223, Figs. 1-6.
     This memoir is very complete on the ear-bones.

FRETS, G. P.—"Uber die Entwicklung der Wirbelsaule von Echidna "hystix" (2 Teil), 14 figs. 1 Tel—Uber die Varietaten der Wirbelsaule bei erwachsenen Echidna, 1908, pp. 608-649. This is a very complete work, and on pp. 649-653 an excellent bibliography of the Monotremes is presented.

EMERY, C.—"Ueber Carpus und Tarsus der Monotremen." (Bologna). Pp. 222-223. Verhandlungen des Gesellschaft Deutscher Naturforchen und Arte. Leipzig, 1900.

Van BEMMELEN, J. F. (Communicated by Prof. C. K. Hoffman).— "Further results of an investigation of the monotreme skull." The Hague. I. Palate. Koninklijke Akad. van Wetenschaffen te Amsterdam. Proc. Sect. of Sciences. Vol. III., pp. 130-133. (June, 1901.) *Ibid.* (July, 1900), pp. 81. Zool. Mr. Hubrecht presents on behalf of Dr. J. F. Bemmelen "The results of comparative investigations "concerning the palatine, orbital, and temporal regions of the Mono"treme skull." (This paper preceded the one last given.) *Ibid.* (pp. 405-407). Third note concerning detail of the Monotreme skull. The Hague. Comm. by Prof. A. A. W. Hubrecht. (Ethmoid and maxillo-turbinate). On p. 133 of the June, 1901, paper, there is presented a figure of "Echidna hystrix; floor of the cerebral cavity, "left side, inner aspect, 2/1." (This is an excellent wash drawing, giving bones, sutures, etc.) On pp. 405-407 in this series, the writer quotes O. Seydel and W. N. Parker "On some points in the struc"ture of the young *Echidna aculeata*." (P.Z.S., 1894.) He also quotes Symington's paper "On the nose, the organs of Jacobson, "and the dumb-bell-shaped bone in the Ornithorhynchus." P.Z.S., 1891, p. 575. (See also Gegenbaur, Harwood-Wiedermann and Zuckerkandi.) See also Verhandlungen des V. Inter. Zool. Cong. zu Berlin, vom. 12-16 Aug., 1901, pp. 596-597. (Discussion). "Ueber das "Ospraemaxillare der Monotremen." Von J. F. van Bemmelen.

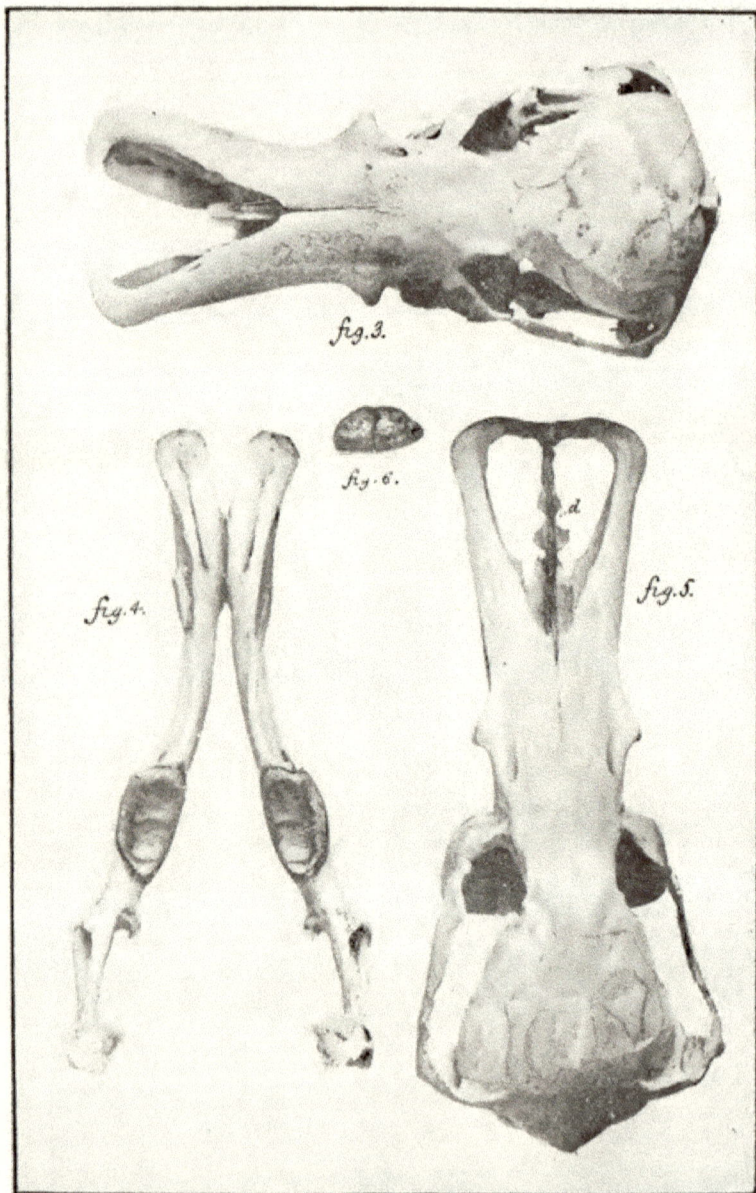

fig. 3.

fig. 6.

fig. 4.

fig. 5.

edition of Flower's *Osteology of the Mammalia*. To be sure, there are a great many special monographs on the skeletology of mammals that are constantly consulted in this line of investigation; but these are not in the same class with a *manual* on the subject—one that essays to give succinct accounts of the bones of the skeleton of mammals in general, such as do the two works mentioned above.

*The Skull in the Adult Duckbill:*—As has already been pointed out by a number of writers on this part of the skeleton in *Ornithorhynchus*, the sutures among the several bones composing it are almost entirely obliterated in the adult, and this is distinctly the case with respect to the skulls of these specimens in the Army Medical Museum. Owen gives us the superior view of the skull of a young Duckbill, wherein the sutures among the bones are in evidence, and it is a very useful cut. (Fig. 205, p. 321).

At *d* in Figures 5 and 9 we have a full view of the much discussed "dumb-bell shaped bone" of authors. Owen speaks of this as a "small prenasal ossicle" (p. 322); while Flower states that "There is a distinct median dumb-bell shaped "ossification in the triangular interval between the diverging "premaxillary bars, placed in front of the anterior extremity "of the mesethmoid cartilage, on the palatal aspect of the "jaw. This bone is not the homologue of the so-called pre- "nasal of the Pig"; but "it corresponds with that part of "the intermaxilla which lies between the incisive canal and "the mesial palatal suture." [6]   (Pp. 243, 244.)

The distal ends of the *premaxillaries* are turned inwards, toward each other and almost at right angles, the interval being about a centimetre. This interval is spanned by a strong, flat ligament, and it is joined, posteriorly, by another ligament, running from the dumb-bell-shaped bone in the median line as shown in Figure 5 of Plate XIX.

On the ventral aspect of the anterior moiety of either maxillary, there is, upon either side, a very shallow, longitudinal groove about two centimetres in length. Horny, pseudo teeth are attached to either of these as shown in Figure 9 of Plate XX. The far more formidable pair is situated considerably further back, each occupying the ventral surface of a *maxillary* upon either side. In the dried skull these structures can easily be pried off, whereupon

---

(6) TURNER, W.—"The dumb-bell-shaped Bone in the Palate of Orni- "thorhynchus compared with the prenasal Bone of the Pig." (Journ. Anat. Phys., XIX., 1885, p. 214.)

ALBRECHT, P.—"Sur la Fente Maxillaire et les quatre Os Intermaxil- "laires de l'Ornithorynque." Bruxelles, 1883.

each has the appearance of Figure 6 of Plate XIX. They take the place of the molar teeth, which, as Flower states, upon either side rest upon the zygomatic process of the maxilla, which is widened inferiorly into an oblong, concave, roughened surface for their attachment. Owen claims that *Ornithorhynchus* has no true malar bone. (P. 322.)

Viewed superiorly, it will be seen that for the most part the cranium of this monotreme is smooth and flat, especially the part anterior to the orbits. There is a conspicuous foramen, on either side, piercing the nasal with a groove leading from it to the front. Laterally, and opposite the broad, thin, and transversely compressed zygoma, the side of the cranium is marked by the temporal fossa; it is shallow, and of equal depth throughout its extent. The narrowest part of the cranium is immediately anterior to this fossa. In the post-basitemporal region there is a pair of large, elliptical foramina, with another smaller pair between them and the posterior nasal apertures.

Between the molar teeth, the surface of the basis cranii is smooth and concaved. On either side may be seen the posterior palatine foramina (Fig. 9), which, next to the interorbital diameter, is the narrowest part of the face. This latter is much flattened, and from behind, forwards, becomes gradually broader, to terminate distally as described in a previous paragraph and here well shown in Figure 5 of Plate XIX. "The infraorbital foramen," as Flower points out, "is "very large, corresponding to the large size of the nerves "distributed to the sensitive sides of the beak. The periotic "has a wide and deep floccular fossa."

The skull belonging to skeleton No. 2639 of the Army Medical Museum has long been broken in two—a fracture that now admits of a view of the interior of the brain case through the absence of the entire anterior wall.

With respect to the general form of the cranial casket, the figures on the plates present more than can be gained through any amount of description. In its interior there is to be noted, however, the small olfactory fossa, pierced at its base by twin foramina, placed side by side transversely. The anteriorly concaved wall rises behind this, the outer angles of which exhibit well developed, posterior *clinoid processes*. Falx cerebri are faintly pronounced and well ossified, especially the postero-median one, which is more or less prominently produced. There appear to be considerable differences in the outline of the *foramen magnum* of the *Ornithorhynchus*; for in the smaller specimen of these two

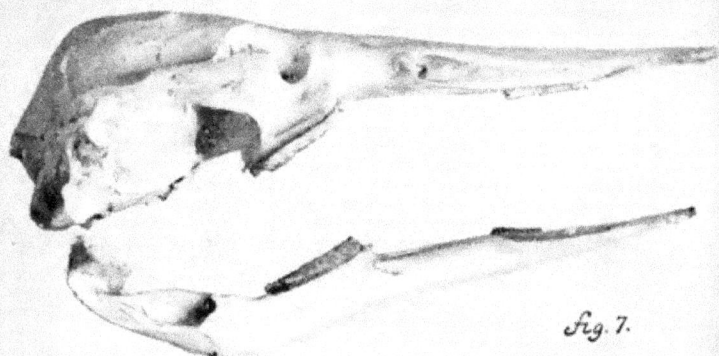

fig. 7.

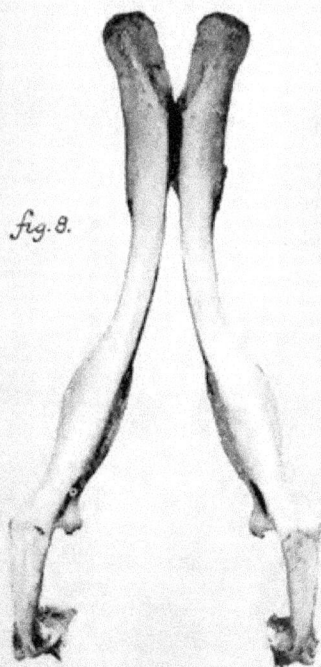

fig. 8.

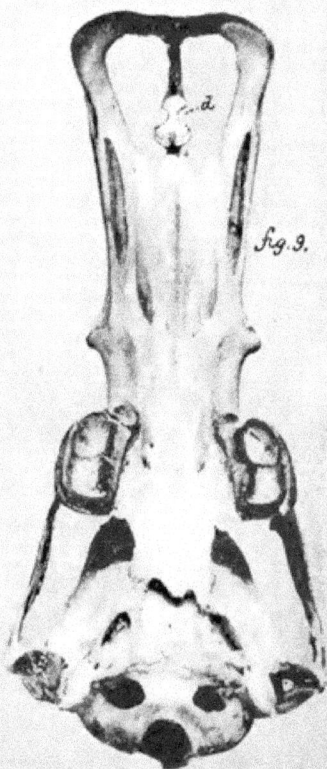

fig. 9.

(2639) this is broad and elliptical, with the major axis horizontal, while in the other specimen it is almost circular. More than this, in the first specimen mentioned there is a well-marked "supraoccipital foramen" present, which is pierced by an elliptical foramen, placed vertically, that opens mesially below by an extremely narrow strait into the superior arc of the foramen magnum. At either side of the cranium the *glenoid fossa* is very pronounced and markedly concave transversely.

As Owen has pointed out, "the *vomer* forms a bony, ver-"tical septum, dividing the nasal cavity from the presphenoid "forward."

Whoever prepared these Army Medical Museum specimens failed to preserve the *hyoidean apparatus* in either of them, so no description of it can be furnished here. Sir Richard Owen does not appear to have described this for either the Echidna or the Duckbill; while Sir William H. Flower, in his "Manual," gives a very excellent cut of the lower surface of the hyoid of the Echidna (*E. aculeata*), and briefly describes it in the text (pp. 242, 243). At this writing I have not at hand a figure and description of the hyoid in *Ornithorhynchus*.

Figures 4, 7, and 8 of the accompanying plates present the three principal views of the *mandible* of the Duckbill; and these, taken in connection with the admirable description by Owen of this remarkable bone (p. 321), leave practically nothing to be desired on this point.

*The Shoulder-girdle and Sternum:*—Both Owen and Flower, in their above-cited work, give quite full accounts of the *shoulder-girdle* and *sternum* in an Echidna and the Duckbill; these accounts are illustrated for the last-named animals, the differences being given in the text. Upon carefully comparing these two descriptions with the corresponding bones of the skeletons at hand, I find that they practically agree in all essential particulars. These parts, in fact, have long been known to comparative anatomists—that is, since Flower published on the subject, for Owen's description is very meagre and unsatisfactory.

Attention is invited to the different way in which the *scapulæ* have been mounted in the two skeletons of the Duckbill. The bones are far apart in No. 1304, while in No. 2639 the upper thirds of these bones have not only been brought, upon either side, flat against the cervical ribs, but actually *wired* in that position. It would appear from the articulations that neither of these is quite correct, and doubtless it is a point that can only be settled through an examination of an adult specimen in the flesh. Personally, I very much doubt that the bones are closely adpressed to the cervical ribs as in the skeleton 2639 (see Fig. 11 for the Echidna).

"In the Monotremata the *Ornithorhynchus*," says Flower, "has a broad presternum, with a small, partially "ossified *pro-osteon* in front of it; three keeled mesosternal "segments, which commence to ossify in pairs, and no xiphi-"sternum, which in *E. bruijni* consists of three metameric "portions.

"The T-shaped bone, *interclavicle* or *episternum* in front "of the presternum, which connects it with the clavicle and is "often completely fused with it, appears to have no homo-"logue among the other Mammalia, and belongs more pro-"perly to the shoulder-girdle than to the sternal apparatus" (pp. 104, 105).

*The Vertebral Column and Ribs:*—Judging from the accounts of various anatomists, the vertebræ and the ribs in the Echidnas and the Duckbill are subject, with respect to number, to very considerable variation in different individuals. [7]

In the work of G. P. Frets, cited above, there are tables presenting the great variation in the number of vertebræ in the Echidna—and so it goes for other authorities.

Flower gives us the following table (p. 89) :—

## MONOTREMATA.

| Species. | Cervic. | Thorac. | Lumb. | Sacral | Caudal |
|---|---|---|---|---|---|
| Echidna— | | | | | |
| Aculeata . . . | 7 | 16 | 3 | 4 | 11 |
| Bruijni . . . . | 7 | 16 | 4 | 3 | 10 |
| Ornithorhynchus ana- | | | | | |
| tinus . . . . . . | 7 | 17 | 2 | 3 | 20 |

Owen makes a brief statement to the effect that "both "the genera have twenty-six 'true vertebræ,' of which seven "are cervical; but the Ornithorhynchus has seventeen and "the Echidna sixteen dorsals, the lumbar vertebræ being "three in the latter, and reduced to the lacertian number two "in the *Ornithorhynchus*," to which statement he makes no exceptions (p. 316).

(7) BROWN, R., M.B., B.Sc.—"Note on an Echidna with eight vertebræ." *Proc. of the Linn. Soc. of New South Wales*, 1900. Vol. XXV., Sydney, 1901. One cut. "Dorsals vary from 14 to 17; lumbars 2 to 4; "sacrals 3 to 4; caudals 10 to 14." This authority also gives some important notes on the *ribs* of the monotremes.

Plate XXI.

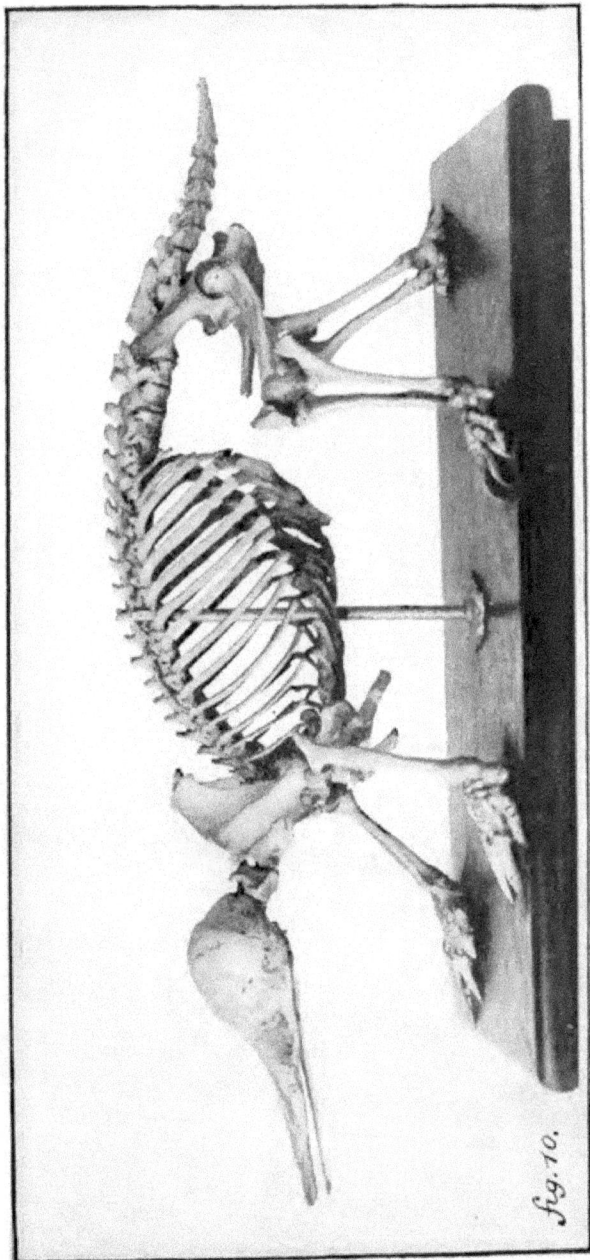

fig.10.

Owen further states that "the sacrum consists of two "vertebræ in *Ornithorhynchus* and three in the *Echidna*. "There are thirteen caudal vertebræ in the Echidna, Fig. "201. The first is the largest, with broad transverse pro- "cesses, the rest progressively diminishing, and reduced, in "the six last, to the central element. The *Ornithorhynchus*, "Fig. 199, has twenty-one caudal vertebræ, of which all but "the last two have transverse processes, and the first eleven "have also spinous and articular processes" (p. 317). The cuts cited are the old figures that illustrated Owen's article on the Monotremes in the third volume of the *Cyclopædia of Anatomy* (1841); they are very crude, especially the one of the Echidna, wherein the number of vertebræ do not agree with the number for the Echidna given in the text, and the cervico-dorsal regions of the spine are altogether too straight.

Flower, in his above cited table, points out that one species of Echidna has eleven caudal vertebræ, and another ten; while in the text in the same work (p. 77) he says:— "The Echidna has 12 caudal vertebræ." Again, in the table, he states that the *Ornithorhynchus* has 20 caudals, while in the text—same page—he informs us that this monotreme "has 20 or 21 caudal vertebræ."

On page 68 he again says that "the Ornithorhynchus has "2 ankylosed sacral vertebræ, and the Echidna 3 or 4." In the table he gives the Ornithorhynchus 3 sacral vertebræ. These discrepancies occur throughout the literature of the subject.

Turning to the vertebræ and ribs of these three Army Medical Museum specimens (Figs. 1, 2, 10, and 11), we find, in the specimen No. 1304, 17 pairs of ribs, the six anterior ones of which articulate with the sternum through sternal or costal ribs. The leading pair of these costal ribs articulate with the extreme outer angles of the presternum; while the last pair, which are very thick for their anterior moieties and more or less flattened posteriorly, articulate with the ultimate joint of the true sternum. Following these, we have 8 ribs that articulate below with costal ribs, the latter being free, very broad, and compressed from above, down-wards. Finally, in the last three pairs of these thoracic ribs are "floating ribs," the last pair being but half the length of the first pair, while the midpair is intermediate in length between these and the first pair. This specimen has *seven* cervical vertebræ; seventeen dorsals; two lumbars; four sacrals; and twenty caudals (counting the terminal one which has been lost).

Turning to the smaller skeleton of these two Duckbills (No. 2639), it is to be noted that the sternal and costal ribs and the vertebræ agree entirely with those of No. 1304, with respect to number and characters.

In his *Osteology of the Mammalia*, Flower has quite fully described the vertebræ of the entire spinal column in the Echidna and the Duckbill; and I find that the specimens here under consideration in no way depart from those descriptions. In these two specimens of *Ornithorhynchus* the *odontoid process* has thoroughly united with its proper vertebræ, which is very good evidence that they are well along in life; and notwithstanding the fact that No. 1304 is much the larger of the two, both having highly developed *spurs* would point toward their both being males.

The *Skull* in the Echidna at hand departs in no way from the descriptions of that part of the skeleton as given by Flower, Owen, and other eminent comparative anatomists, and this is also true of the *sternum* and *shoulder girdle*. The general outline of an Echidna's skull is well shown here in Figures 10 and 11. It is noted for its very feeble and delicately constructed mandible and the general lack of character of the cranium, which is quite devoid of the usual salient apophyses, marked fossæ, and conspicuous foramina.

In the *Ornithorhynchus* the sacrum is of much feebler build than it is in the Echidna, while in both its hinder portion makes an acute angle with the chain of caudal vertebræ. All that Owen has to say about this bone is that "the "sacrum consists of two vertebræ in the *Ornithorhynchus*, "and of three in *Echidna*" (p. 317).

As all three of these skeletons are of adult specimens, it is not possible to decide whether in any of them an *os acetabuli* is present or not. Flower evidently entertained the opinion that the Monotremata lacked this "fourth pelvic "bone," and says of it in general that "its morphological "meaning is as yet unknown, but it can scarcely be consid- "ered as an epiphysis." This authority's description of the *pelvis* in the monotremes agrees with that bone as exemplified in these Army Medical Museum skeletons; he states that "in "the *Monotremata* the pelvis is short and broad. The ilia "are short, distinctly trihedral and everted above. The "ischia are large, and prolonged into a considerable back- "ward-directed tuberosity. The symphysis is long, and "formed about equally by pubes and ischium. The thyroid "foramen is round. The acetabulum is perforated in *Echidna* "as in birds, but not in *Ornithorhynchus*. The pectinal

Plate XXII.

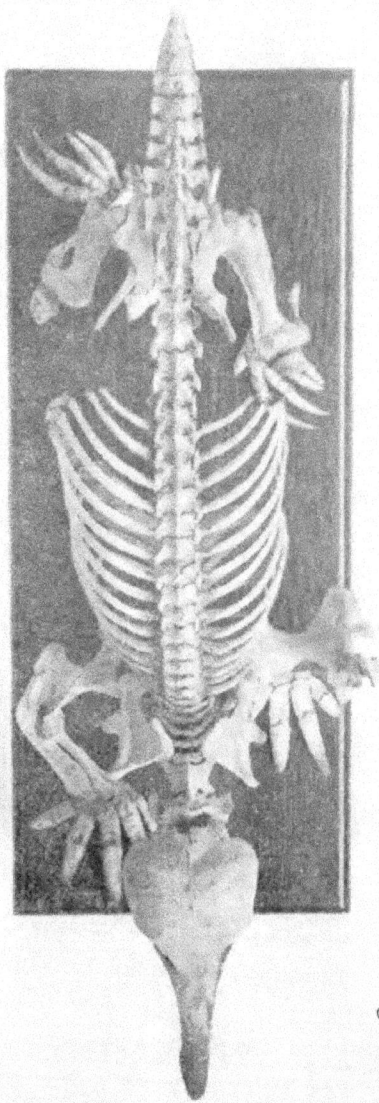

*fig 11.*

"tubercle is greatly developed. There are large 'marsupial' "bones in both genera." These in *Echidna* are longer, narrower, and more divergent than they are in the Duckbill, where they are triangular and broad at their bases. The *sacral vertebræ* fuse with the pelvic bones in these monotremes, and the suture of the pubic symphysis is almost obliterated.

The *Bones of the Limbs* in the *Ornithorhynchus* and the *Echidna* are very fully and quite accurately described by Owen (pp. 323-328), while Flower gives us scarcely anything on the long bones of the pectoral and pelvic limbs, having devoted the most of his space and descriptive matter to *manus* and *pes*, the bones of which are touched upon more or less fully.

In another connection later on it is my intention to take up more in detail some of the special skeletal characters, as exemplified in the *Monotremata*—that is, those that do not fall especially within the scope of the present contribution.

## LEGENDS FOR THE FIGURES.
### PLATE XVIII.

Fig. 1.   Left lateral view of the skeleton of an adult *Ornithorhynchus anatinus*, No. 2639, Army Medical Museum Collection; male; reduced.

Fig. 2.   The same skeleton as shown in Fig. 1, seen directly from above.

### PLATE XIX.

Fig. 3.   Superior view of the skull of the specimen of the *Ornithorhynchus* shown in Figure 1 of Plate XVIII. (No. 2639, Army Medical Museum Collection.) Lower mandible removed. Zygoma of right side missing. Reduced.

Fig. 4.   Mandible of the adult *Ornithorhynchus* viewed directly from above; reduced; male. Specimen No. 1304, Army Medical Museum Collection.

Fig. 5.   Superior view of the skull of an adult male *Ornithorhynchus anatinus*; reduced. Specimen No. 1304, Coll. Army Medical Museum. This is the skull to which the mandible here shown in Figure 4 belongs. The "dumb-bell-"shaped" bone is plainly shown at *d*, between the premaxillary bones, which latter are nearly out of sight below the nasals.

Fig. 6. Horny "tooth" from the left side of the mandible of the specimen shown in Figures 1 and 2 of Plate XVIII.; reduced; superior aspect.

PLATE XX.

Fig. 7. Right lateral view of the skull and detached mandible of an adult male *Ornithorhynchus anatinus*. Specimen 1304 Collection Army Medical Museum. Compare with Figure 4 of Plate XIX. (above), Figure 8 of this Plate for the mandible, and Figures 5 and 9 for the skull.

Fig. 8. Inferior or ventral aspect of the mandible shown in Figure 7; reduced. (See Fig. 4, Plate XIX.)

Fig. 9. Ventral view of the skull of *Ornithorhynchus;* reduced. Same skull as shown in Figure 5 of Plate XIX. (Collection Army Medical Museum.)

PLATE XXI.

Fig. 10. Left lateral view of the skeleton of an *Echidna* (*Tachyglossus*) *aculeata.* Sex? Slightly less than one-half natural size. No. 2639, Coll. Army Medical Museum.

PLATE XXII.

Fig. 11. Direct view from above of the skeleton of an *Echidna* (*Tachyglossus*) *aculeata.* Slightly less than one-half natural size. Same specimen as shown in Figure 10 of Plate XXI. of the present article.

# THE PROGRESS OF GEOLOGICAL RESEARCH IN TASMANIA SINCE 1902.

By

LOFTUS HILLS, M.B.E., M.Sc.,

Government Geologist of Tasmania.

[Originally written for the Hobart-Melbourne Meeting of the Australasian Association for the Advancement of Science, January, 1921.]*

(Read before the Royal Society of Tasmania, 8th August, 1921.)

## I. INTRODUCTION.

On the occasion of the last meeting of this Association in Hobart the late W. H. Twelvetrees presented a paper entitled "The Outlines of the Geology of Tasmania." A period of eighteen years has elapsed since that paper was prepared, and a great advance has been made in our knowledge of the geology of Tasmania during that interval. It, therefore, seems desirable to take the opportunity afforded by the reassembly of the Association in Tasmania of summarising our progress—to take stock of our knowledge and to see what problems still await solution.

It must be stated at once, however, that in spite of the great amount of work accomplished during the period under review, the result, when viewed in relation to the complete geological survey of Tasmania, is to some extent disheartening. This was particularly apparent when the preparation of the Geological Sketch Map of Tasmania was undertaken in 1914 by the Geological Survey of Tasmania. When there had been plotted on the base map the geology of the areas of which geological surveys had been completed, the greater portion of the State still remained blank, and to produce the map as ultimately published, the information contained in R. M. Johnston's original geological map was utilised with sundry modifications. The reason for this is easy to see, for the conditions under which the Geological Survey carries out

---

*Owing to the Shipping Strike the meeting of the A.A.A.S., which was to have been held in Hobart in January, had to be held in Melbourne. As a consequence, numerous difficulties had to be overcome. It was found impossible to bring out the usual Report of the A.A.A.S. meeting, and print all papers. Arrangements were, therefore, made for certain papers to be read before the Society and published in the Papers and Proceedings for 1921.

its work are such as to necessitate detailed investigations of
limited areas, rather than cursory examinations of larger
areas. It must be remembered that the *raison d'etre* of the
Geological Survey is the demand of the Mining Industry for
reports on mineral and coal deposits, and the portions of the
State subjected to such detailed geological examination are
almost wholly confined to our mineral and coal areas. With
the ever-growing demand for examination of mining fields it
has not been possible to pay much attention to the general
geology of the remainder of the Island.

It is not intended to imply that this intensive examination of limited areas is undesirable. In fact, these detailed
investigations are essential to the ultimate elucidation of the
factors controlling ore-deposition in Tasmania, and they have
already enabled important deductions to be made regarding
certain important phases of general geology. The only disappointing feature in regard to them is that indicated above
in relation to the areal geology of the Island.

Before proceeding to deal with the actual progress in
the various branches of geology recognition must be given
to those whose work has made this progress possible.

It is with mixed feelings of admiration and regret that
the writer mentions the name of the late W. H. Twelvetrees
—admiration for the great work he accomplished, and regret
that he was not spared to be present at this meeting and to
be still amongst us. He had looked forward to this meeting
since before its first postponement, and it would have been
very fitting if this summary could have been presented by
him, as it deals very largely with the achievements in geological research by himself and those working under his
genial and able direction. For twenty years the late W. H.
Twelvetrees occupied the position of Government Geologist
of Tasmania, and for seventeen years of the eighteen covered
by this review he directed the acquisition of our knowledge
of the geology of Tasmania. It was he who was responsible
for the initiation of systematic geological surveys of definite
areas in place of the restricted examinations of mining pro-
spects—a change beneficial both to geological science and to
the mining industry. The contributions by this indefatigable
worker to our knowledge embrace all of the branches of geology, but, perhaps, his greatest achievements were in the
domain of petrology. The geological literature of Tasmania
has been greatly enriched as the result of his labours, and
Tasmania undoubtedly must ever remain indebted to him, his
example, and his memory.

Important contributions to our knowledge were made by G. A. Waller, who was Assistant Government Geologist from 1901 to 1904. In addition to his valuable descriptions of many of our ore, deposits and his pioneer work on their genesis, this enthusiastic worker did much to advance our knowledge of the stratigraphy of the Lower Palæozoics on the West Coast, as well as succeeding in throwing much light on the petrology of the associated igneous rocks.

L. Keith Ward, B.A., B.E., during the time he occupied the position of Assistant Government Geologist from 1907 to 1911, was responsible for very great progress in geological research in Tasmania. Immediately after his appointment to the Survey there was instituted the present series of Geological Survey publications which is in accordance with the system in vogue in modern Geological Surveys. His own contributions to this series of publications set a very high standard both as regards literary merit and method of treatment. The thoroughness of his investigations and the illuminating conclusions he drew therefrom have great value both from the importance of the acquired information itself and from the fact that his conclusions and hypotheses supply an invaluable method of approach to many of our petrologic and metallogenic problems.

The work performed by L. L. Waterhouse, B.E., Assistant Government Geologist from 1912 to 1916, has also added to our knowledge. The detailed descriptions contained in the two bulletins prepared by him supply a wealth of information concerning the two areas with which they deal. To this investigator there is undoubtedly due the credit of throwing much light on the detailed petrography of our Devonian granites, and their contact metamorphic deposits, as well as considerable information concerning the factors controlling tin deposition in Tasmania.

To this enumeration of former officers of the Geological Survey of Tasmania, who have materially advanced our knowledge, mention must be made of the present officers of that organisation who are at work on important geological problems. The writer joined the Department in 1912, on the occasion of an increase in the staff of the Survey. Mr. A. McIntosh Reid joined the Geological Survey in 1917, and, together with Messrs. P. B. Nye, B.M.E., and H. G. W. Keid, B.Sc., who were appointed early in 1920, are actively engaged in conducting geological surveys according to the programme authorised by the Honourable the Minister for Mines for Tasmania.

Passing now to those who have contributed towards our knowledge from outside the ranks of the Geological Survey, the name of the late R. M. Johnston, I.S.O., must first be mentioned. The death (in 1918) of this investigator deprived Tasmania of one of her pioneer geologists, and one to whom we are indebted for a great part of our knowledge in regard to the stratigraphy of the Permo-Carboniferous and later systems.

To the late Thos. Stephens, M.A., who died in 1913, we owe appreciable additions to our knowledge of the general geology of the State.

The Grim Reaper has also deprived us of that indefatigable worker in the realms of mineralogy and petrology—the late W. F. Petterd, whose demise took place in 1910. His "Catalogue of the Minerals of Tasmania," published by the Mines Department in 1910, is still the standard work on this subject. In collaboration with the late W. H. Twelvetrees, the late W. F. Petterd contributed largely to our knowledge of the petrography of Tasmanian igneous rocks.

To Professor Sir T. W. Edgeworth David, K.B.E., C.M.G., D.S.O., D.Sc., we are indebted for much advice during the researches of this period under review, as well as for contributions to the literature on the Permo-Carboniferous and Pleistocene glacial geology of Tasmania.

In 1903 Professor J. W. Gregory, D.Sc., visited the West Coast, and his description of the geology and ore-deposits of Mount Lyell, and several other papers on the physiography and glaciation of that portion of Tasmania are valuable additions to our literature.

To Professor E. W. Skeats, D.Sc., is due the credit of definitely determining the Tertiary age of the Port Cygnet alkaline rocks.

Important work on palæontological questions was carried out by W. S. Dun, especially in connection with the age classification of the upper and lower palæozoics. Record No. 1 of the Geological Survey of Tasmania is the work of this palæontologist.

In this domain of palæontology A. F. Chapman, of the National Museum, Melbourne, has assisted us to a great degree in making determinations, and one of his contributions has been published as Geological Survey Record No. 5.

H. H. Scott, Curator of the Victoria Museum, Launceston, has carried out very valuable researches on *Nototherium tasmanicum*, and the results of his labours are embraced by Geological Survey Record No. 4, and that very creditable restoration of the skeleton in the Victoria Museum, Launceston. During the past year this keen investigator, in collaboration with Clive Lord, of the Tasmanian Museum, Hobart, has started the systematic description of *Nototherium mitchelli*, which is the latest discovery in this direction, and the mounted skeleton now on view in Hobart is the work of H. H. Scott.

The late Colonel R. V. Legge did much to increase our knowledge of the topography of Tasmania, particularly the north-eastern portion. His death in 1913 removed another valuable worker in the field of geology.

Professor W. N. Benson, D.Sc., besides contributing towards our petrographical knowledge of our granites and alkaline series, has helped towards the elucidation of the problem of pleistocene glaciation by publishing a study of the Cradle Mountain portion of our highlands.

In addition to these workers in the various branches of geological research, the following have from time to time contributed towards our knowledge:—Fritz Noetling, M.A., Ph.D.; Hartwell Conder, M.A., A.R.S.M.; W. H. Clemes, B.A., B.Sc.; Griffith Taylor, D.Sc., B.A., B.E.; E. C. Andrews; R. C. Sticht; Hyman Herman; H. S. Summers, D.Sc.; Rev. H. H. Anderson, M.A.; Rev. E. D. Atkinson, B.A.; F. Osann; H. Rosenbusch; W. A. MacLeod, B.Sc.; O. E. White; F. P. Paul, Ph.D.

It is thus apparent that the greatest of our unofficial workers have passed the Great Divide, and that the number remaining is lamentably small. Particularly it is noticeable that the number of our Tasmanian observers is limited to two or three—a fact which is much to be regretted, and which must delay the advance of our knowledge to a considerable degree. This lack of geological observers is, in the writer's opinion, very largely due to the fact that for some years past the University of Tasmania has neither provided instruction in the subject of Geology nor held examinations therein, owing to shortage of funds. This neglect of a subject which must inevitably play a very important part in the development of our natural resources is much to be regretted, and every effort should be made to initiate a school of geology at the University. The failure of the University authorities to give this subject the attention which it deserves, both from the utilitarian point of view and from its undoubted educational value, is reflected in our secondary schools, for in the public examinations held last year only two candidates presented themselves for examination in

I

Geology. Under such conditions it is not to be wondered at that there is such a paucity of observers with sufficient knowledge to make observations of value.

The conditions existing in Tasmania at present are, therefore, such that the work of investigating the complex geology of the Island devolves entirely on the Geological Survey. With practically no help from outside, and because of the complexity of our problems, the inclement climatic conditions, the rugged topography, and the heavy forest growth, our progress must be somewhat slow.

## II. PHYSIOGRAPHY.

The advance in this branch of geology has been considerable, but we are still far from a complete understanding of the evolution of the topographic features of Tasmania.

As a matter of fact, there has not yet been produced a topographic map of Tasmania of even approximate accuracy. The existing map of Tasmania is admittedly inaccurate to a marked degree. In fact, there has not yet been completed a trigonometrical survey of the State, as although such a survey was started many years ago, it had not been nearly completed before work on it was suspended, and has not been resumed to date.

The most detailed maps available are the Mineral and Land Charts, which show boundary lines of sections and some of the principal streams and occasional mountain peaks, but even these latter details are to some extent unreliable.

The necessity, therefore, arises of mapping the topography concurrently with the geology in carrying out the work of the Geological Survey. In 1909 the late W. H. Twelvetrees endeavoured to arrange for the addition of a topographer to the Geological Survey staff, but was unsuccessful. The geologists of the Survey, therefore, are compelled to map topographic features as far as opportunity allows or necessity dictates. Under these conditions progress must necessarily be slow.

To Professor J. W. Gregory is due the credit of first recognising the peneplain on the West Coast, which has been so deeply dissected as to make its recognition difficult. The work carried out by the various officers of the Geological Survey since Professor Gregory first drew attention to it has shown that this peneplain extends from northwards of Port Davey to the Mersey River, over an area roughly crescentic in shape, varying in height from 200 to 2,000 feet above sea-level, and having a slope of from 40 to 100 feet per mile. Its age is certainly Pre-glacial, but its relation to the Tertiary basalts has not been satisfactorily demonstrated.

The Central Plateau is clearly a horst as regards its northern, western, and southern precipitous slopes, but recent work by P. B. Nye, B.M.E., has shown that the eastern face is not a fault scarp, but is due to the upthrust of a huge transgressive diabase mass. The work of this investigator in the Midlands has demonstrated that the Midland plain is not a rift valley, as maintained by E. C. Andrews and Dr. Griffith Taylor, but that the diabase masses on either side of this plain are in the approximate positions relatively to the similar rock of the plain which they assumed when originally intruded. It seems, therefore, that the horst must embrace portion of the Eastern Highlands, since undoubted block faulting occurs towards the East Coast. It is hoped that the geological surveys of the East Coast coal-fields at present in progress will definitely settle this question.

A considerable amount of work has been done on the problem of our Pleistocene glaciation, but as this is dealt with in a special report by the Glacial Sub-committee, there is no need to repeat a description of it. Suffice it to say, that a number of glacial cirques have been located and described, as well as lakes of glacial origin, and the maximum descent of the glaciers determined to be 460 feet above present sea level.

Some advance has been made in our knowledge of the Recent oscillations of sea-level on the North and West Coasts, but we are far from being able to outline these with any degree of accuracy. The work of E. C. Andrews, Charles Hedley, and Fritz Noetling must be acknowledged in this connection.

### III. STRATIGRAPHICAL GEOLOGY.

#### (1). PRE-CAMBRIAN.

Since the late W. H. Twelvetrees presented a summary of our knowledge of Tasmanian Pre-Cambrian geology before this Association in 1907, there has been some definite advance in our knowledge. This advance resulted mainly from two exploratory journeys made in 1908 and 1909 by the late W. H. Twelvetrees, in conjunction with L. K. Ward, B.A., B.E., on the route of the proposed Great Western Railway.

In the description of these Pre-Cambrian rocks presented by L. K. Ward, in a paper read before The Royal Society of Tasmania in 1909, the age determination is based on the well-determined fact that they underlie with a marked unconformity the West Coast Range Conglomerate series, which was regarded by Ward as of Lower Cambrian age. It has subsequently been demonstrated, however, that this West Coast Range Conglomerate series is the basal conglomerate of the Silurian System, so that the observed stratigraphical succession gives no more definite age determination than that of Pre-Silurian. The only occurrence *in situ* of rocks of Cambrian Age in Tasmania is that of the Dikelocephalus sandstone near Railton, but as the exact relationship between this series and any other rock series in the vicinity has not been demonstrated, there must be some doubt as to the Pre-Cambrian Age determination. Certainly, the very fresh character of the Cambrian sandstone as compared with the schistose character of the rock series referred to as Pre-Cambrian is suggestive, and the Pre-Cambrian age determination is largely based on lithological character.

That the reference of this rock series to the Pre-Cambrian is most probably correct is indicated by the fact that the following is the definitely ascertained succession:—

*Silurian.*—West Coast Range Conglomerate Series. Diastrophic Period and Erosion Interval.

*Cambro-Ordovician.* — Porphyroid Igneous Complex. Diastrophic Period and Erosion Interval.

*Pre-Cambrian* (?).—Quartzites and Mica-Schists.

Accepting their Pre-Cambrian age, L. K. Ward refers them to the Algonkian, and subdivides them into an Upper and Lower Series—the upper consisting of a relatively gently folded series of white quartzites, and the lower series of intensely crumpled mica and quartz schists, the two being separated by an unconformity. In the vicinity of Point Hibbs the mica-schists contain intercalated beds of dolomitic limestones, this being the only locality in Tasmania where calcareous beds are known to occur in the Pre-Cambrian.

The areas occupied by these rocks have been indicated in the latest geological map of Tasmania. Their greatest development is in the south-western portion of the Island, although isolated areas of much lesser extent occur on the west, north-west, and north coasts. The late W. H. Twelvetrees estimated the total thickness to be 13,000 feet, but in view of the fact that the structural geology has not been

worked out in even approximate detail, this must be regarded
—as the author of it himself regarded it—as a tentative
approximation.

## (2). CAMBRO-ORDOVICIAN.

It is in this system and in the succeeding Silurian system that the greatest progress in Tasmanian stratigraphy
has been accomplished during the period under review.

In 1902 the late T. S. Hall described some graptolites
from the slates in the Dundas district, and determined them
as being Ordovician types. Unfortunately, however, there
is some doubt in regard to the reliability of this determination in fixing the age of the Dundas slates, for repeated
search, both at the locality whence Hall's specimens were
supposed to have been procured and elsewhere in the series,
has signally failed to provide another specimen. Undoubted
Ordovician graptolites have been found in the Permo-Carboniferous glacial till at Wynyard, but with the above exception of the late T. S. Hall's specimens no graptolites have
been discovered *in situ* in Tasmania, in spite of diligent
search.

The Dundas slate and breccia series, of which the typical
rock-type is a finely fissile purple slate, underlie with a
marked unconformity the slates and sandstones definitely
determined as Silurian. They are similarly definitely established as unconformably overlying the mica-schists to which
a Pre-Cambrian age has been ascribed. The series then is
either Cambrian or Ordovician in age, and owing to the
failure to obtain information of the Ordovician determination
by the discovery of further graptolites, it is at present pre-
ferred to refer to them as of Cambro-Ordovician age.

To this dual system are also referred the following
rock series named after the localities in which the chief development of each occurs:—

Read-Rosebery Schists.

Balfour Slates and Sandstones.

Mathinna Slates and Sandstones.

These three series have been described in some detail.
The Read-Rosebery schists have been dealt with somewhat
fully by the writer in Bulletins 19 and 23 of the Geological
Survey. These schists, the origin of which was previously
very obscure, have been now demonstrated to have been
mainly sedimentary in origin, pyroclastic material constituting what is not purely sedimentary. Their structural fea-

tures have been mapped in detail, and their relation to the felsites and keratophyres of the porphyroid igneous complex definitely determined, for the mapping of the structural features has shown that the felsites and kerato- phyres overlie them as effusive lava sheets which have been involved in the same orogenic movement which produced the folds and the schistosity in the schists. It has further been demonstrated that the Read-Rosebery schists conformably overlie the Dundas slates and breccias. The Dundas slates and breccias, the Read-Rosebery schists, and the felsites and keratophyres constitute in fact a con- formable series, having the above ascending order of suc- cession, composed of mixed sediments, pyroclastic accumu- lations, and effusive lava flows. The evidence further goes to show that some at least of these lava flows were sub- marine.

The Balfour slates and sandstones have been described by L. Keith Ward in Geological Survey Bulletin No. 10. They present many similarities to the Dundas slates, but the re- lationship with this latter series has not been determined. They are wholly sedimentary rocks, the pyroclastic members of the Dundas slates and breccias being absent. They have up to the present yielded no fossil remains whatever. Simi- larity of structural features and the close resemblance be- tween certain rock-types of both series seem to indicate that we here have two members of a great sedimentary system.

The Mathinna slates and sandstones, which have been described by the late W. H. Twelvetrees in his reports on the Mathinna field, closely resemble the Balfour slates and sandstones in lithological character and structural features. Although widely separated geographically, they are pro- bably parts of the same sedimentary system. Like the Bal- four series, they are apparently unfossiliferous.

### (3). SILURIAN.

In the account of the Geology of Tasmania presented by the late W. H. Twelvetrees before this Association in 1902, the whole of the metamorphosed igneous rocks now re- ferred to as the Porphyroid Igneous Complex, together with the Read-Rosebery and Mt. Lyell schists as well as the Dundas slates and breccias, were referred along with bra- chiopod sandstones at Middlesex, Zeehan, and Queen River to the Upper and Middle Silurian. The Gordon River lime- stone, together with the Mathinna slates and sandstones were referred to the Lower Silurian.

Since that date it has been satisfactorily demonstrated that the Porphyroid Igneous Complex, the Read-Rosebery and Lyell schists, and the Dundas slates and breccias are separated from the Silurian sedimentary rocks by a period of very pronounced diastrophism. As explained above, these older rocks are referred to as Cambro-Ordovician. The series which are now definitely recognised as belonging to the Silurian system are the slates and sandstones of the Queen River, Zeehan, and Middlesex, and other localities on the West Coast; and the blue limestone, generally known as the Gordon River limestone, but which occurs at numerous localities throughout Northern, Western, and Southern Tasmania. Suites of fossil remains from these series have been examined by W. S. Dun, whose final conclusion was to the effect that the species of the various genera were of Silurian types, but possessed to some extent an Ordovician facies. On the whole, however, this palæontologist concludes that both series are of Silurian age, and most probably Lower Silurian.

And now it is necessary to mention a sedimentary series which is such a prominent factor in West Coast geology, and which has been the subject of much discussion and investigation, being within the last 18 years referred to systems ranging from Devonian to Cambrian. The series referred to is the West Coast Range Conglomerate Series. This series was referred by the late W. H. Twelvetrees in 1902 to the Devonian, and L. K. Ward, mainly on negative evidence, transferred it in 1909 to the base of the Cambrian system. The negative evidence referred to consisted of the non-discovery within the conglomerate of pebbles of rocks of the Porphyroid Igneous Complex. The discovery in 1913 by the writer of numerous pebbles of such rocks in the conglomerate series as developed in the Jukes-Darwin field showed the uncertainty of basing conclusions on negative evidence, and finally determined the Post-Porphyroid age of the conglomerate series. Investigations carried out since that time by the writer, and which are still in progress, have supplied abundant confirmatory evidence.

The age of the West Coast Range Conglomerate Series is by this succession shown to be Post-Cambro-Ordovician. The study of the structural geology of this series and the Silurians, which has been carried out in the Zeehan field by G. A. Waller, and by the writer on the greater part of the West Coast Range, serves to strengthen to almost certainty the conclusion arrived at by G. A. Waller in 1903, that the West Coast Range Conglomerate conformably underlies the Silurian limestone series, and is itself of Silurian age, constituting, in fact, a basal conglomerate series of the Silurian system in Tasmania.

The much-discussed Tubicolar or Pipe-Stem Sandstone belongs to the uppermost horizon of the West Coast Range Conglomerate Series, and is more highly developed in the North than in the more southerly portion of the known occurrences. The limestone immediately succeeds this Tubicolar Sandstone, and is itself conformably overlain by the slates and sandstone series, the Silurian system in Tasmania thus consisting of :—

(3) Slates and Sandstone series of Queen River, Zeehan, Middlesex, etc.

(2) Limestone series of Gordon River, Railton, etc.

(1) West Coast Range Conglomerate series.

### (4). DEVONIAN.

There are no sedimentary rocks so far located in Tasmania which can be referred to the Devonian system.

Consequent on the collapse of the geosynclinal in which the Silurian sediments were laid down, there ensued an orogenic period of considerable intensity. This orogenic movement consisted largely of folding, but thrust faulting on a considerable scale was a marked characteristic. It is this orogenic folding and faulting which is responsible for the very complicated relationships between the older rocks and the Silurian sediments which have been the cause of so many misinterpretations of the geological succession.

The final phase of the orogenic period consisted of the irruption of the principal granitic rocks of Tasmania. The fact that the next sediments to accumulate are of Permo-Carboniferous age, and that they rest in many cases directly on the granite, points to the conclusion that during the Devonian period Tasmania was a land surface, and was subjected to a prolonged cycle of denudation. In fact, work recently carried out by the writer has shown that at the close of the Devonian period this land surface had been reduced to a peneplain.

### (5). PERMO-CARBONIFEROUS.

An important advance in our knowledge of the Permo-Carboniferous system was made by the late W. H. Twelvetrees in 1911, when he demonstrated that the Tasmanite

shale beds of the Mersey basin were the marine facies of
the Mersey (East Greta) Coal Measures. The discovery and
investigation of the Preolenna Coal-field have supplied further evidence of the geological horizon of our Lower Coal
Measures, and the coal seams and the associated kerosene-
shale present much valuable information in regard to sapropelic coals.

The glacial conglomerate forming the base of the Permo-
Carboniferous system in Tasmania has been studied in detail
by Professor Sir T. W. Edgeworth David at Wynyard.

With these exceptions, the work accomplished on our
Permo-Carboniferous system has not been sufficient to give
us greater information than we possessed 18 years ago.

### (6). TRIAS-JURA.

The retention of the above dual nomenclature at once
indicates that we have not to any appreciable extent advanced our knowledge of the Mesozoic sedimentaries as developed
in Tasmania. This is due to the fact that very little actual
geological survey work has been attempted on our coal-fields.
It is, however, very satisfactory to be able to announce that
for the past ten months two geologists of the Geological
Survey have been constantly employed on this work, and will
be so occupied until the close of the summer, and our knowledge in this direction has already been extended. Mr. H. H.
Scott is carrying out some work on the Trias-Jura flora
which is being collected, and it is confidently hoped that
within the next twelve months a somewhat comprehensive
account of both the Permo-Carboniferous and Trias-Jura
systems will be possible.

### (7). TERTIARY.

Beyond the recognition at various localities of deposits
of Tertiary age and the areal mapping of some of them, no
advance has been made in working out the stratigraphy of
Tertiary sediments, either lacustrine or marine.

### IV. PALÆONTOLOGY.

### (1). SILURIAN.

A valuable addition to our knowledge of Silurian fossil
types was made as the result of the study by W. S.
Dun of a suite of specimens collected by the Geological Survey. The resulting determinations are contained in Geological Survey Bulletin No. 8.

More recently, F. Chapman, A.L.S., has studied certain fossils from the Silurian limestone, and has prepared a description of the occurrence of Tetradium therein, which has been published as Geological Survey Record No. 5.

### (2).  PERMO-CARBONIFEROUS.

As the result of the investigations carried out by the late W. H. Twelvetrees in the Mersey basin, our knowledge of the character of the organic component of the Tasmanite shale has been appreciably increased.  In connection with the same examination also, W. S. Dun carried out some palæontological work on the Marine fauna of the Permo-Carboniferous beds in that area, and these are dealt with by that investigator in Geological Survey Record No. 1.

Apart from these increases to our knowledge there has been no advance in our Permo-Carboniferous palæontology.

### (3).  TRIAS-JURA.

No study similar to that carried out in recent years by Dr. Walkom in Queensland has been accomplished in Tasmania.  The systematic geological survey of our coal-fields and other Trias-Jura areas now in progress is supplying material which promises to give important information.  Mr. H. H. Scott is undertaking the palæontological work on these collections, and a contribution is anticipated which will mark a step forward in connection with this field of investigation.

### (4).  TERTIARY.

A considerable amount of work was accomplished by the late Miss M. Lodder on the marine beds of Table Cape.  An indefatigable collector in the same locality was the Reverend E. D. Atkinson, B.A.

A marsupial from this formation—*Wynyardia bassensis*, Spencer—is believed to link the Diprotodonts with the Polyprotodonts.

There has, however, during the period under review been no work whatever accomplished on our particularly rich Tertiary flora, and as far as can be seen at present there is no likelihood of any attention being paid to this most interesting field for research for some years to come.

### (5).  PLEISTOCENE AND RECENT.

The Mowbray Swamp on the North-West Coast has supplied within the last ten years two most valuable and interesting skeletons of *Nototheria*.  It is to the enthusiasm and

perseverance of Mr. H. H. Scott that we owe the excavation
and preservation of these skeletons.  To the same worker
belongs the credit of first describing the *Nototherium tasmanicum*, which is accomplished at length in Geological Survey Record No. 4.  The original skeleton has been mounted
by Mr. Scott, and is now to be seen in the Victoria Museum,
Launceston.

During the past year the second *Nototherium* was discovered, and this has been determined as *Nototherium
mitchelli*.  H. H. Scott and Clive Lord have already presented
preliminary notes on this skeleton before the Royal Society
of Tasmania, and a complete description, as well as the
mounting of the specimen, is in progress.

The discovery of these two skeletons and their immediate
study and description have effected a distinct advance of
knowledge of the *Nototheria* in general.

Another important discovery of marsupial remains was
made in King Island.  The remains are fragmentary, but
sufficient has been found to allow of the recognition by H. H.
Scott of the giant kangaroo—*Palorchestes*.  Further work
remains to be carried out in this direction.

It is very evident from the above resumé of palæontological investigations that the Geological Survey itself has done
very little in the palæontological branch of geology.  This is
only to be expected when it is remembered that the *raison
d'etre* of the Geological Survey is the necessity of intensive
study of our ore deposits, and the demand is for investigations having an obviously practical value.  The significance
of the role played by palæontology in all geological investigations is not realised by the great majority of mining men,
and consequently the palæontological work essential to our
studies in economic geology is carried out more or less sur-
reptitiously, and, in the non-provision of a palæontologist
on the staff, is mostly accomplished by taking advantage of
the keenness and good nature of palæontologists belonging
to other institutions and other States.

## V.  STRUCTURAL GEOLOGY.

Much light has been thrown on the tectonics of Tasmania
during the period under review.  The definite fixing of the
stratigraphical succession has materially assisted in deciphering the structural geology of certain areas, and it is
now possible to form a broad general conception of the tec-

tonics of the Island. Such generalisations must, however, be drawn with care in view of the relatively small areas in which structural geology has been investigated in detail.

The most recent summary of our tectonic geology is that included in Professor Sir T. W. Edgeworth David's Presidential Address to the Linnean Society in 1911. Since that date, however, considerable progress has been made towards supplying data for a more detailed general survey. The writer has dealt with this problem of the mapping of tectonic lines in connection with his work on the Metallogenic Epochs of Tasmania, and has summarised the conclusions which are justifiable on the evidence at present available.

It has been demonstrated that there have occurred in Tasmania at least three, and possibly four, distinct periods of orogenic movement, and one period of block faulting on a huge scale. To these diastrophic movements must be added the intrusion of the diabase, which, although unaccompanied by horizontal thrust, must on the evidence recently obtained by P. B. Nye in the Midlands have been characterised by vertical upthrusting on a very large scale.

The first definitely fixed orogenic period was that which followed the Pre-Cambrian sedimentation. If L. K. Ward's deductions in regard to the subdivision of the Pre-Cambrian are correct an earlier disturbance must be admitted. The direction of the tectonic lines of this Epi-Algonkian orogenic revolution swing in gentle curves from N.N.W. in the South, through N.N.E. near Cradle Mt., back to the N.N.W. to the Northwards, and ultimately end on the north coast with a N.N.E trend. The overfolding is towards the East. There was apparently no batholithic end-point to this Epi-Algonkian orogenic movement.

The period of sedimentation and contemporaneous effusive igneous activity which characterised the Cambro-Ordovician was followed by a pronounced orogenic revolution. The Epi-Cambro-Ordovician trend-lines are N.N.W. in the southern portion, bending to due N. in the neighbourhood of Rosebery, but resuming the general N.N.W. direction north of that locality. No overfolding has yet been observed. A batholithic end-point characterised the close of this orogenic period. The intense alteration and mineralogic reconstitution, which was characteristic of this orogenic movement, gave rise to the fissility of the Dundas slates and the schistosity of the Read-Rosebery and Mt. Lyell schists. The development of the schistose structure was complete at the time the Epi-Cambro-Ordovician plutonics reached their *mise-en-place*.

The close of the Silurian period of sedimentation witnessed the geosynclinal collapse and the occurrence of the Epi-Silurian orogenic movements. The trend-lines are regularly directed N.N.W., and overfolding occurs both to the East and to the West, overthrusting having taken place on a considerable scale. The movements, although undoubtedly intense, did not produce the universal schistose structure which was the result of the preceding diastrophic period. The batholithic phase of this Epi-Silurian orogenic period was one of great importance and size, as it was responsible for the intrusion of our so-called Devonian granites, gabbros, and serpentines, together with their associated congeners.

Since the cessation of the Epi-Silurian orogenic movements there has been no recurrence of compressive forces in Tasmania. The vertical and upwardly directed thrusts of the diabasic invasions at the close of the Mesozoic era apparently gave rise to no horizontal thrusts. This conclusion seems inevitable as the result of the recent researches of P. B. Nye, and the evidence is to the effect that this diabasic upthrust carried upwards to varying heights isolated masses of Permo-Carboniferous and Trias-Jura sediments.

It has been long recognised that the present configuration of Tasmania is very largely due to the effect of tensional faulting on a large scale. During the period under review it cannot be claimed that this conception has been elaborated to any considerable degree. The contention advanced by E. C. Andrews and Dr. Griffith Taylor that the Midlands is a Rift Valley seems to have been disproved by P. B. Nye's recent investigations.

It is undoubtedly true, however, and a mass of confirmatory evidence relating thereto has been collected during the last 18 years, that block faulting has taken place parallel to the general trends of the coast-line. The basal beds of the Permo-Carboniferous system have, for example, been found at sea-level, and 3,000 feet above that level, and a great part of this is due to tensional block faulting, but the exact contribution to this difference of level by the upthrusting during the diabase injections has not been determined. Minor faults of this tensional series have been recognised, but it cannot be claimed that the major breaks have been accurately located. It is hoped that the work now in progress on our coal-fields will result in some valuable data in connection with this problem.

## VI. PETROLOGY.

### (1). Petrography.

The knowledge gained during the period under review of the petrography of the igneous rocks of Tasmania has been considerable. This is not surprising when it is remembered that the late W. H. Twelvetrees was one of the most skilled petrographers of the Commonwealth, and the result of his 18 years' labour, combined with the work carried out by other officers of the Geological Survey, represents a distinct advance towards a complete description of our igneous rocks.

It may at the present time be confidently claimed that the petrographic descriptions of our Epi-Silurian plutonic acid and basic rocks by Twelvetrees, Ward, Waller, Waterhouse, McIntosh Reid, and Professor Benson represent an approach to a complete knowledge of the character of the numerous rock-types of this series.

Similarly it is justifiable to claim that the descriptions of the composition and microscopic structure of the diabase which constitutes such a great proportion of Tasmania, presented at various intervals by Twelvetrees, Petterd, Ward, Professor Benson, A. Osann (Frieberg), and F. P. Paul, constitute an almost complete demonstration of the petrography of this rock.

Completeness in petrographic descriptions also characterises the investigations of our Tertiary basalts, whether they be the normal olivine basalts, the limburgite, or the trachydolerite of Table Cape and Stanley. It is to Twelvetrees, Petterd, and Ward that we owe our detailed knowledge of these.

Although considerable advance has been made in deciphering the variations in rock-types in the Port Cygnet alkaline series and the probably comagmatic nepheline basalts of Bothwell, and the melilite basalt of Sandy Bay—work in which Twelvetrees, F. P. Paul, and Professor Benson have been most prominent—yet there remains a very large amount of investigating to be done before anything approaching the detailed character of our knowledge in regard to the Epi-Silurian plutonics is attained. It is in such a case as this that there is severely felt the handicap to progress which is occasioned by the elimination of the subject of geology from the University curriculum, as the Port Cygnet alkaline series, by reason of both their interest and their proximity to Hobart, must inevitably appeal as a subject of research to an active School of Geology located at Hobart. The most complete description of this series so far published is that by Dr. F. P. Paul, which appeared in 1906. [1]

There now remains to be discussed the advance in knowledge of the Porphyroid Igneous Complex during the last 18 years. The work accomplished in this field is considerable, as is evident when it is remembered that it is during this period that the conception of this Porphyroid Igneous Complex as a distinct igneous rock series has been gradually evolved. The petrographic studies carried out on the innumerable varieties of quartz-porphyries, felspar-porphyries, felsites, syenites, granites, etc., occurring in close association on the West Coast have resulted in a gradual separation of a very large group of these igneous rocks which are characterised by mineralogic reconstitution and evidence of great physical strain, from a group relatively less plentiful in varieties which possess no internal evidence of such dynamic metamorphic action. To the former group the name "porphyroid" was applied by G. A. Waller in 1902, and subsequently this term was adopted as a group name as the result of considerable study by the late Professor H. Rosenbusch, to whom recognition must here be made of very great assistance in elucidating the petrography of this group of igneous rocks.

It is a very difficult task, in view of the mineralogic reconstitution and mechanical deformation which this series of rocks has undergone, to recognise the original character of the several rock-types from petrographic study. Gradual progress in description and in deductions as to original character has been made, mainly by Twelvetrees, Ward, Professor W. Gregory, and the writer, and it is now perfectly clear that in this Porphyroid Igneous Complex we have a comagmatic series consisting of effusive, intrusive, and plutonic types ranging in composition from basic to acid. There still remains, however, a great amount of work to be done in the petrographic study of an almost unlimited number of varieties of this series particularly in the case of the effusive and fragmental types, and also in connection with the basic plutonics.

(1) F. P. Paul: "Beiträge zur petrographischen Kenntniss einiger foyaitisch thiralitischen Gesteine aus Tasmanien" Mineral. petr. Mitteil Band 25, Heft IV., Wien, 1906.

## (2).  PETROGENESIS.

Viewing the igneous rocks of Tasmania from the broader standpoint of petrology and accepting the most comprehensive significance of that word, the questions of chemical composition, structure of the igneous masses, and mode of origin come up for consideration and investigation.

In regard to chemical composition it must be at once admitted that our progress has been practically nil. The number of rock analyses carried out during the last 18 years is practically negligible. It was hoped when the Geological Survey Laboratory was established in 1914 that rock analyses would be systematically carried out if only slowly, but it has been found impossible up to date, owing to the time taken in routine assay work, to devote any time to rock analysis. It is hoped, however, that the conditions will be improved in the near future. The serious hindrance to progress that this lack of rock analyses imposes is so obvious that no further comment is needed.

The petrogenic problems in Tasmania are decidedly complex, and it cannot be said that any near approach has been made to their solution. It can, however, be claimed that some progress has been made.

In regard to the question of geologic age it cannot be more definitely stated of the Porphyroid Igneous Complex than that it belongs to the Cambro-Ordovician. Some of the effusive and fragmental members of that complex are contemporaneous with the larger sedimentary series of that system, while others undoubtedly succeeded the main sedimentation. On the whole the evidence points to the fact that the greater part of the igneous series belong to the closing phases of the Cambro-Ordovician, although this has by no means been completely demonstrated. It is clear, however, that the acid plutonic members represent the end-point of the Epi-Cambro-Ordovician orogenic disturbance, as these show much less crushing than the other members of the complex.

It has been demonstrated by Ward, and confirmed by Waterhouse and McIntosh Reid, although originally suggested by Waller, that the basic and ultra-basic members of the Epi-Silurian igneous series are slightly older than the acid and sub-acid members—in other words, that the basic portion of the magma appeared at the beginning of the petrogenic cycle, while the acid portion followed shortly afterwards. As previously pointed out in this review, this petrogenic period occurred at the close of the Epi-Silurian orogenic paroxysm.

No more definite determination of the Diabase has been made than that it is Post-Trias-Jura and Pre-Tertiary. It is generally referred to the Cretaceous, but there has been no further evidence of this adduced since the late W. H. Twelvetrees wrote his summary in 1902.

An important discovery was made by Professor E. W. Skeats in 1916 when he located a dyke of the Port Cygnet Alkaline Series cutting the diabase near Woodbridge. In a paper read before the Royal Society of Victoria [2] Professor Skeats discusses this discovery and demonstrates the Tertiary age of this most interesting alkaline series. Up to the time of this discovery the series was regarded as of Permo-Carboniferous age.

No data whatever have been obtained from which to determine the relative ages of our olivine basalts, limburgite, trachydolerite, and melilite basalt. We know that they are Tertiary, but our knowledge has not advanced in this direction during the period under review.

In only one district have sufficient investigations of the structural features of the Porphyroid Igneous Complex been carried out to enable definite conclusions to be drawn in regard to the actual structure of the masses of various rock-types of the series. The area referred to is the Read-Rosebery district, in which the writer has mapped the fold axes of the Cambro-Ordovician sediments and the associated igneous rocks, and demonstrated that the felsite or keratophyre which is so well developed in that locality is in the form of an extrusive sheet now characterised by a complex series of folds. Evidence gathered at other localities on the West Coast gives confirmation of this effusive character of many of the porphyries, porphyrites, spilites, etc, but the mapping of the structural geology has not advanced far enough to allow of the definite demonstration of the structure as that of contemporaneous extrusive sheets in the same detail as in the Read-Rosebery district. Neither is it yet possible to give any indication of the order of succession within this petrogenic cycle—an achievement which will only be possible when the structural features of the whole Cambro-Ordovician system have been elucidated.

As indicated above the end-point of the Cambro-Ordovician petrogenic cycle, as well as that of the Epi-Cambro-

---

(2) Proc. Roy. Soc. Vic., Vol. XXIX., Part II. (1917), pp. 155-164.

J

Ordovician orogenic period, was the intrusion of the granite. This granite has been recognised at four localities:—South Darwin, Dove River, Mount Farrell, and Bond's Peak. At the two former localities it is clearly intrusive into other members of the complex, but in the vicinity of Mount Farrell there is a mergence by insensible gradations into members which are clearly extrusive. This very puzzling structure is being dealt with by the writer in his work on the "Metallogenic Epochs of Tasmania," and it seems probable that we have here a possible illustration of "extrusion by de-roofing," as propounded by R. A. Daly. If this is so, however, the granitic phase of the batholithic period is not confined to the end-point alone.

Apart from the areal mapping of the basic and acid members of the Epi-Silurian petrogenic period there has been very little progress, with one noticeable exception, towards arriving at general conclusions in regard to the structure and relationships of the various igneous massifs. The exception referred to is the paper read before this Association in 1911 by L. Keith Ward, entitled "The Heemskirk "Massif—its Structure and Relationships." In that paper the conception is developed that the Heemskirk Massif possesses a definite bottom and is chonolithic in character rather than laccolithic or batholithic. Ward further proceeds to hypothecise two parallel lines of crustal weakness along which igneous intrusion has taken place, and maintains that the various Epi-Silurian igneous massifs, although possibly connected in depth along these lines, are elsewhere quite separate intrusive bodies. Work carried out since the preparation of that paper, however, throws serious doubt on the accuracy of these conclusions. A great difficulty in regard to the acceptance of the existence of the Bischoff and Heemskirk-Middlesex lines of crustal weakness which have been the loci of igneous intrusion lies in the significant fact of the concordance between the orientation of the major axes of the igneous massifs and the Epi-Silurian fold axes. As stated above, the Epi-Silurian trend lines have a bearing of N.N.W.—a direction which is at right angles to that of the two lines indicated by L. K. Ward. Add to this the irregular but wide distribution of the outcrops of both basic and acid massifs of this series, which is obvious from a glance at the Geological Map of Tasmania, and the difficulty of accepting Ward's conclusions is apparent.

The evidence seems to point to the conclusion that the Epi-Silurian magma reached its final resting place in the form of a limited number of composite batholiths. It, moreover, seems possible that there finally resulted one huge batholith underlying the greater part of Tasmania, the cupolas and satellitic injections from which now represent the apparently isolated massifs as we at present see them.

In spite of the great amount of work that has been accomplished, and the numerous descriptions written in regard to the petrography of the Tasmanian diabase, yet, as pointed out by Osann, there is very little in existence descriptive of its field occurrence and structural relationships. We know that it is intrusive and that undoubted sills and dykes occur, and this was the state of our knowledge in 1902 with the addition that other masses had had a laccolithic structure suggested for them. It is therefore disappointing to have to announce that up to the beginning of the past year no material advance had been made in this connection. Certainly L. K. Ward recognised two distinct horizons of intrusive sheets near the King William Range, but no work was done on the larger diabase massifs to elucidate their morphology and mode of origin. During the past year, however, the geological surveys carried out in the Midlands by P. B. Nye, on the East Coast by H. G. W. Keid, and during the last few months by A. McIntosh Reid, have supplied valuable data which, along with that being acquired at the present time in the extensions of those surveys, will probably enable a very complete summary of the field occurrence of our diabase to be prepared. The evidence so far obtained points to our larger diabase massifs being asymmetric laccolithic intrusions possessing an almost vertical face on one or more sides, but grading off into an intrusive sheet on one or more of the others.

Very little work has been done on the field occurrences of the Cygnet Alkaline series and the probably associated nepheline and melilite basalts, and the status of our knowledge in this connection is practically as it was in 1902.

Beyond the areal mapping of some of our olivine basalt areas no advance has been made as to the mode of origin. Certainly the negative evidence provided by the failure to locate a single volcanic cone is valuable but not conclusive evidence of fissure eruptions.

This short review of the progress in petrologic science cannot be complete without a reference to that most interesting discovery—the Darwin Glass. The credit of first bringing this substance under the notice of the Geological Survey belongs to Hartwell Conder, M.A., who in 1912, while acting

as State Mining Engineer, had several fragments presented
to him by one of his prospectors. These fragments were reported to have been derived from the Western portion of the
Jukes-Darwin area, and the assignment of the writer to carry
out a geological survey of that area early in 1913 gave an excellent opportunity for a detailed investigation of the occurrence. The results of such investigation are presented
in Record No. 3 of the Geological Survey, and the conclusion
there indicated that this substance is of cosmic origin and
belongs to the Tektites, being most nearly allied to the Mol-
davites, but differing from the latter in the remarkably
high silica content (89 per cent.). Since the publication
of that official description Dr. H. S. Summers has discussed
the composition in relation to the other members of the
Tektites, and Dr. F. Suess, of Vienna, the world's authority
on this subject, has fully discussed this substance and its
bearing on the whole problem of the Tektites in a paper
entitled "Ruckshau und Veneres uber die Tektitfrage."[3]

The writer would, however, here enter an objection to
the name proposed by Suess, namely, "Queenstownite," on
the grounds that the Darwin Glass does not occur at Queens-
town, the nearest occurrence being ten miles from that town.

## VII. MINERALOGY.

Considerable advance has been made in this branch of
geologic science during the period under review. Most of
the increase in knowledge has been gained during the petrographic researches indicated in the preceding chapter, and
also incidentally to the intensive study of our ore-deposits,
which will be dealt with in the chapter following this.

It is to the late W. F. Petterd that the greatest amount
of credit must be given for our advance in our knowledge
of the minerals of Tasmania. The "Catalogue of the Miner-
"als of Tasmania," published by that enthusiastic mineralo-
gist in 1896, was a valuable contribution, and served as the
standard reference on Tasmanian Mineralogy until 1910, by
which time the increased information acquired necessitated
its re-writing, which was completed early in that year and
published under the authority of the Mines Department.
The advance made in that period is well indicated by the
fact that this second edition contains descriptions of over
one hundred more mineral species than the first compilation.

---

(3) Mitteil der Geol. Sesell. Wien. I., ii., 1914.

The State of Tasmania is further indebted to this investigator by reason of the bequests made by him to the Royal Society of Tasmania of his valuable collection of minerals. This collection, which is the best collection of Tasmanian minerals in existence, and in many particulars quite unique, is now to be seen in the Tasmanian Museum, Hobart.

In addition to this publication, which deals specifically with the subject of mineralogy, there has appeared a wealth of detail as to varieties and some new species in the various publications of the Geological Survey of Tasmania. In regard to one mineral species a special publication was issued as Geological Survey Record No. 2, entitled "Stichtite— "a New Tasmanian Mineral."

An interesting and important discovery was that made by the Geological Survey in 1913 of the occurrence of osmiridium in the parent serpentine rock. Since that date the two varieties of that mineral have been definitely determined— siserskite and nevyanskite. Some very valuable work has recently been carried out by A. McIntosh Reid and W. D. Reid, of the Geological Survey Staff, on the composition of osmiridium and several minerals of the platinum group, including one probably new species.

The most valuable contributions by the Geological Survey since the last edition of the "Catalogue of the Minerals "of Tasmania" in 1910 are those dealing with the paragenesis of the mineral components of our ore deposits rather than with the identification of new species. This type of investigation is in accordance with the recent development of the subject of mineralography, and the application of the latest methods of investigation has already thrown much light on the inter-relationships of the component minerals of our orebodies, and promises to be of even greater utility in the near future. The studies made by L. L. Waterhouse of the contact metamorphic deposits of Stanley River and Heemskirk are valuable contributions to our knowledge of the mineral paragenesis of this type of ore deposit. The complete paragenesis of the complex zinc-lead sulphide ore deposits of Read-Rosebery has been demonstrated by the writer, who is at present engaged on similar investigations in connection with the geological survey of the Mount Lyell field. In this connection it must be noted that Gilbert and Pogue, of the American National Museum, have carried out a mineralographic study of some of the ore of the Mount Lyell field forwarded to them by Mr. R. C. Sticht.

## VIII.   ORE-DEPOSITS.

### (1.)   THE DEVELOPMENT OF THE INVESTIGATIONS.

It is in this domain that our greatest advance has been made.  This is not surprising, in view of the fact that the study of our deposits of economic minerals is the *raison d'etre* of the Geological Survey.

The earlier portion of the period under review witnessed intense mining activity in Tasmania, and it is to the developments resulting from such work, together with the concurrent demand for geological examinations, that we owe the opportunities for research which have been productive of appreciable results.

The year 1902 saw the late W. H. Twelvetrees and his assistant, G. A. Waller, busily engaged examining active mining fields and preparing incomplete geological maps of those areas.  The work performed by Waller in the Zeehan field constitutes the first complete geological mapping of a mining field executed in Tasmania.  There was gradually evolved at this period by both investigators the conception of a genetic connection between the plutonic igneous rocks and our ore-deposits, particularly between the granitic rocks and our tin, lead, zinc, and iron deposits.

After the resignation of Waller in 1904 the late W. H. Twelvetrees continued the examination of ore deposits, without, however, having the opportunity of carrying out detailed mapping.  With the appointment in 1907, however, of L. Keith Ward as Assistant Government Geologist, an opportunity was afforded of initiating systematic studies of our ore-deposits, accompanied by the detailed geological research which is essential to an understanding of their genesis.  The old ground traversed by Twelvetrees and Waller was retraced and new ground broken as opportunity offered, and these repeated examinations of our more important mining fields and their ore-deposits have continued up to the present time, with the result that the knowledge we now possess of these ore-deposits is considerable.

### (2).   THE GALENA LODES OF ZEEHAN.

The earlier investigations by G. A. Waller on the ore deposits of the Zeehan field were elaborated in detail by Twelvetrees and Ward, and the composition, structural features, and genesis thoroughly elucidated.  The galena-bearing lodes are grouped into two belts—the Pyritic Belt and the Sideritic Belt.  The difference in mineralogic composition

has been determined by zonal precipitation, each zone representing certain limiting ranges of temperature and pressure
which characterised the conditions during actual deposition
of the mineral species from the ore-bearing solutions. The
origin of the ore-bearing solutions is ascribed to the differ-
entiating igneous mass which gave rise to both them and
the underlying granitic mass.

L. K. Ward elaborated this conception of zonal precipitation in a paper read before this Association in 1911, entitled
"An Investigation of the Relationship between the Ore-
"bodies of the Heemskirk-Comstock-Zeehan Region and the
"Associated Igneous Rocks." His conception demonstrates
three zones—the Granite Zone; the Contact Metamorphic
Zone; and the Transmetamorphic Zone—the latter being
subdivided into the Pyritic and Sideritic Belts. The factor
determining the amount and kind of precipitation from the
outwardly migrating ore-bearing solutions is the decrease
in temperature and pressure as distance is gained from the
magmatic hearth.

It must be here pointed out, however, that A. McIntosh
Reid has recently adduced evidence which shows that the
Comstock magnetite deposits, classed as contact-metamorphic
by Ward, are magmatic differentiations within the basic
phase of the Epi-Silurian plutonic period. There are, however, undoubted contact metamorphic magnetite and hæmatite deposits around the periphery of the granite, and Ward's
conception of zonal distribution is not affected in general
principle.

### (3) THE READ-ROSEBERY ZINC-LEAD SULPHIDE DEPOSITS.

These deposits have been studied in detail by the writer,
and their composition, structural features, mineralogy, and
genesis are fully delineated in Bulletins 19 and 23 of the
Geological Survey. The northern extension of this belt is
described by A. McIntosh Reid in Geological Survey Bulletin
No. 28.

It is shown that the zinc-lead sulphide ore-bodies are
metasomatic replacements of schistose calcareous beds in the
Read-Rosebery schist series, which, as previously indicated
in this review, are predominantly sedimentary in origin. The
component beds of this schist series have been thrown into
a series of complex folds by the same stress which brought
about their schistosity. The axes of the two series of folds
are at right angles to each other, and the more important of
these have been mapped. The actual structure observable

is that of a series of irregular domes and basins, so that at any mine level the outline of the ore-bodies is irregularly lenticular.

The origin of the ore-bodies is ascribed to ascending magmatic waters genetically associated with the Epi-Silurian quartz-porphyry and granite-porphyry dykes in the vicinity.

## (4). THE TIN DEPOSITS OF NORTH-EAST DUNDAS.

These were examined in detail by L. K. Ward in 1908, and their structural features, composition, and genesis are described in Bulletin No. 6 of the Geological Survey. Some of the later developments in the various mines are dealt with by Hartwell Conder, M.A., in Bulletin No. 26.

The tin deposits are grouped by Ward under two heads—Pyritic-Cassiterite deposits and Quartz-Tourmaline-Cassiterite Veins. The composition and structural features have been somewhat completely elucidated, and the genesis referred to the associated granite-porphyry and quartz-porphyry dykes of Epi-Silurian age. However, it cannot be stated that the exact relationship to the pyritic-lead deposits, the garnet actinolite veins or the axinite veins, which occur associated with the tin-deposits, has been demonstrated. Neither can it be claimed that the mineralography of the pyritic-cassiterite ores has been closely studied, especially in regard to those of dense stanniferous pyrrhotite.

## (5). THE ORE DEPOSITS OF THE MOUNT FARRELL
### DISTRICT.

The investigation carried out by Ward in 1907 on the ore-deposits of this district was an elaboration of previous examinations by Twelvetrees and Waller.

Ward's description of these deposits, contained in Geological Survey Bulletin No. 3, shows three types of lead deposits—Sideritic-Galena lodes, Pyritic-Galena lodes, and Barytic-Galena lodes. No attempt, however, is made at a zonal classification similar to that evolved for the Zeehan field.

Certain types of copper ores, as well as iron ores, are described, and the genesis of all of the ore deposits is ascribed to the Epi-Silurian plutonic period. However, the relationship between the lead-deposits, those containing copper, and the hæmatite and magnetite deposits is not elucidated, so that a common genetic origin for them all is by no means certain.

(6).  THE TIN DEPOSITS OF THE STANLEY RIVER DISTRICT.

These have been described in detail by L. L. Waterhouse in Bulletin 15 of the Geological Survey, following upon previous work by G. A. Waller.

The deposits are mainly of the Quartz-Tourmaline-Cassiterite type and what are termed Stanniferous Contact Metamorphic Deposits. These are both described in detail in regard to structural features, composition, and paragenesis. It is important to note that it has been demonstrated by Waterhouse that the cassiterite in the contact metamorphic deposits is later than the contact metamorphic minerals. The origin of the ore-bearing solutions is shown to be the Epi-Silurian granitic plutonics strongly developed in the field.

Sufficient evidence, however, is not available to establish the definite relation between the two types of tin deposits, nor between these and the zinc and lead veins.

(7).  THE HEEMSKIRK TIN DEPOSITS.

G. A. Waller described these deposits in considerable detail in 1902, and L. L. Waterhouse carried out a more comprehensive survey in 1914. The description of this field is contained in Bulletin No. 21 of the Geological Survey, and the description of the ore deposits is presented in meticulous detail.

The tin deposits are classified into six types:—

     (1) Quartz-Tourmaline-Cassiterite Veins;

     (2) Quartz-Quartzose Deposits;

     (3) Pyritic Cassiterite Deposits;

     (4) Pinitoid Veins;

     (5) Greisen Veins;

     (6) Pipe Formations.

The structural features, composition, and paragenesis of all of these types are described in detail. In addition, contact metamorphic deposits are described, as well as zinc and lead deposits and nickel ores. It is shown that certain of the zinc and lead deposits are variants of certain of the tin veins, and zonal precipitation is given as the explanation of the change in character with increasing distance from the magmatic hearth.    The contact metamorphic deposits preceded the tin deposition.

The whole of the ore deposits in the field are shown to be genetically connected with the Epi-Silurian plutonics.

(8). THE ORE DEPOSITS OF MOUNT BALFOUR.

These were examined by L. K. Ward, and described in Geological Survey Bulletin No. 10.

Two groups of deposits are shown to exist—the Copper Group and the Tin-Tungsten Group. Both are described, and a zonal distribution in relation to a hypothetical granite core to the Balfour Range is suggested, although not definitely established. However, it is assumed that they are both genetically connected with the Epi-Silurian granite of the district, although the evidence for the copper deposits is by no means conclusive.

(9). THE ORE DEPOSITS OF JUKES-DARWIN.

Following upon the work carried out by the late W. H. Twelvetrees twelve years before, the writer in 1913 made a thorough investigation of the ore deposits of this region. The results of this investigation are contained in Geological Survey Bulletin No. 16.

The ore deposits are classified into the following groups:—

(1) Copper-Silver-Gold Ore-bodies;

(2) Hæmatite and Magnetite Deposits;

(3) Blue Hæmatite-Bornite Veins;

(4) Barytes Lodes;

(5) Quartz Lodes;

(6) Epidote Veins.

The composition, structural features, and paragenesis of these deposits are described. It is shown that the hæmatite and magnetite ore-bodies are genetically connected with the granite of the porphyroid igneous complex. The problem of metallogenesis is discussed at some length, but the evidence was at that time not found sufficient to justify definite conclusions as to which metallogenic epoch or epochs the remaining groups were to be assigned.

(10). THE ORE DEPOSITS OF THE MIDDLESEX-PELION
AREA.

These have been described in successively greater detail by G. A. Waller, the late W. H. Twelvetrees, and A. McIntosh Reid.

The late W. H. Twelvetrees was the first to recognise the true nature and origin of the garnet rock which forms the country rock of the tin-wolfram-bismuth lodes of the S.

& M. Mine, Moina. The description of this rock and the structure, composition, and paragenesis of the lodes are presented in Geological Survey Bulletin No. 12. The origin is assigned to the adjacent Epi-Silurian granite, which gave rise to the garnet-magnetite rock as a contact metamorphic rock as a metallogenic phase preceding the tin-wolfram-bismuth phase.

The galena ore-bodies at Round Hill are also assigned to the same source as their origin, and are shown to have a saddle structure similar to the Bendigo saddles. They are assigned to an outer zone of the tin phase of the Epi-Silurian metallogenic epoch.

A. McIntosh Reid has described in Bulletin No. 30 the wolfram and copper deposits of the Pelion District. In the relatively undeveloped state of these deposits complete descriptions are not possible. The genesis of the wolfram is definitely assigned to the Epi-Silurian granite, but the evidence for the age determination of the copper deposits is not as conclusive.

### (11). THE ORE DEPOSITS OF SCAMANDER.

These are described by the late W. H. Twelvetrees in Bulletin No. 9 of the Geological Survey. The structural features and composition are described, and they are grouped as follows:—

    (1) Wolframite and Cassiterite Veins;

    (2) Arsenopyrite-quartz-chalcopyrite lodes;

    (3) Arsenopyrite-quartz-argentiferous lodes.

The distribution of these groups is interpreted as indicating a zonal precipitation outwards from the Epi-Silurian magmatic hearth in the order indicated above.

### (12). THE OSMIRIDIUM DEPOSITS.

The occurrence of osmiridium in alluvial deposits has been known for many years, and its origin from serpentine was regarded as almost proved, but it was not until the year 1913 that this mineral was definitely established as being an original component of the serpentine rock. In that year the discovery of what were termed "osmiridium lodes" was responsible for the examination of the Bald Hill area by the late W. H. Twelvetrees, and as a result of this investigation the occurrence of osmiridium as a constituent of serpentine was definitely established. This is described in Geological Survey Bulletin No. 17.

During the summer of 1919-20 A. McIntosh Reid carried out a very thorough investigation of the occurrences of osmiridium in Tasmania, and his bulletin dealing with the questions of composition, mode of occurrence, and genesis is now in the Press. In this bulletin the differentiation of the basic phase of the Epi-Silurian plutonic period is studied in detail, and it is shown that the osmiridium is confined to the ultra-basic olivine-rich differentiates now converted to serpentine. It is further shown that the distribution within the serpentine masses is controlled by the occurrence of definite contraction fissures.

### (13) Ore Deposits of Various Districts.

In addition to the ore deposits in the districts mentioned above which have been investigated in detail, there are a very large number of isolated deposits which have been subjected to more or less complete examinations without completely elucidating their relation to the general geology. It may in fact be claimed that we possess a good general knowledge of the mineralogic composition of the great majority of the ore-deposits of Tasmania. It cannot, however, be claimed with equal justification that either the structural features, paragenesis, or genesis of the deposits, other than those specifically mentioned above, have yet been completely elucidated and described. It is certainly a fact, however, that sufficient material is available, either published or unpublished, to enable such an elucidation and demonstration to be effected, and the writer is attempting this undertaking in his work on "The Metallogenic Epochs of Tasmania."

### (14). Metallogenic Epochs.

It was recognised by the late W. H. Twelvetrees in 1909 that there have been at least two metallogenic epochs—one genetically associated with the porphyroid petrogenic cycle, the other with the Epi-Silurian batholithic epoch. Since that date additional material for the genetic classification of our ore-deposits has been acquired, and the writer is presenting such a complete genetic classification in his above-mentioned work, in addition to demonstrating the various phases and zones of the several metallogenic epochs.

## IX.  SOME PROBLEMS AWAITING SOLUTION.

### (1).  Areal Mapping.

The total area of Tasmania is 26,215 square miles. The areas of which geological maps have been made as the result of definite surveys measure in all 2,122 square miles. There, therefore, remain to be mapped 24,093 square miles. This, it must be admitted, is a big task.

In addition, it must be pointed out that the greater part of those geological maps already prepared are approximate only, and the more accurate survey of these areas is a problem for the future.

### (2). PHYSIOGRAPHY.

(a). A more detailed description than anything attempted heretofore of the topographic features of Tasmania is a desideratum. A large amount of field work yet remains to be done before such an account can be completed. Particularly does this apply to the south-western portion of the Island.

(b). The exact relationship between the more prominent topographic features and geologic structure must be worked out. Particularly does this apply to the problem of the respective rôles played by the diabasic upthrust, Tertiary tensional faulting, and erosion in the evolution of our Diabase Highlands. A similar problem confronts us in the origin of those "inland seas," Macquarie Harbour and Port Davey, as well as the D'Entrecasteaux Channel and the Derwent Estuary.

(c) Some of our highland lakes are of glacial origin, but the problem of the origin of the greater number of our lakes is still to be solved.

(d). The evolution of the drainage system of Tasmania has yet to be traced. Incidental to this is the problem pointed out by Dr. Griffith Taylor, in his "Australian Environ-"ment," of the pronounced bends in some of our largest rivers.

(e). The exact limits of the Darwin peneplain have yet to be determined. Does it extend to the North-East and East Coasts? What is its relation to the Tertiary tensional faulting?

### (3). GENERAL GEOLOGY.

(a). The stratigraphy and structural geology of the old sedimentary system at present termed Pre-Cambrian yet remain uninvestigated in detail. This is undoubtedly an undertaking of considerable magnitude, necessitating, as it obviously will, explorations in uninhabited and heavily timbered and mountainous country. Correlation of this rock system with the Pre-Cambrians of the Australian mainland is a step which can only follow such an investigation.

(b). The relationship of the Dikelocephalus sandstone series to the other rock systems still remains to be determined. It seems highly desirable that the series should be thoroughly searched for a complete suite of fossils, and these examined in detail in order to definitely establish, or otherwise, the Cambrian age determination.

(c). The rock system now termed Cambro-Ordovician requires more exact age determination. Particularly should search be directed in the sedimentary members for fossils which so far have escaped observation.

(d). The stratigraphic relationship between the Dundas slates, the Balfour slates and sandstones, and the Mathinna slates and sandstones yet remains to be determined.

(e). The structural geology of the whole of the Cambro-Ordovician system must be worked out on the lines already accomplished in the Read-Rosebery district. In this connection it will be important to deduce from the strike and dip of the planes of schistosity of the schistose members of this system the position of the drag folds, and from these to determine the location of the axes and dimensions of the major folds.

(f). The petrology of the porphyroid igneous complex must be studied in greater detail, and the effusive and pyroclastic members distinguished from the intrusive and plutonic. With the solution of the structural problem will then come the opportunity of finally determining the order of succession within the petrogenic cycle. Incidental to this is the relationship between the Read-Rosebery and Mt. Lyell schists, which are probably different facies of the same geologic horizon.

(g). The sapropelic coals of the Permo-Carboniferous system are deserving of minute investigation, as they promise to throw much light on the natural history of coal. The exact details of the transition from these coal beds to the Tasmanite shale marine facies of the same horizon still remain to be determined.

(h). The stratigraphy and more definite age determination of our Trias-Jura system both demand attention. Particularly a detailed study of our Trias-Jura flora and comparison with that of the mainland must be undertaken. It is important also to determine whether the break between the Permo-Carboniferous and Trias-Jura is an unconformity or a disconformity, or whether there is a conformable succession.

(i). The study of the stratigraphy and the abundant flora of our lacustrine Tertiary beds is a desirable and attractive undertaking, and it is surprising that this has not been attempted in view of the very strong development of these beds at our second largest centre of population.

(j). The detailed mapping of the glaciated areas of Tasmania is a task yet before us, although some progress has been made. The location of the ice-sheets and the glaciers descending therefrom has only been partially effected, but the final solution of this problem necessitates work in some of the wildest and most inhospitable parts of the Island.

(k). The details of the separation of Tasmania from the Mainland have yet to be determined.

(l). The mapping of the Port Cygnet alkaline series has not yet been accomplished, and the order of succession within this petrogenic cycle yet remains to be determined.

(m). The study of the field occurrence of the diabase so long neglected has only recently been undertaken, but as this rock covers such a large proportion of Tasmania the amount of work to be accomplished on this problem is very considerable.

(n). The investigation of the structural relationships of our Epi-Silurian plutonics is an important one, and still remains to be satisfactorily dealt with.

(o). The determination of the exact relationship between our trachydolerites, limburgites, and normal olivine basalts.

(4.) ECONOMIC GEOLOGY.

(a). The detailed description of some of our most important ore deposits yet remains to be accomplished. This applies particularly to the copper deposits of Mt. Lyell, the tin deposits of Mt. Bischoff, and the galena lodes of the Magnet district.

(b). The mapping and description of the ore deposits of various types in many districts not yet examined in detail represent work for some years to come.

(c) The genetic classification of those of our ore deposits which have been examined to any appreciable extent is very desirable. This must entail the recognition of the metallogenic epochs, and in addition the greater refinement of the various phases within each epoch. This is the problem on which the writer has been engaged in preparing his thesis on the "Metallogenic Epochs of Tasmania."

(d)   Much work remains to be done on the determination of the extent and value of our coalfields.

(e).   No work of importance has been attempted in regard to our building stones. This is a subject for valuable study.

(f).   The investigation of our deposits of the raw materials in the ceramic and glass-making industries is badly needed.

(g).   An important mineralographic study awaiting attention is that of the stanniferous pyrrhotite ore-bodies of North Dundas. The determination of the mode of occurrence of the tin and its exact relationship to the pyrrhotite is an important preliminary in any metallurgical research on these ores.

(h).   The whole problem of the genesis of our ore deposits and the factors controlling their deposition fairly bristles with intricate problems which are too numerous to attempt to indicate in this paper. Suffice it here to say that the progress already made is only a very small portion of the work necessary before anything approaching a complete elucidation of the factors controlling the distribution, extent, and value of our valuable mineral deposits can be attained.

### (5.)   CORRELATION.

With the exception of that accomplished in regard to the Permo-Carboniferous and Trias-Jura systems, practically no work has been done on correlating our Tasmanian systems and rock species with those of the mainland. This is important work which will only become possible of complete accomplishment as our investigations extend in Tasmania. Much, however, can be done at present, and it is very desirable that the first opportunity should be seized of summarising the conclusions which are possible on present evidence.

# FRANCE AND AUSTRALIA.

## THE "PRISE DE POSSESSION."

## A NEW CHAPTER IN OUR EARLY HISTORY.

By THOMAS DUNBABIN, B.A. (Oxon.), M.A. (Tasmania).

[Originally written for the Hobart-Melbourne Meeting of the Australasian Association for the Advancement of Science, January, 1921.]*

(Read before the Royal Society of Tasmania, 8th August, 1921.)

When Ernest Scott, Professor of History in the University of Melbourne, was working on his *Life of Flinders*, he employed a copyist to obtain material from the Paris archives. The copyist found so much about Australia that the charges mounted very high. So Professor Scott pointed out to the Commonwealth Parliamentary Library and the Mitchell Library that they ought to have copies of these valuable historical documents. The authorities agreed, and the cost of Professor Scott's material was one-third of what it would otherwise have been.

This partial overhaul of the Paris archives by an intelligent copyist has thrown a flood of light on the early relations of France and Australia. An examination of the papers in the Commonwealth Library, made by the courtesy of the Speaker, reveals the hitherto unpublished fact that a French expedition did, in 1772, take formal possession of Western Australia.

It is not in France alone that material may be found. Hidden away in some dusty corner in Portugal, Spain, or possibly Holland, there may be documents which upset accepted ideas about the obscure but fascinating subject of early exploration in Australasian regions. For the history

---

*Owing to the Shipping Strike, the Meeting of the A.A.A.S., which was to have been held in Hobart in January, had to be held in Melbourne. Many difficulties had to be overcome, and it was found impossible to publish the usual full report of the A.A.A.S. Meeting and to print all papers. Arrangements were therefore made for certain papers to be read before the Society and published in the Papers and Proceedings for 1921.

K

of the early days of settlement, too, there may be valuable material awaiting research. American vessels played a great part in the early trade of Australasia, and in the whaling and sealing which were the greatest industries of those days. In the twenty years from 1792 to 1812 over fifty American vessels called at Sydney, while many others visited Australasian waters without going to Sydney. There may be much of Australian interest in the ships' logs and other records of the old New England whaling towns. Even Russia is not too far afield to have possibilities. Several Russian expeditions visited Australia in the early days, including that of Bellingshausen, one of the greatest of Antarctic explorers, who paid two visits to Sydney in 1820.

## THE FEAR OF FRANCE.

France might have been a serious rival for the possession of Australia. To a large extent the early history of Australia was shaped by the fear of French rivalry. This fear caused the founding of the first settlements in Tasmania, in Western Australia, and in tropical Australia. It led to the sending of Collins' Expedition to Port Phillip in 1803, and to the temporary settlement of Westernport in 1826.

French interest in the South Seas goes back to a date nearly a century before the first British Settlement. From 1699 onwards projects for exploration and colonisation in the far South were continually being put forward in France. Two years after Cook had taken formal possession of the Eastern part of Australia for Great Britain a similar ceremony was carried out on the Western Coast on behalf of France.

## DE VOUTRON'S VOYAGE OF 1687.

Just as the voyage of Cook was but the greatest of a series of English voyages to the South Seas of which the earlier ones are now almost forgotten, so French interests in the New World of the South by no means began with Marion's voyage of 1772. Take, for instance, the letter which de Voutron, a French sea captain, wrote to the Minister for Marine from La Rochelle on February 10, 1699. In this he offers to lead an expedition to explore, with a view to colonisation, that part of the Terres Australes called by the Dutch New Holland. He states that he and his brother-in-law, Duquesne, had sighted this land in 1687 while on a voyage to Siam. They made their land fall in latitude 31 deg. south (a little to the north of the Swan

River), and coasted the country for some distance, keeping
two or three leagues off shore, and finding an open sea,
though such charts of this region as they had showed a mass
of rocks and reefs extending for 12 or 15 leagues out to sea.
"According to appearance the lands are habitable and im-
"portant," wrote De Voutron.  He asserted that the Dutch
knew much more of this country than they chose to tell, and
states that their pilot had been strictly forbidden on pain of
punishment to give to foreigners any information about these
coasts.    He asked for two vessels of medium size and a
smaller craft for use in shallow water, and mentioned the
end of April or the beginning of May as the best time for
an exploring expedition to set out from France.   De Voutron
urged that a port on the Australian coast would be of great
value to the French trade with the far East.

On October 8, 1699, de Voutron renewed his request.
His scheme was backed by one Renan, who describes him as
a "man of stout heart who would not be repelled by difficul-
"ties, one accustomed to deep sea voyages, as he had been
"several times to the Indies."

## SOUTH SEA BUBBLES.

It was in this same year that the British Admiralty
sent out William Dampier in the *Roebuck* to explore the
Australian coast, but de Voutron was less persuasive, or
less fortunate than that eminent buccaneer.   Interest in
de Voutron's suggestion was apparently revived a few years
later.    Bouvet states in a memorandum written in 1735,
that but for the death of du Vivier, the Captain who was to
have taken command, a French vessel would in 1708 have
been sent to explore the "land discovered by Dampier."

The year 1699 was marked by a great stirring of French
interest in Southern exploration.   Another document of
that year is a "Memorandum on the Discovery of the Terres
Australes" by Saint Marie.   Saint Marie accepts as correct
the alleged discovery in 1503 by a Norman Sea Captain
named de Gonneville of a Southern Land which he, like
others, is inclined to identify with Australia.   De Gonneville stated that he had brought back to France a native of
the new-found land named Essomeric, a chief's son, who
settled in France and founded a family there.   But even
in France the de Gonneville story found critics.   In a document written in 1738 Bernard de la Harpe claims that the
story contains contradictions and impossibilities, and con-
siders it more probable that de Gonneville, if he made the

voyage at all, reached some point on the South American coast.

In a later memorandum, undated, but written after 1745, since it states that in that year the English sent two vessels, the *George* and the *California*, to seek for a north-west passage to the Pacific, de la Harpe tells us that at the beginning of the 18th century there was a very active French trade with the Pacific coast of South America. He states that between 1703 and 1720 the inhabitants of St. Malo sent ninety-two vessels to the South Pacific. One of these, the *Francois*, was commanded by Marion du Fresne, no doubt of kin to the more famous Marion who visited Tasmania and New Zealand in 1772, and was the first white man to meet the aborigines of Tasmania. This earlier Marion was at Concepcion in Chile in 1714, when the Captain of a Spanish vessel told him that 400 leagues to the west and in latitude 38 deg. south he had fallen in with a high land and coasted along it for a day. De la Harpe received without question the theory that there was a great southern continent, quite distinct of course from Australia, a belief generally held until Cook proved that such a continent, if it existed, was confined to the Antarctic regions. Of this continent New Zealand, de la Harpe thought, formed part, and he conjectured that its inhabitants had crossed from Australia or Van Diemen's Land to New Zealand. Like de Voutron, he thought that a French Settlement in these Southern lands would largely control the trade "with India, "China, and the South Seas."

While de la Harpe was sceptical, Bouvet fully accepted the de Gonneville story. Bouvet tells us that in 1734 he had, in the *Dauphin*, bound to the East Indies, run down the easting till he sighted the Australian coast, "as almost all "the English now do." He urged the planting of a colony in the Terres Australes du Saint Esprit. In 1738 Bouvet set out in two vessels to search for the great southern continent armed in a model form for taking possession. But he searched in the stormy seas southward of the Cape of Good Hope. and found only Bouvet Island. In a memorandum written in 1767, Bouvet proposed another voyage, but nothing came of it. Incidentally Bouvet complains that Bougainville had stolen his ideas.

## ACADIANS FOR SOUTHERN COLONIES.

In later years the English suspected the French of designs on Australia which apparently they did not enter-

tain.   In these earlier days the French sometimes thought
that the English ideas about expansion in the South Seas
were far more definite than was actually the case.     Bougainville, writing from the Falkland Islands, apparently in
1764, says: "The views of the English about forming estab-
"lishments in the South Seas and in the neighbouring coun-
"tries have long been known, but it is above all since the
"relation of the voyages of Anson that the English have
"decided to follow seriously the execution of these views."
Bougainville states that they intended to seize the Island
of Juan Fernandez.

Though Bougainville did not visit Australia, he anticipated a proposal made when the British did actually begin
to think of settling in Australia.    It was urged by James
Maria Matra in 1783 that the American Loyalists expelled
from the United States should be sent as settlers to Australia.   Owing to delays and to other causes the idea came
to nothing, though one or two United Empire Loyalists did
reach Australia.   We are, for instance, told of James Reid,
who came out as a superintendent of convicts in 1789, that
he had been a planter in America.    Bougainville's idea was
to use the Acadians of Longfellow's "Evangeline," expelled
from the maritime province of Canada by the English, to
found a new French Colony in the far south.    He wrote
in 1763: "As the modest funds of the owners of the vessel
"do not allow them to embark, at their own cost, large crews,
"they would ask the King for forty men, half soldiers and
"half Acadians.   The soldiers should be men who have
"served in Canada, and are therefore accustomed to live in
"the woods, to rove and to traverse unknown countries.   The
"Acadians are sailors and fishermen, and are the more re-
"commended by the strong and constant proofs of attachment
"to France given since the Peace of Utrecht.    They are
"most suitable men for founding a flourishing settlement.
"The Acadians who had made the voyage would determine
"their compatriots to transfer themselves to the south."

Bougainville had served under Montcalm in Canada, and
had conceived the idea of indemnifying France for her losses
in the New World by calling into existence French colonies
in the "third part of the world" in the south.    Unluckily,
he took his colonising expedition and his Acadian settlers to
the Falkland Islands, the Iles Malouines of the French, and
as the result of Spanish objections the French colony was
withdrawn after three years.

## KERGUELEN'S VOYAGES.

In the year 1772 two French expeditions visited Australasia. The story of the voyage of Marion du Fresne and Crozet from Mauritius to Tasmania and New Zealand is well known, but a strange oblivion has fallen on the activities of Saint Allouarn on the western side of Australia. The name of Saint Allouarn is preserved by an island near Cape Leeuwin, and there are one or two casual references to his voyage, but no one seems to have suspected that he actually took formal possession of part of Australia for France.　Saint Allouarn was a companion of Ives Kerguelen, who had set out from France to seek for the southern continent.　This was the vast continent supposed to exist in the temperate regions of the southern hemisphere, the continent whose existence Cook finally disproved, a work which he considered of far more importance than the mere charting of the east coast of "New Holland."　Had Cook had a better vessel he might never have visited Australia at all.

While Cook decided in 1770 that there was not much to be found between New Zealand and the Cape of Good Hope, though he had yet to prove that no southern continent existed between New Zealand and Cape Horn, Kerguelen was in 1772 still searching for a southern continent south-east of the Cape of Good Hope.　After a visit to Mauritius he sailed to the Southward on January 16, 1772, in the *Fortune*, accompanied by Saint Allouarn in command of the *Gros Ventre*, a 300 ton vessel carrying 14 guns and a crew of 105 men.　On February 13, they reached Kerguelen Land, which Kerguelen named La Nouvelle France, and took to be part of the long-sought continent.　Next day a storm separated the two vessels.　Kerguelen returned to Mauritius, but St. Allouarn bore away for Australia.　Of his voyage two accounts are preserved in the Commonwealth Library.　One is the log of the *Gros Ventre*, the other the Diary of Rosily, properly an officer of Kerguelen's vessel, who was on the *Gros Ventre* by accident.　He had been sent in the sloop to sound on February 14, and managed to reach the *Gros Ventre* when the storm broke.　The log tells us the land near Cape Leeuwin was sighted on March 17, 1772.　Next day St. Allouarn sent a boat to reconnoitre, but those in it were unable to land.　They caught many fish, but saw no signs of inhabitants.　The *Gros Ventre* then sailed northward along the coast, missing the Swan River, discovered in 1697 by Vlaming, until March 30. The vessel was then in latitude 25 deg. 25 min. south, or somewhere about Shark Bay.

## WESTERN AUSTRALIA CLAIMED.

The log continues: "At ten o'clock this morning M. de "Saint Allouarn sent a boat with an officer to reconnoitre "this land, supported by the boat's crew and five soldiers. "They effected a landing at a bay to the south south east, "and penetrated about three leagues into the country without "seeing à living soul. This land is sandy, and covered with "bushes and small scrub, as at the Cape of Good Hope. "M. de Mings, on returning to the coast, took possession of "the land, hoisting a flag and causing a notification of the "fact that he had taken possession to be read in the form "usual in such cases. The document was put in a bottle "and buried at the foot of a little tree. Near it were put "two crowns of six francs each. In the afternoon the sloop "went on shore with many persons. They traversed a space "of three leagues without finding any one. They returned "on board in the evening. They found on land traces of "some quadrupeds, and saw a kind of little fox. At 6 o'clock "in the evening the captain sent the boat on shore to bury "one Massicot, a gunner's mate, who had died that day of "scurvy. They were to pass the night and to see if they "could catch turtles in the great bay, but none came on "shore."

The log refers to this Bay as the "Baie de Prise de "Possession." It mentions that on April 1 the vessel entered the "Baie de Bricarloge," which no doubt means the bay of Dirk Hartog, or Dirk Hartog's Road, as Vlaming calls it, the Bay in which Dirk Hartog had anchored in 1616.

## DESCRIPTION OF THE COUNTRY.

Rosily was evidently one of those who went ashore at the Baie de Prise de Possession. He says that with much difficulty they climbed up a steep sand hill covered with scrub. "From the top of this," he writes, "we perceived a "landscape extending away for seven or eight leagues. The "land rose imperceptibly, and we penetrated for about two "and a half leagues inland. We saw there many burnt "trees and others where it appeared that one had set fire to "the foot of them. I do not believe that it is the heat of "the sun that sets fire to these trees, for they are very green, "and in the night there is a very heavy dew that refreshes "them and gives them nourishment. We thought that we

"saw traces of men and of children, but we could hardly
"distinguish them, because of the very shifting nature of
"the sand.　There was in particular one place as if it
"appeared that people had danced in a ring.　We saw there
"animals like makis (long tailed monkeys) and others like
"mangoustes (the ichneumon or Pharaoh's rat), and several
"birds, including a kind of goose which had difficulty in
"flying, but never allowed us to approach within gun shot.
"Generally speaking, all the animals that we saw were very
"wild.　We found no water at all.　I believe that the
"animals drink only at night, taking advantage of the dew.
"We found on the beach thousands of little tortoises no
"bigger than your hand.　The persons who passed the night
"in catching them saw a large animal in the shape of a
"dog which was scratching in this place in a search for the
"eggs of the tortoises.　We caught many very good fish with
"the line, but could not succeed with the seine, the shore
"being very steep."

Rosily states that the *Gros Ventre* was detained for
eight days before she could get out of the Bay which she
entered on April 1.　She lost two anchors there owing to
the strength of the currents.

The *Gros Ventre* left the coast on April 11, being then
in latitude 23 deg. 44 min. south, and sailed by way of Timor
and Java to Mauritius, which she reached on September 5.
There Francois Alesne de Saint Allouarn, who had long been
grievously sick, died a few days later, at the age of thirty-
five.

## KERGUELEN'S DOWNFALL.

As may be judged from the remarks of Rosily, about
the lack of water, and the look of the country generally,
Saint Allouarn's officers were not enthusiastic about the
region round Shark's Bay of which possession had been
taken.　Kerguelen Land, on the other hand, was for the
moment looked on as part of a great continent, and a discovery of capital importance.　"In two months M. Ker-
"guelen has discovered for France a new world," wrote M.
Poivre, the Intendant at Mauritius, on March 21, 1772, when
Kerguelen had just returned.　In another note, however, M.
Poivre wrote, "I have the honour to observe that the cost of
"these expeditions ordered by the Court should not be borne
"by the Colony."　There was a fear that the English would
try to get hold of the new "Continent."　In a memorandum
dated August 2, 1772, it is urged that Kerguelen should be

sent back without waiting to see what had become of the *Gros Ventre*. "A pressing incentive," says the anonymous but apparently official writer, "is the necessity of forestalling "the English, who, on the reports spread abroad of this dis-"covery, might seek to trouble at its inception our possession "of these lands of which the Commander of the *Gros Ventre* "has probably taken possession in the name of His Majesty." This refers, of course, not to Western Australia, of which Saint Allouarn had actually taken possession, but to Kerguelen Land. Kerguelen asked for three good ships, stating that the English were equipping four for an expedition to the South Seas. After a good deal of delay he went down to Kerguelen Land again, but was so buffeted by gales and beset by the ice and snow of that inhospitable region that he ran north to Madagascar, and then to Mauritius, and reported sadly that New France "offered no resources." Perhaps he would have tried the Australian coast for a change, but wine and wassail at Port Louis led to trouble. Eventually Kerguelen was tried by a court-martial, broken, and dismissed from the Navy. A book which he wrote was suppressed, and a score of years after his voyage, in the days of the revolution, he was still seeking to make good a claim to justice. There was a new Intendant at Mauritius by the time of Kerguelen's second Expedition, one Maillart Dumesse, and he had no sympathy with these explorations. In language of a kind not unfamiliar in our own day he urged that the first consideration should be the promotion of 'payable enterprises. Agriculture at Mauritius should be encouraged by importing negro slaves from Mozambique and cattle from Madagascar. "Our expedition," wrote Dumesse, in complaining of Kerguelen's requisitions for supplies, "should have no other objects than blacks and beasts "(neirs et bestiaux)."

French activity in Australasian seas continued for many years after this. It is enough to mention the great voyages of La Perouse, who put into Botany Bay when Sydney was a few days old, of D'Entrecasteaux and of Baudin, with later voyagers like Dumont d'Urville. But Saint Allouarn was the first and last to claim for France a foot of the soil of Australia.

# TASMANIAN STATE RECORDS.

By J. MOORE-ROBINSON, F.R.G.S.

(Librarian and Publicity Officer, Chief Secretary's
Department, Tasmania.)

[Originally written for the Hobart meeting of the Australasian Association for the Advancement of Science, January, 1921. Revised, and in part re-written, and read before
the Royal Society of Tasmania, 8th August, 1921.]*

A careful consideration of all facts concerned compels
the belief that, ranking in prime importance among State
functions, is a proper preservation of State Records. Other
processes being normally in a continual state of progression
or development, can never share the innate quality of
Records. Records do not develop—they are the imprint of
current events. They stand alone in the world of Science.

Records have not been well treated by Australia since
she took her place among the living entities of the earth.
It is the exception to find important Records explicit and
reliable. For instance, the very date of Captain Cook's discovery of the N.S.W. coast is now called in question, owing
to an alleged error by the Great Navigator in his calculations
in crossing the 180th Meridian, while sailing westward from
Tahiti in 1770. It is true that December 1st, 1642, has never
been challenged as the day on which Tasman cast anchor
on Tasmania's coast; yet many different dates have been
assigned to Bowen's Settlement at Risdon in 1803. The
almanacs up to 1893 give the date of Bowen's landing as
August 10th, 1803. In those of the following year that date
is altered to September 12th, and later September 13th, 1803,
is adopted. Curiously enough, in *Walch's Red Book* for
1920 the date is assigned as September 14th, owing probably
to an error in copying. So careful an author as James
Backhouse Walker writes ("First Settlement of the Derwent," *Early Tasmania*, p. 26):—

"I have searched in vain hitherto in printed
"accounts for the correct date of Bowen's Settlement.

* Owing to the Shipping Strike, the Meeting of the A.A.A.S., which
was to have been held in Hobart in January, had to be held in Melbourne.
Many difficulties had to be overcome, and it was found impossible to
publish the usual full report of the A.A.A.S. Meeting and to print all
papers. Arrangements were, therefore, made for certain papers to be
read before the Society and published in the Papers and Proceedings
for 1921.

"The dates given vary from June to August, but I think
"we may henceforth consider it settled, on the authority
"of official documents, that the birthday of Tasmania
"was Tuesday, the 7th day of September, 1803."

Walker's conclusion is not correct, and his error is due,
not to lack of examination on his part, but to the careless,
inconclusive, and incomplete Records of the period. Bowen
himself reported that he arrived at Risdon "on Sunday.
"September 12th, 1803." As a matter of fact he made an
error in the day of the month. The correct dates of that
important event are:—

> *Lady Nelson* (tender) arrived at Risdon Cove at
> 6 p.m. on *Thursday*, September 8th, 1803.

> *Albion* (with Bowen on board) arrived at 8 a.m. on
> *Sunday*, September 11th, 1803.

Proof of these dates is given by Dr. F. Watson, Editor of the
*Australian Historical Records*, Series III., Vol. I., and to
that author much credit is due for patient investigation and
careful examination. In these circumstances it is pleasant
to be able to state that the Records of the Tasmanian Government give great promise of affording not only verification
of disputed statements, but the discovery of new and important facts.

One specific instance of the latter will suffice on this
point. The exact history of Port Arthur has always been
regarded as a lost possibility owing to the non-existence of
earlier Records of the famous Settlement. It was loosely
stated "that Port Arthur was born in 1830." The Tasmanian
Historians, West (1862) and Fenton (1884), totally ignore
so important a point. Since commencing the work of
indexing the MS. Records in the Chief Secretary's Department, I have been fortunate enough to find:—

> (1) Governor Arthur's autographed Minute dated
> September 7th, 1830, giving instructions to found Port
> Arthur.

> (2) The Report to Arthur of Assistant Surgeon
> John James Russell, the first Commandant, dated from
> the Settlement October 2nd, and giving details of his
> landing there on September 22nd, 1830.

> (3) Several other documents relating to the same
> subject.

These documents establish with authority, not only the exact date of the Settlement's birth, but the more important fact that at least in the beginning it was not designed as the ultra or super-penal station into which it afterwards developed, and from which it has derived its somewhat unenviable fame. The dates and facts given in these documents are explicit, and though their detail is not as full as might be desired, they afford a sufficient ground on which Port Arthur's story may be accurately based. They establish the fact that Port Arthur was primarily designed as a timber station, which might indeed be worked by prisoners more suitable (owing to their bad conduct) for life away from convicts of better dispositions. But Russell's testimony is clear:—

> "Port Arthur," he writes, in the first Despatch referred to, "forms a fine capacious harbour, and from "the quantity of *good Timber* with which its Coast "abounds, I have no doubt but that it will answer *the* "*main object* of its establishment as a settlement."

Therefore, Port Arthur was designed and opened as a Timber station such as others then in existence at Birch's Bay and elsewhere.

Take another instance, that of Drake, England's greatest adventurer. Old Fuller, in his immortal *Worthies*, thus describes Drake: "A very religious man towards God and "His Houses, chaste in his life, just in his dealings, true of "his word, and merciful to those under him." Truly a model panegyric. Yet Drake had been accused not only of being a Pirate, but of being the murderer of his friend, that courtly gentleman Thomas Doughty. And but for the accidental discovery of a 16th Century Record, Drake's name might never have been freed from this suspicion. A lady, Mrs. Zelia Nuttall, student of Mexican Archæology, a few years ago, was pursuing her researches in the National Archives of Mexico, when she chanced on a dust-covered tome. On examination this proved to be the declaration of Nuno da Silva concerning his compulsory association with "Francisco Drac," who, it will be remembered, captured da Silva, and used him as a Pilot while on the Spanish Main. In his Declarations to the Spanish Inquisitors da Silva stated that Doughty challenged Drake's authority to behead him, and that Drake in reply, produced

> "some papers, kissed them, raised them to his forehead, "and read them with a loud voice."

All present recognised these as the warrants of Elizabeth of England, granting Drake, in terms similar to those used in the case of Richard Grenville, absolute power of life and death over all who sailed under him.

Thus has a Record—the musty Record of the Spanish pilot—proved the judicial execution of Doughty, and scouted the attainters of England's Sea Hero. Instances like this might be multiplied, but I am sure these two are sufficient to lend insistence to my claim for the completion and preservation of Records.

After this somewhat lengthy exegesis of Records in general, let me state the position relative to the Early Records of the Tasmanian Government.

Subsequent to the 24th of May, 1824, when Colonel George Arthur assumed the Lieut.-Governorship of Tasmania, the State Records are reasonably ample and complete, both in MS. and printed forms, and in narrative and in statistical styles. Prior to that period the Records are meagre, non-sequential, and altogether inadequate. Thus we have two prime Epochs with which I shall deal separately:—

## FIRST EPOCH. PRE-ARTHUR.

This Epoch may be conveniently classified in three subdivisions:—

(a) *Discovery*, 1642-1803. This period begins with Tasman's discovery of Van Diemen's Land, and includes the successive discoveries and surveys effected by Marion du Fresne (1772), Furneaux (1773), Cook (1777), possibly La Perouse (1788), Cox (1789), D'Entrecasteaux (1792-3), Hayes (1794), Bass and Flinders (1793), and Baudin (1802). So far as Tasmanian ownership is concerned, no MS. exists of the work of these Early Voyagers. All we know of them has been learned from Records belonging to other peoples and nations. Not one stroke of the pen exists in Tasmania from the hands of this galaxy of illustrious Navigators.

(b) *Settlement*, 1803-4. The three names prominent in this period are those of Lieut. John Bowen, who on September 11th, 1803, landed at Risdon to form the first Settlement in Tasmania; Lt.-Col. David Collins, who on the 21st February, 1804, founded the present capital of Tasmania; and Lt.-Col. Wm. Paterson. The latter arrived at Port Dalrymple (River Tamar) on November 4th, 1804, in H.M.S.

*Buffalo*, but that ship dragged her anchor during the night in a strong gale from the North-West, and went aground. As a consequence, seven days were lost before Col. Paterson came to a safe anchorage, and on November 11th, 1804, effected the beginning of Settlement in the North of this Island, which he named George Town.

To these three names, or perchance more fairly to the Navigators of the Discovery Period, should be added the name of William Collins. This officer (later Hobart's first Harbour Master), who came out with Governor Collins to engage in the Seal Fishing, was despatched from Port Phillip to examine Port Dalrymple, and landed there from that famous ship in Tasmanian history, the *Lady Nelson*, on January 1st, 1804, three and a half months after Bowen had landed at Risdon. Wm. Collins spent three weeks examining the Tamar, and was much impressed, claiming its beauty to be "not surpassed in the world." The credit of this voyage, however, must be shared between Wm. Collins and Lieut. Symons, who commanded the *Lady Nelson*.

Of this period, too, Tasmania possesses no written Records. We have at our disposal only the Records of other States, which, however, are sufficient to give us a fairly clear view of all the leading events. But these, even the official Reports and Despatches, are lamentably lacking in those details which the Historian finds so necessary to enable him to obtain correct colour and evolve an accurate perspective.

(c) *Occupation*, 1804-1824. It is a period of marked laxity in almost every Department of Government, a laxity in none more marked than in that designed for the preservation of official Records. I do not desire to place individual blame, for that would be manifestly unfair. Circumstances fortuitously guided to an unfortunate end. Official jealousies, the lack of instructions, personal weakness, the vacillations of the Home Government, and many other forces active and passive, combined to the unhappy result, the which it is no part of my purpose to enter into here. Our Records, official and private, of this period are hopelessly inadequate, especially when we reflect that it is the real foundation on which the fabric of Tasmanian History should be built. A few Garrison Orders of Collins, the Journal of that worldly divine, the Rev. Robt. Knopwood, some transcripts of letters and despatches by Governor Sorell, some second-hand statements, generally garbled, concerning Commandants Giel, Murray, and others, the incidental light shed by Despatches from the Governor in

Chief to the Home Government; a few Court Documents and
Survey Records, and the terse official notes and notices of
the *Hobart Town Gazette*, which began publication on June
1st, 1816; these, and a few odds and ends, are the main
bases on which the story of the years 1804 to 1824 has to
be founded.

I will tabulate those that have come under my own
notice:—

(1) Our Survey Department has some interesting
Records of Land Grants, Buildings and Allotments, Statements of Fees, etc., which are being indexed, and so made
available.

(2) We have a priceless original Land Grant dated
December 18th, 1805, signed by Philip Gidley King, devising
that "Henrietta Farm" of 100 acres on the banks of the
Derwent, to Henry Hayes. This is, I believe, the oldest land
document extant relating to Tasmania. In the Chief Secretary's possession.

(3) A MS. Map dated 1803 of the country East of the
Derwent, by James Meehan, with that Surveyor's Field
Books. In possession of Lands and Survey Department.
This map, the oldest extant of Tasmania, has some curious
and interesting features. These are dealt with in my
*Tasmanian Nomenclature* published in 1911, and by Mr. T.
Dunbabin in some articles published in *The Mercury* in 1912,
and headed "In the Map Room."

(4) Two type-written copies (in the possession of the
Royal Society of Tasmania) of some of Governor Sorell's
Letters and Despatches dated 1818.

(5) A Book half full of Drafts and Letters to Home
Government Departments by various Governors from 1818 to
1824. His Excellency the Governor has kindly allowed me
to peruse this book, which is in his official possession.

(6) A book of some of the Records of the Judge
Advocates Court. It is endorsed "No. 7," and dated from
June 2, 1823. This is in the Chief Secretary's Vaults.

(7) Sundry Deeds and Bonds, fragmentary and dis-
connected, dated from 1819 onward. In the Chief Secretary's
Vaults.

(8) Some unexamined Files of Correspondence which
Dr. Watson and I recently found at George Town, and which
are now in the possession of the Chief Secretary.

(9) A complete File of the *Hobart Town Gazette* (Government), commencing with Vol. I. on June 3rd, 1816. In the Chief Secretary's Vaults.

(10) Some Muster Rolls recently discovered at Launceston.

## SECOND EPOCH.  ARTHUR AND ONWARDS.

*MS. CORRESPONDENCE.*  In the vault of the Chief Secretary, we have an invaluable collection of MS. official documents, filed from the beginning of his Regime, by Tasmania's most noteworthy Governor, Col. George Arthur. Counting to the beginning of the present century, these form a library of about 2,600 volumes, averaging about 270 pages. I am engaged in preparing these for careful investigation by compiling a Card Index of Subject, Authors, and including, where possible, the names of such prominent persons as appear. Owing to the pressure of other work, progress has been slow, but the Commonwealth has given assistance, and I am hopeful of proceeding much faster this year, and expect to have the bulk of the work done inside two years. Certain Indices and Registers exist in reference to this MS., but they are not of great value owing to (1) confused method of indexing, (2) missing files, (3) the cumbrousness involved in such a system when the dates of Files range over nearly eighty years. These disadvantages will disappear under a consecutive Card system.

These 2,600 volumes contain certain correspondence of a most valuable character (as, for instance, the beginnings of Port Arthur, referred to above), and I am hopeful that a careful search will reveal matter of utmost importance. Original Shipping Records are bound up indiscriminately in these Files, and when collated should afford intensely interesting side-lights, indeed lights of primary importance, on our early history.

*GOVERNOR'S DESPATCHES.*  In the vault, too, is a complete series of Governor's Despatches, outward and inward, from 1824 to 1856. These, as might be expected, form a reasonably complete epitome of official acts and observations during the period covered. They have never been carefully examined, and when indexed may be expected to yield a vast number of facts, some quite new to the Historian. Some of them are the duplicate copies sent to the Secretary of State; others original copies, and some copies for filing. I do not know how the first named were returned to Tasmania, or by whose authority.

*NEWSPAPERS.* The vault contains bound volumes of Tasmanian Newspapers. The earliest of these are the *Colonial Times* of 1826 to 1856, the *Hobart Town Courier* of 1827 to 1859, the *Australasian* of 1824, *The Tasmanian* of 1826, *The Cornwall Chronicle* of 1835 to 1880, *Bent's News* of 1834 and 1837-38. The Volumes of these Newspapers are numbered and catalogued, but otherwise the information they contain is only available after arduous and exhausting search, "Page upon page, and line upon line."

*HOBART TOWN GAZETTES.* The Government has also a complete set of these from No. I., Vol. I., June 1st, 1816, to the present date. This set is a veritable mine of information, which, like that of the old newspapers, is not readily available. If these Volumes and the Newspapers were indexed in regard to news items, even up to the year 1850, some surprising facts would be brought to light. It is a work that I hope to see done.

*THE BONWICK TRANSCRIPTS.* No list would be complete without reference to the result of Mr. James Bonwick's work, undertaken at the request of the Tasmanian Government, and completed in 1892. Mr. Bonwick copied papers, some in the official custody of the Imperial Government, and others preserved in the British Museum. These include valuable documents relating to the discovery and settlement of Tasmania and New South Wales. Among them is to be found a copy of *Tasman's Journal* in Dutch (British Museum) and a copy of Woides' translation of it. The latter contains three several points quite new to History. I am hopeful of seeing it in print in the near future, as it is too good to be lost. The transcripts were largely used by the late James Backhouse Walker in preparing that series of monographs read before the Royal Society, and published in a Memorial volume called *Early Tasmania*, which entitled their author to be counted among the chief of Tasmania's historical writers. Much of the matter contained in these Transcripts is being published in that valuable Commonwealth enterprise, *The Historical Records of Australia*, under the able editorship of Dr. Frederick Watson, referred to above.

*PARLIAMENTARY PAPERS.* It is, I suppose, hardly necessary to state that the vault contains a complete set of Parliamentary Papers since Responsible Government in 1856, and the enactments of the earlier Legislative Council from 1837.

L

*GAZETTES OTHER THAN TASMANIAN.* Our collection of these is interesting and valuable, although rarely used. It includes:—

(1) *SYDNEY Gazette*, 1833 to 1864.

(2) *LONDON Gazette* (bound), 1839 to 1874. Unbound to date.

(3) *WEST AUSTRALIA Gazette*, 1824 (No. 287) *et seq.*

(4) *SOUTH AUSTRALIAN Gazette*, 1842 (No. 212), *et seq.*

(5) *VICTORIAN Gazette*, June, 1852, *et seq.*

(6) *QUEENSLAND Gazette*, 1860, 1861, 1863, 1864, 1865, 1866, 1867.

(7) *NEW ZEALAND Gazette*, 1843 to 1866.

(8) *AUCKLAND, WELLINGTON, SOUTHLAND and OTAGO Gazettes*, various dates from the fifties.

(9) *CAPE OF GOOD HOPE Gazette*, January, 1847, *et seq.*

## SOME SUGGESTIONS.

I do not wish to close this paper without suggesting practical application of its main purpose. I am certain that if Governments realised the value, actual and historical, of their old Records, they would have them properly indexed and available for use.

I think that a useful first step would be for all the State Governments to get into communication with a view to each having returned to its possession any documents now held by another Government.

The next step would be to arrange that all historical matter held by State Governments should be arranged, collated, and indexed on a system common to all. This is an important aspect, which will be appreciated most by those who have had the task of hunting up information in more than one State.

A further step would be an endeavour to obtain re-possession of any official documents which by one means or another have strayed from official custody.

I need scarcely stress the great advantages which would accrue if the State officers in charge of Historical Records were to be in constant communication with each other.

By these means Australia would gradually build up a solid, authoritative, and complete foundation upon which Australia's historian, when he eventuates, would be enabled to construct an historical fabric worthy of our Commonwealth, and worthy, too, of those indomitable spirits who, preceding us, have shaped for us so goodly an heritage.

## CONCLUSION.

It is impossible to conclude this paper without making reference to the interest, no less than the courtesy and kindness, of the Honourable the Premier of Tasmania (Sir Walter Lee) in regard to its subject matters. The Government of which Sir Walter Lee is Premier has taken a keen interest in the Historical Records of the State, and has kindly conceded to me the privilege of committing to paper for the first time in the State's History the facts concerning Tasmania's Records, set out here. I feel this to be a great boon. The Under Secretary (Mr. D'Arcy Addison, I.S.O., M.V.O.) and Mr. Charles F. Seager (Acting Under Secretary) have been equally sympathetic.

It only remains for me to express the hope that, in the not far distant future, the secrets held latent in Government Vaults will be unveiled for the credit of the giants whose doings the Records chronicle, and the profit of those of this generation who tread the tracks they hewed out for us with so much labour.

# JUNGERMANNIA STYGIA, HOOK. F. ET TAYL.

By Wm. Hy. Pearson, M.Sc., A.L.S.,

Plate XXIII.

(Read 19th September, 1921.)

In Mr. Rodway's interesting and useful List of Tasmanian Hepatics (Proc. Royal Scc. Tasm., p. 74, 1916) reference is made to this species, and also to *Cesia erosa*, Carr. et Pears.

The following notes will clear up some misunderstanding with reference to these species.

In Hooker's *Flora Antarctica, Jungermannia stygia* is described and figured as follows:—"Perpusilla, caule erecti, "laxe caespitoso ramoso, foliis erectis, subimbricatis, "appressis, obovatis, integris v. emarginatis, perichaetiis "rotundatis, caule duplo latioribus. (Tab. LXII., Fig. IV.)

"Hab. Campbell's Island, on rocks on the hills, growing "amongst other Hepaticæ and Mosses.

"Caules 2-3 lin. longi, crassiusculi, superne fusco v. atro-"purpurei, inferne fusco-olivacei, vage ramosi; ramis divari-"catis. Folia minima, subsecunda, alterna, vix imbricata "obovata v. oblonga, apices versus obtusos late emarginata, "segmentis obtusis, rarius integra, margine superiore inter-"dum scariosa. Perichaetia subrotunda, foliis imbricatis, "latiusculis, ad apices albidos, pleurumque scariosis.

"A very inconspicuous little species approaching J. con-"cinnata (Lightf.), of which it is probably the representative "in these islands; the leaves are, however, more distant, never "bifid at the apex, the stem slenderer, and the perichætia "sessile and round. Its colour is like *Gymnomitrium adustum*, "Nees, a German plant, with short and simpler stems."

In the Manchester Museum there is an original specimen of *Jung. stygia* from Campbell's Islands, and I have had the opportunity of microscopically examining the same; it is composed of two quite different species, one, which is figured by Hooker, being a round-leaved species, probably a *Jamesoniella*, and a *Gymnomitrium*, which it would be difficult to distinguish from *Gym. concinnatum* (Lightf.). Evidently the two species have been described as one, but with Hooker's

Fig. 1. Copy of Hooker's figures from *Flora Antarctica*, Pl. LVII., fig. IV.

Fig. 2. *Gymnomitrium stygia* (H. et T.) Pears: x 50.

Fig. 3. *Jungermannia*, growing with *G. stygia*; x 50. (Campbell's Island, Hooker, original, ex herb. Manchester Museum.)

notes in English, that his *Jung. stygia* is related to *Gym. concinnatum* and *Gymn. adustum*, we may reasonably conclude that the stems of *Gymnomitrium* were his type of the species, so, as I have been unable to distinguish them from *Gymn. concinnatum*, I consider it as a synonym of that species.

Further, Mr. Rodway writes under *Gymn. concinnatum* (Lightf.), Corda (Trans. Roy. Soc. Tasm., p 74, 1916):—"In "exposed situations on mountains the leaves more closely "appressed and entire; marginal cells elongated and irregular, "forming an erose colourless border.—*Cesia erosa*, C. et P." With this opinion I cannot agree.

The late Dr. Carrington, who was one of the most careful students of the Hepaticæ, and who spent endless time in their study, and before publishing anything as new would for weeks and months let his mind play freely round any species he was studying, had an undoubted opinion that *C. erosa* was a good and new species. I candidly admit that the specific name is misleading. One would naturally infer by the term "erosa" that the leaves were weathered, hence its name; on the contrary, although the leaf margins are irregular, they are bordered by a row of acute elongated cells, somewhat similar to those on the margin of the leaves of *Gymn. crenulatum* (G.). It certainly has no similarity to *Gymn. concinnatum* (Lightf.), to which Mr. Rodway refers it; this species is diœcious, whereas *Gym. erosa* is monœcious.

Stephani (Sp. Hep., vol. II., p. 3, 1906), under the generic name of *Acolea*, places *G. erosa*, C. et P., as a synonym of *Acolea stygia* (H. & T.) St.   The above notes will show how mistaken he is.

He also refers *Gymn. vermiculare*, Schiffner (Ex. Gazelle, IV., p. 2), to *Acolea stygia*. Generally Schiffner's figures are very illustrative, but in this case it is difficult to make out what the species is; however, Schiffner is well able to defend the specific value of his species.


EXPLANATION OF PLATE XXIII.

Fig. 1.   Copy of Hooker's figures from *Flora Antarctica*, Pl. LVII., fig. IV.

Fig. 2.   *Gymnomitrium stygia* (H. et T.), Pears; x 50.

Fig. 3.   *Jungermannia*, growing with *G. stygia*; x 50 (Campbell's Island, Hooker, original, ex herb. Manchester Museum.)

# DESCRIPTION OF TWO TASMANIAN ABORIGINAL CRANIA.

By W. Lodewyck Crowther, D.S.O., M.B.

and

Clive Lord (Curator of the Tasmanian Museum).

Plates XXIV. and XXV.

(Read 10th October, 1921.)

In a previous paper (P. and P. Roy. Soc. Tas., 1920) we compiled a complete list of the osteological specimens, relating to the Tasmanian Aborigines, contained in the Tasmanian Museum.*

Two of the specimens mentioned in the published list present features worthy of comment, and in the present instance we desire to place on record a short description of the specimens catalogued as No. A. 298 and No. A. (E.H.) 558.

Both are crania which have been added to the Museum collection in recent years. The former was discovered at Tasman Island, and presented to the Museum by the Marine Board of Hobart. It was found in a penguin (*Eudyptula*) rookery, and was not in association with any other bones, careful search in this direction yielding nothing. Apart from the anatomical details of the skull, the locality of its discovery is of interest.

Tasman Island is in reality an enormous outcrop of rock lying off the South-East corner of Tasmania. Its cliffs, in most cases, rise for hundreds of feet sheer from the sea. The coast of the mainland, for several miles in both directions from the island, presents a massive bastion of diabase—an inhospitable coast upon which the surges of the Southern Ocean beat with relentless force. Between the island and the mainland the narrow channel is usually seething with the force of the tide rip.

In view of the foregoing, one cannot but wonder how the Tasmanian woman, whose skull is now included in our national ethnological collection, was able to reach the island

---

*Since that list was published the Tasmanian Museum has obtained five additional crania, three by purchase and two by exchange.

at all. Did she set out in one of the rough bark rafts of the natives to satisfy her curiosity as regards the island, or was she blown off shore by accident, and managed to swim to the island and climb its cliffs? Such questions naturally arise, but to a large extent they must remain unanswered. All we know is that the islands off the coasts were certainly visited by the natives, and that Tasman Island, despite the difficulties to be overcome, was no exception to the rule. This is proved by the fact that numbers of aboriginal stone implements are to be found on the island.

As regards the second cranium (No. A. (E.H.) 558), we are again at a loss to account for the fate of the Tasmanian male and the party to which he belonged. The cranium formed part of the Eaglehawk Neck discovery, the facts in connection with which have already been placed on record in the Papers and Proceedings of the Royal Society of Tasmania for 1918 (p. 118).*

In both cases the crania were very friable and worn by sand and exposure. Some slight restoration had, of necessity, to be made in order to provide for the adequate preservation of the specimens. Such restorations were carried out as carefully as possible, and done in such a manner as to interfere as little as possible with the correct anatomical details of the specimens.

## TASMAN ISLAND SKULL.

### (Tasmanian Museum, No. A. 298.)

The skull is that of an adult woman, and comprises the greater part of the cranium and face, as well as the mandible, the latter being in two portions.

The remains lying for many years on the left side, and being gradually uncovered, the wind and weather have disintegrated and removed the greater part of the right side of the cranium.

This has also happened to the face; the right malar and part of the external surface of the maxilla being wanting. The right parietal, almost in its entirety, and part of the left are also absent. Of the frontal, the outer table and greater part of the right half of this bone have disappeared, as also have the greater part of the occipital and right

---

*Since the first discovery further detailed examination of the site has been made by Mr. W. H. Clemes, with the result that a chipped stone implement has been found.

temporal. The *Pars glabellaris* is of interest. Here the outer table has weathered away, and no air cells or sinus are to be made out. In this respect, the specimen differs very materially from the more strongly developed cranium from Eaglehawk Neck (A. (E.H.) 558), also described in this paper. Sexual characteristics of the crania would explain this at least in part.

In spite of the absence of the cells, which might very reasonably be assumed to have a considerable part in the formation of the prominent glabella, this latter feature is as typically marked as in the average Tasmanian skull.

The mandible, recovered at the same time, wants portion of the right ramus, and has been broken into two fragments. This has since been restored.

The great interest of this skull, apart from the locality of its discovery, lies in the palate, together with the superior and inferior dental arches. The teeth are perfect, all 32 being in position. The general conformation of the palate and arches, with the tendency to elongation, and the parallel nature of the alveolar borders are points of much interest. (Plate XXIV.)

It has already been noted that the extinct Tasmanian race approaches more closely to the anthropoid apes than other races do, in the arrangement of the molar teeth and their tendency to be set in approximately parallel rows on each side of the palate. Such characteristics are well shown in the specimen at present under review.

The following measurements are given:—

Palato-maxillary, length[*] .. .. .. .. .. .. 64 mm.

Measurements between outer borders of 3rd molars .. .. .. .. .. .. .. .. .. 61 mm.

Measurements between outer borders of 1st molars .. .. .. .. .. .. .. .. .. 57 mm.

Combined length of molars and premolars (R.) .. .. .. .. .. .. .. .. 48.5 mm.

Combined length of molars and premolars (L.) .. .. .. .. .. .. .. .. 47.5 mm.

The whole palate has an excavated appearance, the horizontal processes being deeply set.

Depth at 3rd molars .. .. .. .. .. .. .. .. 12 mm.

---

[*]Margin of error in this measurement owing to the disintegration of the process of superior maxilla, posterior to 3rd right molar.

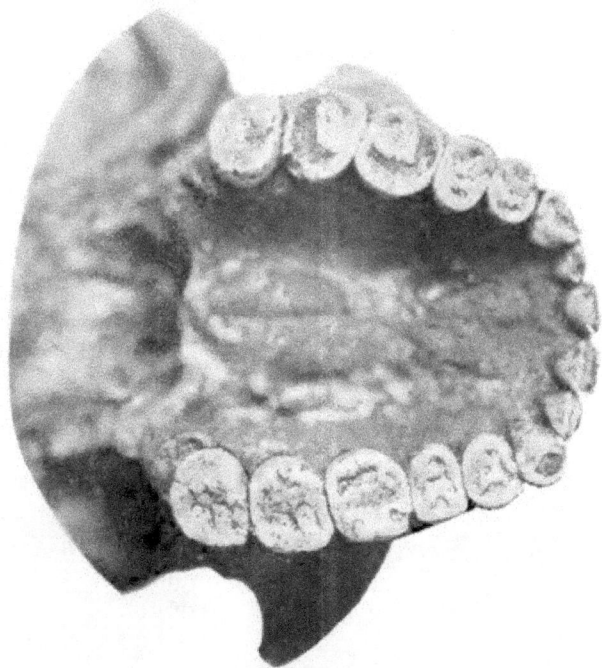

Palate of Skull of Tasmanian Aboriginal from Tasman Island
(Tas. Museum A. 298.)

Interval between internal margins of
   3rd molars .. .. .. .. .. .. .. .. 35.5 mm.
Interval between internal margins of
   1st premolars .. .. .. .. .. .. .. 28 mm.
Maximum length of skull .. .. .. .. .. 178 mm. (Approx.)
Maximum height of skull .. .. .. .. .. 128 mm. (Approx.)
Maximum breadth of skull (Impossible to measure with
   accuracy, owing to disintegration.)

## EAGLEHAWK NECK SKULL.

### (Tasmanian Museum, No. A. (E.H.) 558.)

This cranium consists of the greater part of the Frontal,
right and left Parietal, and Occipital bones. Two small
portions of the temporal articulations have been recovered
and replaced in their correct positions. The calvarium itself
is in very fair preservation. In several places the outer
table is wanting.

Inferior to the right temporal ridge; immediately above
the glabella; and in the sagittal suture 55 mm. posterior to
the bregma, are cavities throughout the whole thickness
of the bone. The loss of bone above the glabella enables
the conformation of the frontal sinus to be made out, and
shows this to consist of three large and several smaller air
cells, the largest of these being over 20 mm. in length by
14 mm. in breadth. This central space is connected directly
with the large cell of the right side, but not apparently with
that of the left. The disintegration of the orbital and nasal
portions of the bone allows only parts of six air spaces to
be identified.

It appears that in this cranium the great development
of the glabella is associated with and is proportional to the
marked development of the air cells of the frontal sinus.

The frontal eminences are not marked, and no remains
of the frontal suture are to be made out, nor any flattening
immediately behind the glabella. The superciliary ridges,
like the glabella, are well marked. The supra-orbital notches
are represented by two shallow grooves 5 and 7 millimetres
broad, on the right and left sides respectively.

Passing backward in the median line, and 45 mm. anterior to the lambda, is a large parietal foramen, 1 mm.
to the right side of the sagittal suture. The thickness of
the vault is 4 mm. The cerebral fossæ are deep and circular
rather than ovoid in shape.

The feature of greatest interest in the skull is its
remarkable resemblance, in point of general configuration

and actual measurements, to that of *Homo primogenesis*, as represented by the Neandertal skull. As instancing this, the following measurements are given:—

|  | Homo primogenesis (Neandertal) (From Munro's Prehistoric Britain) | Homo tasmanensis. (Tas. Mus. No. A. (E.H.) 558) |
| --- | --- | --- |
| Ant.-Posterior (Max. Dia.) .. | 200 mm. | 205 mm. |
| Transverse (Max. Dia.) .. .. | 144 mm. | 148 mm. |
| Frontal (Minimum) .. .. .. | 106 mm. | 115 mm. |
| Frontal (Maximum) .. .. .. | 122 mm. | *117.5 mm. |
| Cephalic Index .. .. .. .. .. | 72 mm. | 72.19 mm. |

The points that the Tasmanian skull emphasised more thoroughly than any recent race were the prominent glabella, superciliary ridges, and narrowing (post-orbital) of the frontal bone. It will be seen how these compare with the Neandertal skull, the actual measurements of the two skulls being very similar. The Tasmanian skull does not, of course, present the marked flattening of the cranial vault which is so characteristic of *Homo primogenesis*. The *Pars glabellaris*, whilst very prominent and pronounced, has not the rugged projection of the Neandertal skull; in consequence, the narrowing of the frontal bone is not thrown into such strong relief as in the latter.

Not having the actual measurements of the Neandertal calvarium we are not able to compare the superior portions of the occipital of A (E.H.) 558 with it. Attention has, however, been drawn to the depth and shape of the cerebral fossæ.

## EXPLANATION OF PLATES.

### PLATE XXIV.

Palate of Tasmah Island skull (Tas. Mus. A. 298).

### PLATE XXV.

Fig. 1.  Reduced outline (*Norma lateralis*) of Tasmanian Aboriginal skull (Tas. Mus. A (E.H.) 558).

Fig. 2.  Reduced outline of Neandertal skull, from cast in the Tasmanian Museum.

(Note:—In the absence of a dioptograph these outlines were obtained from actual photographs of the Specimens.)

---

*Between existing processes.

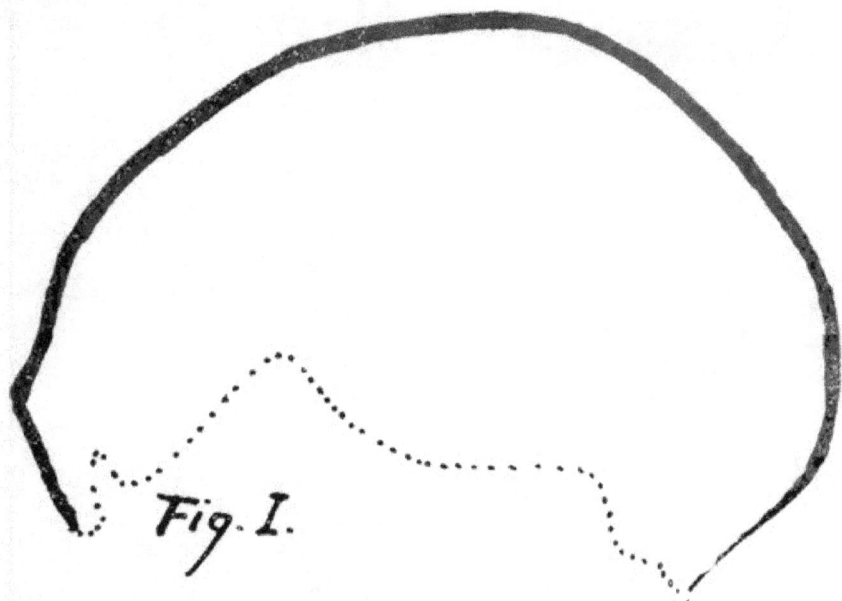

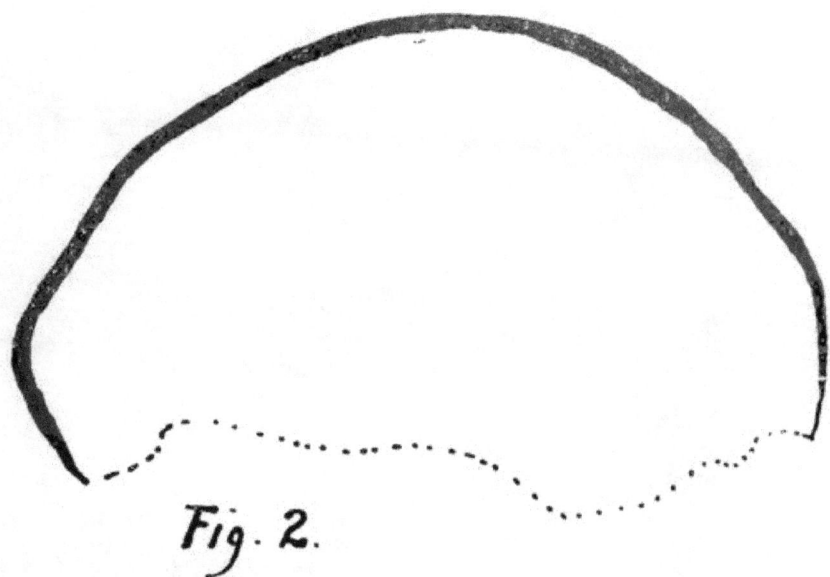

Fig. 1. Outline of Tasmanian Aboriginal Skull (Tas. Museum A. (E.H.) 555.)

Fig. 2 Outline of Neandertal Skull.

# BRYOPHYTE NOTES.

## By W. A. WEYMOUTH and L. RODWAY, C.M.G.

### (Read 10th October, 1921.)

In the description of the Mosses of Tasmania recorded in Papers and Proceedings for 1913, a specimen of *Ephemerum cristatum*, H.f.W., not being available, Mitten's description was used. This is vague and insufficient to assist the junior student. The plant is minute, barely one millimetre in height, the capsule is globose as in *Acaulon*, but the leaves are very distinct. These are of thin texture, ovate-acuminate, the margin and midrib armed with relatively long simple or compound spinous processes. The cells are rectangular, but very irregular in size and shape. This description is from a specimen gathered at Bellerive by A. J. Taylor in 1886.

Mitten described a plant and named it *Trematodon flexipes*. It was gathered at Cuming's Head, Western Mountains. For some reason Dr. Brotherus, in Pflanzenfamilien, refers it to *Campylopodium* as *Campylopodium flexipes* (*Mitt.*) *Broth.*, though it has the typical arcuate capsule with a long apophysis of *Trematodon*.. The plant described under Brotherus' name in the description of Tasmanian Mosses above referred to, is *Campylopodium euphorocladium* (*C.M.*), *Besch.* The true *Trematodon flexipes*, *Mitt.*, does not appear there at all. Mitten's plant is:—Small, subulate, entire leaves, with a broad nerve occupying the upper three-fourths of the leaf, margin entire. Seta about 5 mm., flexuose; capsule inclined, oblong, 1 mm., with a long slender apophysis; lid with an inclined slender beak slightly longer; calyptra dimidiate, inflated. Peristome with deeply cleft teeth.

The following are new to Tasmania, and determined by H. W. Dixon:—

*Trematodon mackayi* (*R. Br. Ter.*), *Dixon.* Stem 2-3 mm. Leaves with a broad sheathing base and a long subulate lamina 4 mm. Seta straight, 10 mm. Capsule narrow oblong, inclined to arcuate, 2 mm., tapering into a slender apophysis 3 mm., lid with a slender rostrum 1 mm. Peristome, none.

West Coast. T. B. Moore. Also New Zealand.

*Pottia heimii* (*Hedw.*), *Feurn.* Small, erect, 6-10 mm. Leaves narrow-ovate, acuminate, acute, 2 mm., with a few serrations towards the apex; nerve slender, continuous, or vanishing below the apex. Seta slender, erect, 12 mm.; capsule erect, oblong, 1 mm., peristone none, mouth broad; lid with a slender rostrum.

Locality unrecorded. W.A.W.

Differing from *P. subphyscomitrioides*, chiefly in the serrate margin and non-excurrent nerve. Range, cosmopolitan.

*Pottia melbourniana, Dixon.* Small, seldom exceeding 2 mm. Leaves oblong-spathulate obtuse, but apiculate, margin entire but closely revolute below, nerve bold, dissolved in the apiculate apex. Seta erect, 3-4 mm.; capsule broadly oblong, with a wide mouth barely 1 mm., lid with an oblique rostrum.

Glenorchy. W.A.W. Also Victoria.

*Ditrichum punctulatum, Mitt.* Slender, in dense cushions, about 2 cm. long. Leaves narrow linear-subulate from a long, narrow, sheathing base, 5 mm., acutely serrate towards the apex, nerve broad, cells oblong, shining and twisting when dry. Seta 1.5 cm.. capsule erect, narrow cylindric, 2 mm., mouth constricted. Peristome teeth short, slender, unequal. "In *D. elongatum* the leaves are dull and "little twisted, otherwise they scarcely differ at all. But the "fruit is different" (Dixon).

Navarre Plains, near Mt. King William.　　Also Mt. Field.

*Dicranum trichopodum, Mitt.* Yellow-green tufts on bark. Leaves slender, little secund, 6 mm., nerve broad, flat, excurrent, and occupying the upper half of the leaf, wings narrow, cells oblong above, longer towards the base, strongly incrassate, more or less serrate towards the apex, a broad auricle of numerous brown quadrate cells. Seta slender, capsule erect, narrow, lid with a very long rostrum.

Cradle Mountain. Also New Zealand.

*Mnium rostratum, Schrad.* In loose, dark green trailing tufts with short erect fertile stems. Leaves shortly decurrent, broadly obovate, those of the coma spathulate (Braithwaite). Margin limbate generally serrate above, nerve continuous into a short apiculus or lost just below the apex. Seta long, slender, capsule pendulous, elliptic, 2.5 mm., lid shortly rostrate, exostome and endostome typical.

Gould's Country. W.A.W. Also England.

*Macromitrium rodwayi, Dixon.* Dark purple-brown, in dense masses on wet diabase rock on sea coast, apex yellow-green. Stems 1-2 cm., densely covered with leaves· Leaves linear-lanceolate, acute, 2 mm., nerve solid usually excurrent in a short smooth point, margin entire.   *

On dripping rock at the entrance to Port Arthur.

Mr. Dixon notes that it is near *M. peraristatum, Brotherus,* of Lord Howe Island.   From this it differs in being a much smaller, denser plant.   "But the leaves differ "in one or two ways, which I think are of importance.   In "your plant the narrow basal cells occupy only a small por-"tion of the leaf; while in *M. peraristatum* they are extremely "narrow and sinuous, and occupy more than half the leaf, "sometimes considerably more.   In addition to this, the leaves "in *M. rodwayi* taper gradually to a very acute apex, and "the nerve becomes indistinct near apex, and does not appear "to be excurrent, whereas in *M. peraristatum* the apex is "rapidly narrowed and scarcely acuminate, while the nerve "runs out very distinctly into a longish cuspidate point." H. N. Dixon.

*Leucobryum brachyphyllum, Hampe.*   This moss has the habit, structure, and fruit of the common *Leucobryum candidum,* but very different foliage.   With the latter the leaves are narrow lanceolate, tapering to an acute apex, and about 4 mm. long, but with *L. brachyphyllum* the leaves are lanceolate to oblong, with a short, serrate apex or apiculus, and mostly but 2 mm. long.

Weldborough.   W.A.W.

# ON *POLYPORUS PULCHERRIMUS.*

## By L. RODWAY, C.M.G.

### (Read 10th October, 1921.)

*Polyporus pulcherrimus, n.s.* Dimidiate sessile, simple bracket or irregularly proliferate, generally about 10 cm. diameter, bright crimson throughout, fleshy, very watery, the dorsal surface roughly verrucose-strigose with no distinct dermis. Pores very irregular mostly about one millimetre diameter, dissepiments very thin and irregular at the mouth. Spores hyaline, very broadly oblong, 6 x 5 μ diameter.

Commonly on the trunk of our Evergreen Beech, rarely on a Eucalypt. It is a wound parasite, but spreads to the living wood. Mr. C. G. Lloyd, to whom I submitted this fungus, points out the close relationship to *Polyporus confluens*, from which it differs in the absence of a differentiated dermis, crimson colour, growing on trees, more watery consistency, and rather larger oblong spores.

# A SUPPLEMENTARY NOTE TO

# A PRELIMINARY SKETCH OF THE GLACIAL REMAINS PRESERVED IN THE NATIONAL PARK OF TASMANIA.

By A. N. Lewis, *M.C.*

(Read 14th November, 1921.)

In a paper read by me before the Royal Society of Tasmania on 11th July, 1921, on the above subject, I stated: "As far as can be ascertained, the glacial remains on the "Mt. Field ranges have never been described. They do not "appear to have been observed, or at least their existence "recorded, before the proclamation of the area as a National Park. There is, therefore, no previous literature on the subject to which to refer."

Since publishing these statements my attention has been drawn to a paper, entitled "Climatic Cycles," published by Dr. (now Professor) Griffith Taylor, of the University of Sydney, in the American Geographical Review of December, 1919, in which, at pp. 292-3, he mentions the existence of glacial remains, cirques, moraines, etc., in the National Park, and also to the fact that an outline of the subject was compiled by the same author in January, 1919, for inclusion in a Tourist Department guide book, which, however, has not yet been published.

I regret that my ignorance of the existence of these articles caused the omission of any reference to Professor Taylor's researches in the Mt. Field district, and should, therefore, like the paragraph quoted above to be amended to read as follows:—

"The only previous literature on the subject of glaciation "in the National Park is a mention of the existence of traces "of glaciation in a paper, entitled 'Climatic Cycles,' published "in the American Geographical Review of December, 1919, "by Dr. Griffith Taylor, D.Sc., and a hitherto unpublished "account of the glacial features by the same author to be "incorporated in a handbook of the Park, the publication of "which is contemplated by the Government Tourist Depart-

"ment. We are also indebted to Dr. Taylor for a map and a "relief model of the area."

The general lack of knowledge on the subject of past glacial action in Tasmania, and the necessity of a general survey of our present information on the subject both recorded and unrecorded, is illustrated by a statement published by no less an authority than Professor Walter Howchin, F.G.S., of the University of Adelaide, in the Official Year Book of the Commonwealth of Australia, No. 13 of 1920, at page 1,135, of which the learned author says: "(c) "Glaciers of Tasmania—No expedition for the specific object "of investigating the Pleistocene Glacial remains has been "undertaken, but incidental observations bearing on the "subject have been made by several travellers who were "visiting the country in pursuit of other objects . . . . "etc."

The actual state of affairs is that this subject has been largely written upon by all our Government geologists and most of our outstanding geological observers. In the Papers and Proceedings of the Royal Society of Tasmania for 1916, Dr. W. N. Benson, at the end of his paper on the geological features of the Cradle Mountain district, at page 40, published a "Bibliography of Pleistocene Glaciation in Tasmania," containing 45 references. Of these, twelve (viz., references Nos. 8, 9, 10, 11, 12, 17, 25, 33, 35, 43, 44, and 45) are detailed and extended accounts of the glacial phenomena within the area described, the remainder being references to the occurrence of such phenomena. Also, it is far from the truth to suggest that these observations were made by "travellers who were visiting the country in pursuit of other "objects." Only nine of the references (viz. Nos. 4, 7, 14, 15, 24, 25, 28, 29, and 41) were written by gentlemen who were not domiciled Tasmanians. In the recently published R. M. Johnston Memorial volume one paper by the late Mr. Johnston on the Pleistocene Glacial Epoch extends over 80 pages.

For the sake of completeness, and for the benefit of anyone studying this subject, I should like to add the following references to Professor Benson's bibliography:—

10. 1893. R. M. Johnston. "The Glacial Epoch of Australasia," Proc. Roy. Soc. Tas., 1893, republished R. M. Johnston Memorial volume, 1921, pp. 16-96.

19a. 1894. E. J. Dunn. Proc. Roy. Soc. Vict. (new series), Vol. VI. (1894), pp. 133-138.

46. 1916. W. N. Benson. "Notes on the Geology of the Cradle Mountain District," Pap. and Proc. Roy. Soc. Tas, 1916, pp. 34-40.

47. 1918. Hartwell Conder. "The Tin Field of North Dundas," Geol. Surv. Tas. Bull. No. 26, pp. 8, 9, and 26.

48. 1918. A. McIntosh Reid. "The North Pieman, Huskisson, and Stirling Valley Mining Fields," Geol. Surv. Tas. Bull. No. 28, pp. 15-18.

49. 1919. A. McIntosh Reid. "The Mining Fields of Moina, Mt. Claude, and Lorinna," Geol. Surv. Tas. Bull. No. 29, pp. 10, 21, and 43.

50. 1919. A. McIntosh Reid. "The Mt. Pelion Mineral District," Geol. Surv. Tas. Bull. No. 30, pp. 14-17.

51. 1919. Griffith Taylor. "Climatic Cycles." American Geographical Review, Dec., 1919, pp. 292-3.

52. 1920. A. McIntosh Reid. "Osmiridium in Tasmania," Geol. Surv. Tas. Bull. No. 32, pp. 69, 83, and plans.

53. 1920. W. Howchin. "Past Glacial Action in Australia," Official Year Book of Comm. of Aust., No. 13, p. 1,133.

M

# STUDIES IN TASMANIAN MAMMALS, LIVING AND EXTINCT.

## No. VI.

## CETACEAN REMAINS FROM THE FOSSIL BEDS AT WYNYARD.

By

H. H. Scott, Curator, Launceston Museum,

And

Clive Lord, Curator, Tasmanian Museum.

(Read 5th December, 1921.)

We desire to place on record a few notes relating to the discovery of certain Cetacean remains from the assumed Miocene beds at the Wynyard Cliffs, North-West Tasmania.

Our latest additions consist of parts of the embedded centra and processes of some twenty vertebræ, which in superficial osteology agree fairly closely with those of the modern *Globicephalus* whales, and depart, as equally, from such *Squalodont* remains as we have handled from this locality.

Early in the year 1914 Messrs. E. D. and R. N. Atkinson presented to the Launceston Museum a small slab of rock, much infiltrated with silicon, containing a fossil that was determined as the supra-orbital portion of a Delphinoid skull that had been stripped of its overlying maxillary wing, prior to its inclusion in the matrix. The donors, upon extended research, were able to unearth, at some distance from the first discovery, a piece of fossil bone that presented every appearance of being the missing maxillary wing, it having evidently been swept hither and thither upon the old Miocene beach until it eventually found a resting place.

These remains were plotted out in terms of modern Cetaceans and were found to agree in several points with the Round Headed Dolphin, and in this connection the agreements noted were as follows:—

(1) The frontal bone was excavated for the reception of the coronoid process of the mandible. This character is retained in *Globicephalus* but not in *Delphinus* or *Tursiops* to any extent.

(2) The single vertebra and scrap of the mandible found with this skull also agree with *Globicephalus* as far as they were available for comparison, but their fragmentary nature made a close study quite impossible.

(3) Upon the assumption that the rest of the skull indicated parts of the frontal bone curving upwards to form the fronto-occipital ridge and a moiety of the posterior upper wall of the temporal fossa, with a forward extension to the maxillary region, the whole of the find was accounted for.

The recent acquisition by the Tasmanian Museum of some twenty vertebral remains, previously mentioned, seems to confirm the idea of these being related to a whale of *Globicephalus* class, and we provisionally record them as such.

At a future date we hope to give extended details, together with illustrations of the two discoveries. This paper must therefore be regarded as a preliminary recording note only. It is most unfortunate that both of the Atkinsons, father and son, have passed away without leaving any exact data as to the spots from which the fossils were obtained. The recently instituted Government protection of these fossil cliffs should prevent such situations arising in the future.

# THE CONCAVE STONE IMPLEMENTS OF THF TASMANIAN ABORIGINES.

By George Horne, V.D., M.A., M.D., CH.B.

Plates XXVI-XXVIII.

(Read 5th December, 1921.)

The following paper seeks to deal with these implements as they are found in Tasmania, and to institute a comparison with those found in S.E. Victoria.

This is the last part of Australia to be united to Tasmania, and here, if anywhere, resemblances should be found.

When we take into consideration the daily life of the aboriginal, a considerable part must have been spent in the making, smoothing, sharpening, and maintaining of his wooden weapons.

These were two in number—the spear and the throwing stick. All the secondary or finishing work on them was done with the concave stone implements.

## DIFFERENT GROOVES FOR DIFFERENT PURPOSES.

Two sorts of grooves would, of course, be necessary, and two sorts are found for preparing these two weapons. There is the short semi-circular groove (Fig. 1a.), usually small in diameter. This was evidently for the smaller circumference of the spear or for the sharpening of points of either implement. Then there was the long hyperbolic curve (Fig. 2b.), which is, as a rule, larger and stouter. It appears to have been used in the earlier work on implements. (In my collection, this variety is the commoner form of the two in Tasmania.)

## VARIETIES OF GROOVES.

1. *The Worked Groove* (Fig. 2a.).—The chipped markings along the edge show plainly that the groove has been worked; and this is the commonest form of Tasmanian concave implements.

In S.E. Victoria one finds the working developed further into crenulations. These must have acted like so many teeth, and would have been most effective in the first cutting action when getting the wooden implements into shape. I have not seen this form amongst Tasmanian specimens.

2. *The Smooth Groove* (Fig. 3).—This is relatively rare

Fig 1A.

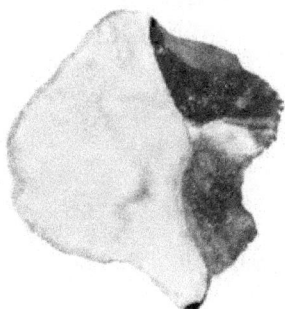

Fig. 1B

Fig. 2A.

Fig. 4.

Fig. 2B.

Fig. 5A.

Fig. 3.

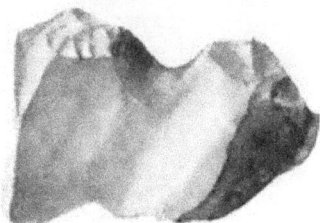

Fig. 5B.

in Tasmania, but is very common in S.E. Victoria. It is made by the pressure of a rounded wooden weapon on the thin edge of the stone.

This concave implement is often also concave in transverse section, and is like the covers of a closed book which stand out beyond the leaves. Gradually friction reduces these sharp edges (which are quite thin, and in this also resemble the covers of a book). Generally, however, a shadow can be seen running longitudinally along the face of the groove, which shows that at first there is a part untouched by friction.

The absence of any chipping or irregularity would impart smoothness to the weapon being worked. The sharp, thin outside edges are the best possible thing for scraping action.

3. *The Channel Groove* (Fig. 4) is the third variety, and consists of a concave gutter sometimes 24 mm. long (13 mm. is the longest noted amongst Tasmanians). This gutter frequently dips down at its outside edge, *i.e.*, it is bevelled at the gutter's end. This bevelling would be made by rubbing the implement on the spear with long sweeps, when its edge would turn over to a slight extent.

A variant of the channel groove is found in the *underneath groove* (Fig. 5). In this the groove, instead of being made on the narrow surface of the stone, is upon its under surface.

The Tasmanian concaves differ from the Victorian chiefly in the coarseness, strength, and power of the former and the delicacy and fineness common in the latter.

The Victorian as a rule (though not always) made his concave scraper out of a flake that was chipped first, and had, therefore, always a suitable edge for making this groove upon.

### METHODS OF USE.

Amongst the Australians a common method is the (1) *two-handed* or spokeshave method as in the illustration of the Aluritja man (Fig. 8).

For this photograph I have to thank Dr. Basedow, from his *Australian Tribes*. This method was sometimes used by the Tasmanians as is seen in Fig. 2b., which shows two thumb-marks for gripping the spokeshave. The Victorian often made a long flake first, and chipped marks on it subsequently for steadying fingers or thumbs. They would then break in the concave grooves which completed the spokeshave.

Sometimes the position of the groove tells that it was for (2) *one-handed* use. The concave is in this case at the end of a stone which may be quite long, or it may be near the end at one side, or it is on such a round thick stone as appears improbable for a spokeshave.

The channel grooves appear to have been used by the (3) *overhand* grip, as in the illustration of the Wonkanguru man (Fig. 9), for which I have to thank Mr. Aiston. The man is here using a flat smoother on a boomerang, but the method of employment is the same.

### OTHER IMPLEMENTS USED.

The Tasmanians frequently made, upon a straight edge, a curved excrescence or a sharp point. The protuberance was chipped all round, or, if a point, on both sides. With its use this article does not deal. The angle, where this curve or point joined the straight edge, was often used to form a concave scraper.

If both sides of the curve or point were so used, a (1) *"duck-bill"* (Ling Roth) was made (Fig. 6).

The illustration shows a chalcedony specimen from Lisdillon, near Little Swanport, where one angle of the chipped curve has been so employed.

Just as other implements were often used as concave scrapers in Australia, the Tasmanian would also pick up the first stone to hand if he sought to plane down his throwing stick, or to put a point on his spear. For him the (2) *scraper* with its thinner edge and especially with its chipped margin would be particularly suitable; therefore, it is this implement that was most frequently used.

The comparatively (3) *thin knives* of the Tasmanians are made quite readily into concave scrapers, and, although this is not seen as often as it is North of Bass Straits, yet relatively they are quite as frequent. The Victorians frequently used the little "chipped-back knives" (Etheridge) as sharpening implements, and even the minute, round, chipped scrapers (6 mm. in diameter) are sometimes grooved for that purpose.

*The disc-shaped scraper* (4), which has one flat side (Fig. 1a and b), and the other side either flattened or in a ridge, or conical, is in 16 per cent. of my cases made into a concave scraper. Mr. Clive Lord draws my attention to the fact that dents in its edge are frequently worked in concave implements. It is singular that a similar employment by the Victorians is not noted. Out of 60 (not selected) specimens, not one had been so employed.

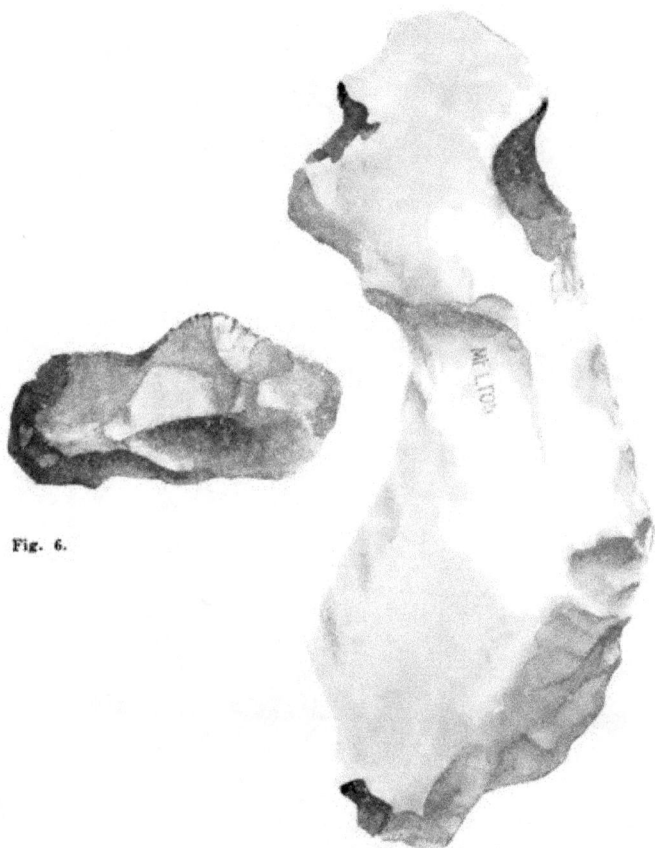

Fig. 6.

Fig. 7.

Fig. 6. Chalcedony specimen from Lisdillon.

Fig. 7. Specimen from Melton Mowbray.

## PART OF THE STONE USED.

The chipped stones that are used as implements have, more or less, a definite shape. They have the one side more or less flat, and the other side raised, tending to form a pent house, ridge, keel, or cone. Mr. Scott, whose brother lived long amongst Tasmanian aboriginals, was the first (P. & P. R.S. Tas., 1873) to point out that the flat side was always used with the thumb upon it. The keeled or conical side supported the fingers. On the edge of this finger side was the chipping. The concave groove, especially when it was worked, was never straight across the stone. It was always on the same side as the chipping and sloped up from the margin on to this finger-side. This holds good for the first groove that was made in an implement, but frequently two grooves were made. This was, generally, in stones that were more or less flat on both sides. Here both sides were treated as if they could be thumb-sides, and the second groove was therefore cut on the opposite side of the stone to the first groove.

It has been asserted (Noetling, P. & P. R.S. Tas., 1909) that this was an accident, and arose from a mistake on the part of the native. However, my investigations over a small group of concave scrapers show that in 84 per cent. of cases (not including duck-bills) the grooves are on opposite sides of the stone, and only in 16 per cent. upon the same side. In cases where they are chipped, the chipping is on the opposite side, but in the concave and also on the stone around. Apparently the groove which was first made was placed opposite that side which was most plainly the thumb-side.

It is impossible to say why this particular device to work on opposite sides of the stone existed in the Tasmanian. A somewhat similar habit exists in Australians, not indeed in concave scrapers, but in those irregular chunks of stone used as scrapers.

The concave scrapers of S.E. Victoria, in picking up at random 100 double-grooved stones, I find to be in 26 per cent. on opposite sides, whilst 74 per cent. are on the same side. Why this should be it is difficult to say. One might hazard a guess that the Australian frequently used his concave scraper with two hands, that is, as a spokeshave, and he therefore from the start made a tool that would work in that way.

## NUMBER OF GROOVES.

The number of grooves that may be made in any stone of course varies; but, as one might guess from the casual habits of the native, one groove was made, it was used, and the stone then dropped. The following table was made from a random 100 concave scrapers:—

Concave scrapers with 1 groove .. ..    44 per cent.

        2 grooves .. 20 „ „

        3 or more

        grooves .. 36 „ „

As many as six grooves I have found on one stone, but such a large number is uncommon.

Amongst the Victorians large numbers of the smooth grooves are the rule, whereas almost invariably single concaves are found where a pebble is used, and worked grooves are either single or not numerous.

## MATERIAL.

Any material, just as any implement, may serve the Tasmanian in making a concave scraper; but by far the commonest in use is the blue-black metamorphic mudstone, called hornstone by some writers.

This stone has the peculiarity that its surface, in certain conditions, alters. It changes with decomposition to a light buff colour, but it still remains hard and its outlines are still sharp. It is not a real patina, but a decomposition of the rock. Some implements, that I have, are heavily thus patinated, but have other concave grooves worked in them that are blue-black and sharp (Fig. 7).

The difference between the age of the grooves covered with patina and those grooves with no patina would be interesting.

Unfortunately, the patina is acquired in varying times according to the moisture, etc.

All one can say is that some considerable time has elapsed since the first chips were made. How long we can guess at, but a guess it must remain.

## EXPLANATION OF PLATES.

### PLATE XXVI.

| Fig 1A. | Fig. 2B. | Fig. 2A. | Fig. 2B. |
| Fig. 3. | Fig. 4. | Fig. 5A. | Fig. 5B. |

Fig. 8    Aluritja man using two-handed spokeshave.    (Illustration from
          Dr. Basedow's *Australian Tribes*.)

Fig. 9.   Wonkanguru man using flat smoother.   (From photograph by
          Mr. Aiston.)

## PLATE XXVII.

Fig. 6.          Fig. 7

### Fig. 6.

Chalcedony specimen from Lisdillon, East Coast.

### Fig. 7.

Specimen from Melton Mowbray.


## PLATE XXVIII.

### Fig. 8.

Aluritja man using two-handed spokeshave.    (Illustration from Dr. Basedow's *Australian Tribes*.)

### Fig. 9.

Wonkanguru man using flat smoother.    (From photograph by Mr. Aiston.)

# SOME GEOGRAPHICAL NOTES ON A MODEL OF THE NATIONAL PARK AT MT. FIELD, TASMANIA.

By Professor Griffith Taylor, D.Sc., B.E., B.A., F.G.S., F.R.G.S.

Plates XXIX., XXX., and Five Text Figures.

(Read 5th December, 1921.)

Early in February, 1919, I had the pleasure of visiting the Tasmanian National Park with a party organised by the Hon. Secretary to the Park Board. The whole journey was filled with interest to the geographer, especially as my suspicions of a glacial topography were abundantly verified by the fine examples of cirques, moraines, erratics, and glacial lakes which I identified on the plateau.

I collected topographic data sufficient to construct a rough contour map (Plate XXIX.), using the reconnaissance survey of Mr. Propsting and others as a basis. From this on my return I constructed the model which is illustrated in Plate XXX. Owing to the pressure of other research, I was unable to complete a memoir on the glacial features, and these have since been worked out with great care and success by Mr. A. N. Lewis, M.C. [1]

There are a few aspects of the problem which do not appear in his lengthy memoir, and I feel that the geographical literature of Tasmania is so scanty that these brief notes may not be out of place.

The most striking feature of the region perhaps is the marked parallelism of the valleys. The Plateau is so dissected that in plan it is somewhat like a gridiron (see Fig. 1), with three or four main ridges all trending north-west to south-east. Almost the whole area consists of one geological formation, a medium-grained dolerite or diabase, so that we are not concerned here with dip or strike topography. Jointing is a more probable cause, and a reference to Tasmania as a whole shows that the major tectonic features have the same direction. I have elsewhere (p. 176, "Australian Environment," 1918) drawn attention to this "grain"; which is well seen in the three main lines of weakness in the island. These are the Tamar-Macquarie lineament, the Lake St. Clair-Derwent lineament and the Macquarie Harbour-Gordon lineament. (See Fig 1.)

---

[1] P. & P. Roy. Soc. Tas., 1921, pp. 16-36.

# SKETCH   MAP
## MOUNT FIELD. NATIONAL PARK. TASMANIA
### BY DR GRIFFITH TAYLOR  BE.BA.FGS.FRGS

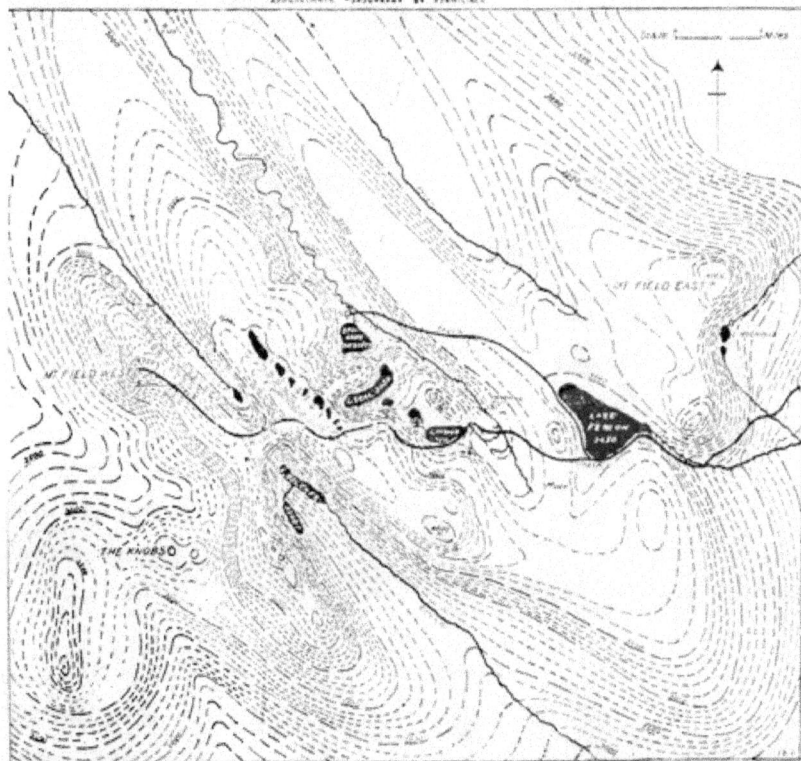

NOTE.—Lakes shown black, thick lines are main tracks.    Form-lines only approximate.

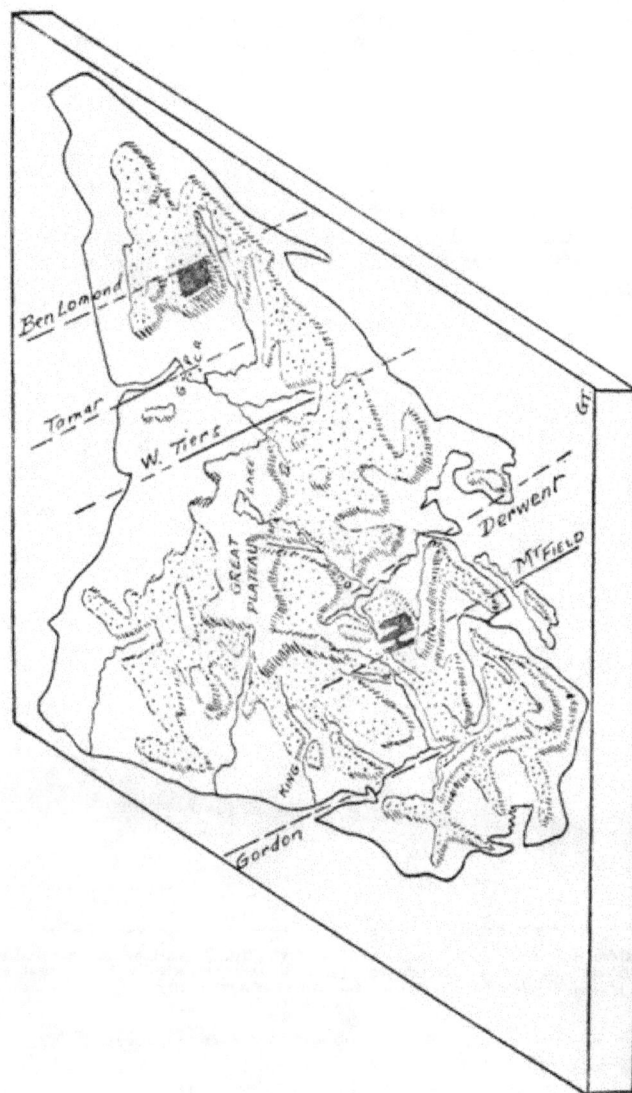

Fig. 1.—Block diagram illustrating some of the main "lineaments" of Tasmania. The Mount Field Plateau is the black "gridiron" in the south. Ben Lomond Plateau is the black rectangle in the north-east. The Gorge, Punchbowl, and Corra Lynn at Launceston are indicated. The 1,000 foot and 3,000 foot contours are shown by the dotted and a higher plain "layers."

The trellis-work drainage of the summit of Ben Lomond[2] seems to show that this diabase plateau is dissected along a similar series of fault-planes running northwest to south-east. There is here, however, also a set of cross-faults, and together they have determined the rectangular shape of the top of the plateau.

My belief is that the whole island is dominated by fault-blocks and fault-planes, some of which are no doubt later than the intrusion of these diabase sills. Hence the Mount Field Plateau offered unequal resistance to the agents of erosion, with the result stated. This theory must of course be tested further in the field.

The second problem concerns the agents which have

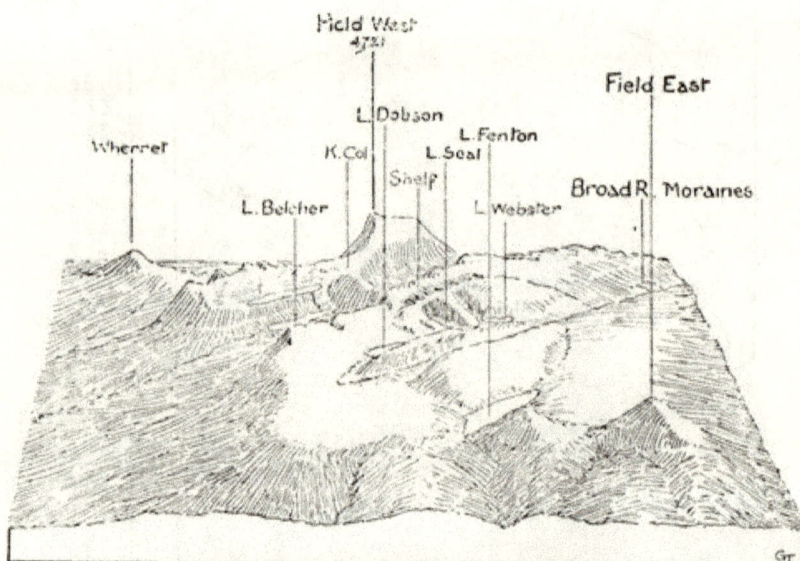

Fig. 2.—Block diagram of the Plateau looking west. The parallel arrangement of the valleys and lakes is apparent. Notice the "shelf" of tarns, the cirque of Lake Seal, and "K" Col. A glacier 5 miles long descended the Broad River Valley.

given rise to the remarkable topography (see Fig. 2). We have here offered to us the same difficulties as are met with so generally in the elevated portions of the temperate zone. The special facies of the region is due to glacial

(2) P. & P. Roy. Soc. Tas., 1913. Map by Colonel Legge.

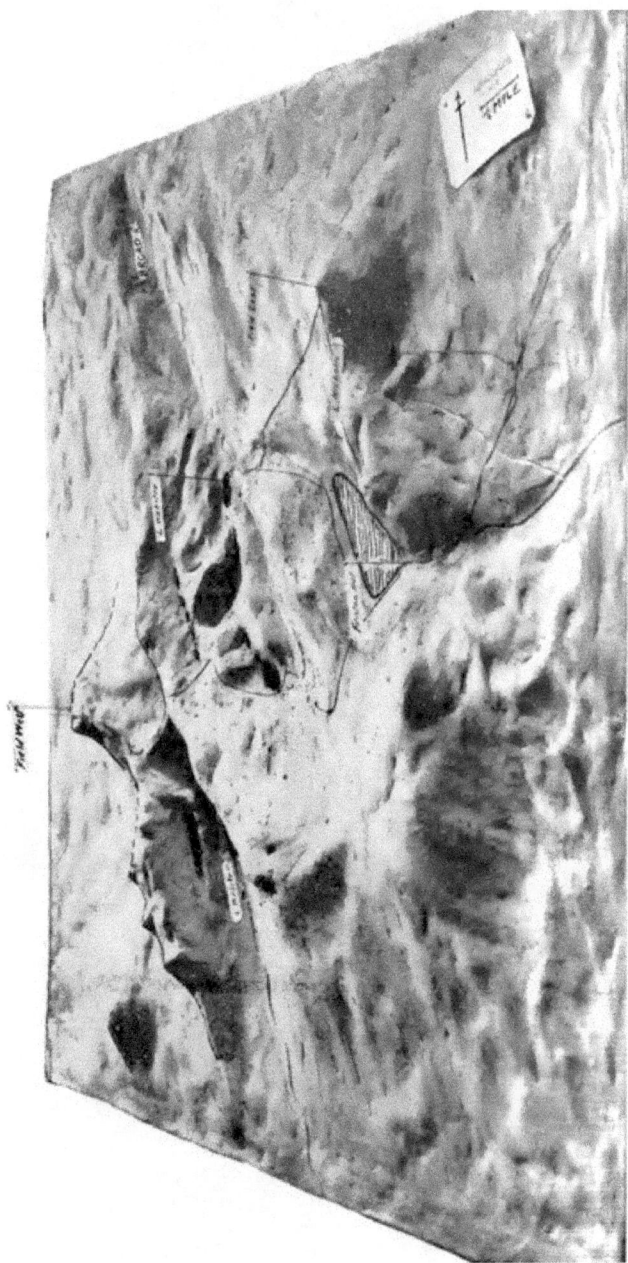

erosion; but how much erosion by ordinary streams preceded
the advent of the Ice Age? And further, was the glacial
erosion due to glacier *planation* (*i.e.*, by the rasping and
plucking due to debris cemented on the sole of the glacier)
or to the method which has been termed "*nivation*"?

Evidence as to the great amount of erosion accomplished
since the last period of uplift is obvious throughout Tasmania. The gorge of the Ouse is cut down 1,200 feet, while
the King River canyon is even more striking. A better-
known example lies in the suburbs of Launceston, and offers
a wonderful study to the Tasmanian geographer. Here the
South Esk enters the Tamar estuary through a most pic-
turesque notch giving the clearest evidence of late uplift;
though later subsidence[3] has drowned the mouth of the
gorge. Probably Corra Lynn gorge and the Punchbowl, a few
miles to the south-east, are due to the same differential
movement between the Tamar estuary and the environs of
Launceston. The positions of these most interesting examples appear on Figure 1.

We may therefore, I think, postulate a considerable
amount of erosion in the pre-glacial period, giving rise to
valleys, perhaps 500 feet deep, where now flow the Broad
River and the creeks draining north and south from K Col,
through Lake Hayes and Lake Belcher. These pre-glacial
valleys would be of a juvenile type with V cross sections,
and the thalweg would fall rapidly in the first mile of each
stream. (See Fig. 3.)

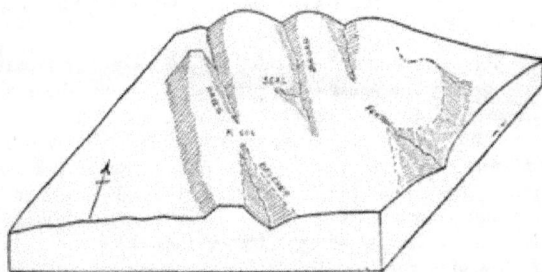

Fig. 3.—Block diagram illustrating approximately the pre-glacial
drainage of the Plateau.

It will be seen, therefore, that the striking cirque valleys
of Lake Hayes, Lake Belcher, and Lake Seal were originally

(3) Daly would explain this drowning as due to the melting of the
world's ice caps after the Ice Age.

not unlike the steep valley which leads from Fenton Hut
down the outer slope of the Plateau towards Russell Falls.
There was, therefore, a good deal of material to be removed
during the Ice Ages before these valleys developed the
characteristic cirque-heads of to-day.

In each of these three typical cases the cirque has a
maximum wall of about 1,000 feet, lying approximately between the 3,000 and 4,000 feet contours.

It is further to be noted that these cirques lie largely
on the sheltered easterly aspect of the ridges, so that they
are protected from the hot afternoon sun.

To understand the way in which the ice has eroded
these valleys we must, I think, further consider two aspects
of the problem.  Firstly, the alimentation of the glaciers;
and secondly, the life history of the latter.  We shall then,
I believe, see that nivation probably played a more important
part than planation in carving out the main cirques.  This
type of erosion also helps to explain the interesting shelf-
tarns above Lake Seal, and the unusual position of Lake
Belton "perched" above Lake Belcher.

The snow-fields nourishing the glaciers of the plateau
must have been very circumscribed.  The collecting ground
for the Hayes and Belcher glaciers was the original K Col
and the adjacent narrow ridges.  It seems to me unlikely
that the Belcher glacier resulting from this meagre snowfield
had sufficient power to gouge out a bowl-shaped hollow *right
at its head* to the depth of one thousand feet.  The same
objection applies to the Hayes glacier, and to a lesser degree
to the Seal glacier.

On the other hand, if we adopt the principle of *nivation*,
as developed by the Americans, Matthes, Johnson, and Hobbs,
the process of erosion becomes much more intelligible.  In
nivation the alternating freezing and thawing of water in
the interstices of the rocks is the prime agent of disintegration.  The glacier plays a somewhat passive part in the
erosion, but supplies much of the water for the nivation by
the melting of its periphery.  Its surface, however, acts as
a vehicle which very slowly carries away debris to the lower
end.  The thaw-water streams at the side of the glacier also
are of great importance in eating down the rock edges of
the valley.  The glacier also acts something like the scour-
wall at a river mouth which directs the removal of debris.
(See the paper on Antarctic Glaciology by the writer—
Geogr. Jnl., 1914, p. 562.)

In my brief report[4] on the glaciology which I made in February, 1919, I wrote as follows:—

"In the early days of the Ice Age a great drift of
"snow occupied a shallow valley where now is Lake Seal.
"Freezing and thawing took place continually around
"this snow-drift, and broke down the structure around
"the drift.  Small streams surrounded the drift, and not
"only supplied the ice wedges, but carried away some of
"the debris.  The sapping extended outward by slow
"degrees as the snow-drift increased, and gradually a
"flat valley was eroded, much like the embryo cirque on
"the 4,300-foot level above (and south of) Lake Seal.
"(See Fig. 5 at A.)  The deepening process would ad-
"vance into the hill at the foot of the snow-drift and
"would be especially strong during the dwindlnig of the
"ice-slab (into which the snow would soon be converted)
"as the Ice Age passed away."

It is important to realise that the oncoming and waning of the Ice Age were both gradual.  Hence the controls determining the erosion varied more or less continuously.  The major control was, of course, the temperature; and the point is not sufficiently stressed in glacial literature, that there is an optimum temperature as far as frost-action is concerned.  It is obviously near the melting point of ice, and probably from 32 deg. to 35 deg. F. (or around 34 deg. F.) is about the most favourable temperature.  One of the most striking results of my Antarctic investigations was to find that the temperature in the Antarctic is too cold for the maximum glacial erosion.  There is infinitely more of this erosion going on in New Zealand than in latitude 78 deg. South.

We must therefore imagine this layer of favourable temperature slowly settling down on to the plateau as the Ice Age is ushered in.  At present the temperature layer of 34 deg. F. lies at 6,000 feet above sea level and about 3,000 feet above Lake Seal.  Here we may assume an average annual temperature of about 44 deg. F. at the present time. (See Fig. 4.)

If now we imagine a cooling of about 10 deg. F. at the maximum of the Ice Age, this "nivation-layer," as we may term it, will descend to the level of Lake Seal, and the maximum amount of frost action will occur at this level.  Above

(4) A report prepared for the Tasmanian Government Tourist Bureau.

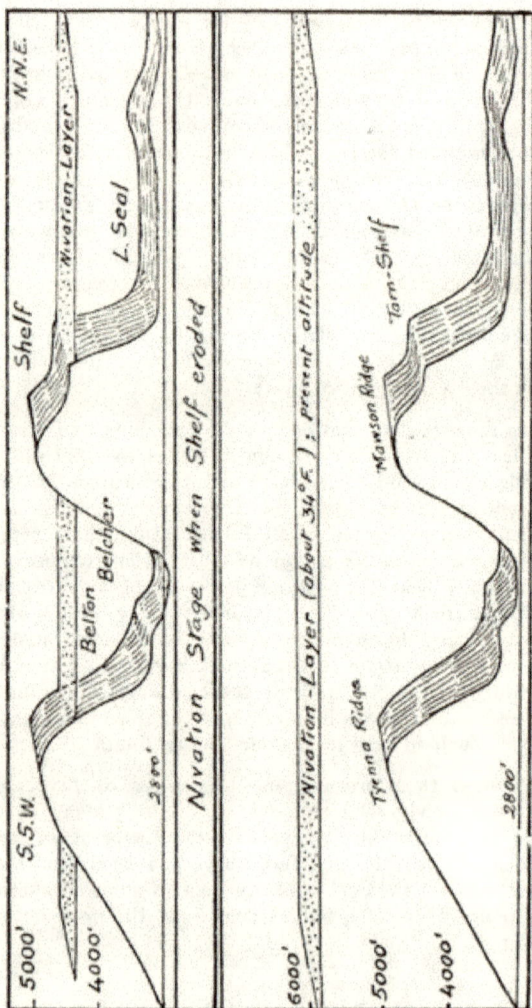

Fig. 4.—Block diagrams showing the movements of the layer of maximum sapping ("nivation-layer"). Upper figure, in Ice Age, when 4,300 feet above sea level. Lower figure, at present time. At maximum of Ice Age it descended to 2,800 feet.

this level the temperature will be somewhat too cold for the maximum effect, and below this level it will be too warm for ice to form.

We know that there were colder and warmer stages during the Pleistocene Ice Ages. This implies that the nivation-layer halted at various elevations in its descent from and ascent to its present elevation of 6,000 feet above sea level. I imagine that we have evidence of two such phases in the topography of the Plateau. At the maximum cold period the layer was at its lowest; and the low-level cirques of Lakes Seal, Hayes, and Belcher were cut out while the great Mount Field glacier moved down the river valley for some five miles as the beautiful moraine crescents [5] clearly show. At this period the edges of the Broad River Valley were "cleaned out" and the cross-section converted from a V into the catenary curve of the glacial type. All the lower moraines were laid down also at this phase. Two well-marked halts are indicated however by the grouping of the moraines, above and below the two enormous erratics in Broad Valley (which I learn from the paper by Mr. Lewis have been named after myself). This stage would be indicated in Figure 4 if we imagine the nivation-layer at the lowest level in the section.

The seven tarns named after Johnston and Newdegate lie on a shelf (see Figs. 4 and 5) whose origin can best be explained in a similar fashion, I think. They are at an elevation of 4,300 feet, or 1,200 feet above the floors of the cirques described previously. The shelf is about one mile long and varies in width from 80 yards in the south to a quarter of a mile at the somewhat lower northern end. The whole shelf is jewelled with rocky tarns lying in the hollows between rounded rock hummocks whose surface has certainly been smoothed by ice action. Their most striking feature, however, is the way in which some of the lakelets have two openings, one passing *along* the shelf to the north, and the other opening directly *over* the great thousand-feet cliff. Large erratics perch precariously on sloping platforms just as they were dumped by the ice. All this indicates that no long interval has elapsed since the topography was initiated, for the longitudinal drainage of the seven tarns must suffer capture in the near future by the streams flowing directly over the edge.

---

(5) These were, I believe, first identified on February 3rd, 1919. See my brief report in American Geographical Review, December, 1919.

N

Fig. 5.—Sketch looking north-east over the tarns on the "shelf" above Lake Seal, showing the thousand feet of drop to Lake Seal. On the right at A is an immature cirque.

There are two possible explanations of this unusual shelf with its rock-tarns. One involves the filling of the whole Broad Valley with ice, so that the lateral drainage flowed to the north along the position of this shelf and so cut a notch between the glacier and the containing ridge to the west. This is not well supported by the field evidence, though it accounts for the shelf sloping to the north.

The more plausible explanation involves the nivation-layer which I have described above. I imagine that for some long period this layer with a temperature around 34 deg. F. halted at the 4,300 feet level, possibly both in the advancing and retreating hemi-cycles of the Ice Age. (See Fig. 4 above.) The shelf was favourably situated for collecting snow, which was not readily removed by the sun from its sheltered position. A series of cirques were sapped out in the course of time, and these became apposed sideways in much the same fashion as Nussbaum has described in the Swiss Alps.[6]

A shelf is thus produced by the sapping action of seven adjacent cirques. The ice-slabs are competent to carry the erratics to the positions noted, and also to round the rocks forming the rim of the shelf. Since a cirque glacier "*burrows*" *into the hill* (as Hobbs has shewn in his "Characteristics of Existing Glaciers") rather than erodes the valley under its snout. we see why the edge of the shelf remains almost entirely unaffected by the shelf glaciers.

The evolution of Lake Belton, perched some 300 feet up the side of the Lake Belcher Valley, may be partly explained in a similar fashion, but this demands much more field work than I was able to give to this locality.

It is in the hope that these brief notes will stimulate local interest in the innumerable geographical problems of Tasmania that I have written the paper.

## LIST OF ILLUSTRATIONS.

### PLATE XXIX.

Sketch survey of the Park. The form-lines are approximately correct near the routes marked, but are only filled in from sketches, etc., elsewhere.

---

[6] Die Taler der Schweizer-Alpen; Berne, 1910.

## PLATE XXX.

Model of Mt. Field Plateau, National Park, Tasmania.
A key to the model appears in Text fig. 2. (Photo. by J. W.
Beattie.)

## TEXT FIGURES.

# ROYAL SOCIETY OF TASMANIA

## ABSTRACT OF PROCEEDINGS
### 1921

14th MARCH, 1921.

*Annual Meeting.*

The Annual Meeting was held at the Museum on 14th of March, 1921. Sir N. E. Lewis, K.C.M.G., presiding.

The Annual Report and Statement of Accounts were read and adopted.

The following were elected as Members of the Council:—Dr. A. H. Clarke, Dr. W. L. Crowther, Rt. Rev. Dr. R. S. Hay, Messrs. W. H. Clemes, W. H. Cummins, J. A. Johnson, L. Rodway, and Major L. F. Giblin.

Mr. R. A. Black was appointed Hon. Auditor.

*Paper.*

*Nototheria* and Allied Animals. By H. H. Scott and Clive Lord.

*Illustrated Lecture.*

Early Hobart. By L. Rodway, C.M.G.

*Conversazione.*

After the business of the meeting was concluded an adjournment was made to the Art Gallery, where a Conversazione was held.

11th APRIL, 1921.

The Monthly Meeting was held at the Museum on 11th April, Mr. L. Rodway, C.M.G., presiding.

Mr. J. Moore Robinson was elected a Member of the Council.

*Lecture.*

"Education in Fetters." By S. R. Dickinson, M.A.

### 9th MAY, 1921.

The Monthly Meeting was held at the Museum on 9th May, His Excellency Sir W. L. Allardyce, K.C.M.G., presiding.

Mr. Clive Lord exhibited a series of fossils, including marsupial bones, which he had recently obtained from the Mole Creek Caves.

#### Papers.

"The Native Feeding Grounds at Little Swanport, East Coast." By W. L. Crowther. D.S.O., M.B.

"The Historical Records of Tasmania." By J. Moore Robinson, F.R.G.S.

### 13th JUNE, 1921.

The Monthly Meeting was held at the Museum on 13th June, Mr. L. Redway, C.M.G., presiding.

#### Papers.

"New Species of Fossil Mollusca." By W. L. May.

"Studies in Tasmanian Mammals." *Zaglossus harrissoni*, sp. nov." By H. H. Scott and Clive Lord.

"The Fossil Remains at Mole Creek." By H. H. Scott and Clive Lord.

#### Lecture.

"The Coastal Camps of the Australian Aborigines." By George Horne, M.A., M.D.

### 11th JULY, 1921.

The Monthly Meeting was held at the Museum on 11th July, Mr. L. Rodway, C.M.G., presiding.

#### Papers.

"Description of a New Species of *Loricella*." By Edwin Ashby, F.L.S.

"The Glacial Remains in the National Park." By A. N. Lewis, M.C.

"Australian *Bombyliidæ* and *Cyrtidæ*." By G. H. Hardy.

#### Illustrated Lecture.

"Fiji." By His Excellency Sir W. L. Allardyce, K.C.M.G.

## 8th AUGUST, 1921.

The Monthly Meeting was held at the Museum on 8th August, Mr. L. Rodway, C.M.G., presiding.

### Papers.

"The completion of the General Magnetic Survey of Australia by the Carnegie Institution of Washington." By Captain Edward Kidson, O.B.E., M.Sc.

"Skeletons of the Monotremes in the Collections of the Army Medical Museum at Washington." By Dr. R. W. Shufeldt, C.M.Z.S.

"The Progress of Geological Research in Tasmania since 1902." By Loftus Hills, M.B.E., M.Sc.

"France and Australia—The 'Prise de Possession.'" By Thomas Dunbabin, M.A.

"Tasmanian State Records." By J. Moore Robinson, F.R.G.S.

### Illustrated Lecture.

"The Geology of the National Park." By A. N. Lewis, M.C.

## 19th SEPTEMBER, 1921.

The Monthly Meeting was held at the Museum on 19th September, Mr. L. Rodway, C.M.G., presiding.

### Paper.

*Jungermannia stygia.* By H. W. Pearson, A.L.S.

### Illustrated Lecture.

"The Application of Science to Warfare on the Western Front." By Loftus Hills, M.B.E., M.Sc.

## 10th OCTOBER, 1921.

The Monthly Meeting was held at the Society's Room, Museum, on 10th October, His Excellency Sir W. L. Allardyce, K.C.M.G., presiding.

### Papers.

"On *Polyporus pulcherrimus.*" By L. Rodway, C.M.G.

"Bryophyte Notes." By W. A. Weymouth and L. Rodway, C.M.G.

"Description of Two Tasmanian Aboriginal Crania." By W. L. Crowther, D.S.O., M.B., and Clive Lord.

## 14th NOVEMBER, 1921.

The Monthly Meeting was held at the Museum on 14th November. Mr. L. Rodway, C.M.G., presiding.

### *Paper.*

"An Additional Note to a Preliminary Survey of the Glacial Remains preserved in the National Park of Tasmania." By A. N. Lewis, M.C.

### *Illustrated Lecture.*

"The Structure of the Atom." By Dr. L. McAulay.

## 5th DECEMBER, 1921.

A Meeting was held at the Museum on December 5th, Dr. A. H. Clarke presiding.

### *Papers.*

"The Concave Stone Implements of the Tasmanian Aborigines." By George Horne, V.D., M.A., M.D., Ch. B.

"Cetacean Remains from the Fossil Beds at Wynyard." By H. H. Scott and Clive Lord.

"Some Geographical Notes on a Model of the National Park at Mount Field." By Professor Griffith Taylor, D.Sc., B.E., B.A., F.G.S., F.R.G.S.

# ANNUAL REPORT
## 1921

### The Royal Society of Tasmania

---

**Patron:**
HIS MAJESTY THE KING.

**President:**
HIS EXCELLENCY THE GOVERNOR OF TASMANIA
(SIR W. L. ALLARDYCE, K.C.M.G.)

**Vice-Presidents:**
L. RODWAY, C.M.G.
A. H. CLARKE, M.R.C.S., L.R.C.P.

**Council:**
(Elected March, 1921).

A. H. CLARKE, M.R.C.S., L.R.C.P.          L. F. GIBLIN, D.S.O.
*(Chairman)*
W. H. CLEMES, B.A., B.Sc.                 Rt. Rev. R. S. HAY, D.D.

W. E. L. CROWTHER, D.S.O., M.B.           J. A. JOHNSON, M.A.

W. H. CUMMINS, A.I.A.C.                    L. RODWAY, C.M.G.

J. MOORE-ROBINSON, F.R.G.S. (elected April, 1921)

**Standing Committee:**
A. H. CLARKE, L. F. GIBLIN, L. RODWAY.

**Hon. Treasurer:**
L. RODWAY.

**Editor:**
CLIVE LORD

**Auditor:**
R. A. BLACK.

**Secretary and Librarian:**
CLIVE LORD.

# LIST OF MEMBERS

## Honorary Members:

David. Sir T. W. Edgeworth, K.B.E., C.M.G., B.A., F.R.S., F.G.S., Professor of Geology and Physical Geography in the University of Sydney. The University, Sydney.

Mawson, Sir Douglas, B.E., D.Sc. Adelaide.

Shackleton, Sir Ernest H., Kt., C.V.O., F.R.G.S., F.R.A.S. 9 Regent-street, London, S.W., England.

Spencer, Sir W. Baldwin, K.C.M.G., M.A., D.Sc., Litt.D., F.R.S. Melbourne.

## Ordinary, Life, and Corresponding Members:

"C," Corresponding Member.

"L," Member who has compounded subscriptions for life.

\* Member who has contributed a Paper read before the Society.

† Member who has been elected a member of the Council.

| Year of Election. | | |
|---|---|---|
| 1916 | | Ansell, M. M., B.A.  The University, Hobart. |
| 1920 | | Arnold, T. P.  37 Cromwell Street, Battery Point. |
| 1921 | | Atkinson, C. W., M.A., L.D.  117 St. John Street, Launceston. |
| 1918 | L | Avery, J.  52 Southerland Road, Annandale, Melbourne, Victoria. |
| 1921 | | Allen, D. V., B.Sc.  Principal Launceston Technical College. |
| 1908 | L | Baker, Henry D.  C/o American Consulate, Hobart. |
| 1921 | | Baker, H. S., LL.M., M.A.  York Street, Sandy Bay. |
| 1887 | | Barclay, David.  143 Hampden Road, Hobart. |
| 1921 | | Barr, J. Stoddart, M.D., Glas.  Lower Sandy Bay. |
| 1890 | | *Beattie, J. W.  1 Mt. Stuart Road, Hobart. |
| 1918 | | Bellamy, Herbert, City Engineer.  Town Hall, Hobart. |
| 1901 | C | Benham, W. B., M.A., D.Sc., F.R.S., F.Z.S.  Professor of Biology, University of Otago, Dunedin, N.Z. |
| 1903 | | Bennett, W. H.  Ashby, Ross. |
| 1918 | | Bennison, E. A.  Napoleon Street, Battery Point. |

| Year of Election. | | |
|---|---|---|
| 1921 | | Bertouch, V. Von. Wellington Square Practising School, Launceston. |
| 1920 | | Bernacchi, A. G. D. Maria Island. |
| 1921 | | Bethune, Rev. J. W., B.A. Church Grammar School, Launceston. |
| 1921 | | Birchall, J. A. 118 Brisbane Street, Launceston. |
| 1912 | | *Black, R. A. Chief Clerk, Department of Agriculture. |
| 1909 | | *Blackman, A. E. Franklin. |
| 1920 | | Blaikie, T. W. Practising School, Elizabeth Street, Hobart. |
| 1918 | | Bowling, J. "Barrington," Tower Road, New Town. |
| 1892 | C | Bragg, W. H., M.A., F.R.S. Professor of Physics in the University College, London. |
| 1920 | | Brett, R. L., B.Sc. 160 Macquarie Street, Hobart. |
| 1917 | | Brettingham-Moore, E., M.B., Ch.M. Macquarie Street. |
| 1911 | | Brooks. G. V. Director of Education, Education Department, Hobart. |
| 1921 | | Brown, Mrs. Justin. 10 Welman Street, Launceston. |
| 1907 | | Brownell, F. L. "Leura," Main Road, Moonah. |
| 1921 | | Bruce, L. S. Tourist Bureau, Launceston. |
| 1918 | | Bryer, J. R. Taroona. |
| 1918 | | Burbury, Alfred. "Glen Morey," Antill Ponds. |
| 1918 | | Burbury, Frederick. "Holly Park," Parattah. |
| 1919 | | Burbury, Charles. "Inglewood," Andover. |
| 1919 | | Burbury, Gerald. "Syndal," Ross. |
| 1919 | | Burbury, T. J. "Park Farm," Jericho. |
| 1920 | | Burdon, R. S., B.Sc. The University of Tasmania. |
| 1909 | | †*Butler, W. F. D., B.A., M.Sc., LL.B. Bishop Street, New Town. |
| 1921 | | Butler, Rev. W. Corly. The Parsonage, Melville Street. |
| 1917 | | Butters, J. H. Chief Engineer and Manager State Hydro-Electric Department, Hobart. |
| 1921 | | Camm, Dr. Carlyle. George Street, Launceston. |
| 1920 | | Cane, F. B. 90 High Street, Sandy Bay. |
| 1920 | | Canning, R. W. The University. Hobart. |
| 1919 | | Chapman, A. D. 105 Macquarie Street. |

1912　　　　　Chapman, J. R.　Holbrook Place, Hobart.

1901　C　　Chapman, R. W., M.A., B.C.E.　Elder Professor
　　　　　　　　　of Mathematics and Mechanics in the
　　　　　　　　　University of Adelaide.　The University,
　　　　　　　　　Adelaide.

1913　　　　　Chepmell, C. H. D.　Clerk of Legislative Council,
　　　　　　　　　Hobart.

1920　　　　　Clarke, W. I., M.B.　Macquarie Street, Hobart.

1896　　　　†*Clarke, A. H., M.R.C.S., L.R.C.P.　St. Helens,
　　　　　　　　　Tasmania.

1918　　　　　Clarke, T. W. H.　Quorn Hall, Campbell Town.

1887　　　　†Clemes, Samuel.　Principal Leslie House.　Clare
　　　　　　　　　Street, New Town.

1910　　　　†*Clemes, W. H., B.A., B.Sc.　Leslie House School,
　　　　　　　　　New Town.

1917　　　　　Copland, D. B., M.A.　Lecturer in History and
　　　　　　　　　Economics.　The University, Hobart.

1920　　　　　Cranstoun, Mrs. F. A.　6 Gregory Street, Sandy
　　　　　　　　　Bay.

1917　　　　　Cullen, Rev. John.　Macquarie Street, Hobart.

1918　　　　†*Cummins, W. H., A.L.A.C.　Lindisfarne.

1919　　　　†*Crowther, W. L., M.D., D.S.O.　Macquarie Street,
　　　　　　　　　Hobart.

1919　　　　　Davis, H. Warlow, C.E. Abermere, Mt. Stuart.

1908　　　　†Dechaineux, Lucien.　Principal of Technical
　　　　　　　　　School, Hobart.

1903　　　　　Delany, Most Rev. Patrick.　Archbishop of Hob-
　　　　　　　　　art.　99 Barrack Street.

1892　C.　　Dendy, A., D.Sc., F.R.S., F.L.S.　Professor of
　　　　　　　　　Zoology in the University of London
　　　　　　　　　(King's College).　"Vale Lodge," Hamp-
　　　　　　　　　stead, London, N.W.

1921　　　　　Douglas, O. Gordon.　27 Patterson Street, Laun-
　　　　　　　　　ceston.

1921　　　　　Dryden, M. S. 13 Hillside Crescent, Launceston.

1921　　　　　Eberhard, E. C.　Charles Street, Launceston.

1919　　　　　Elliott, E. A., M.B.　Macquarie Street, Hobart.

1918　　　　　Ellis, F.　Education Department, Hobart.

1921　　　　　Elms, E. A.　Post Office, Launceston.

1913　　　　　Erwin, H. D., B.A.　Christ's College, Hobart.

1921　　　　　Emmett, E. T.　Director Tasmanian Government
　　　　　　　　　Tourist Bureau, Hobart.

1918      Evans, L.    Acting Director of Agriculture, Hobart.

1921      Evershed, A. E.    65 George Street, Launceston.

1921      Eyre, H.    Manual Training School, Launceston.

1902      Finlay, W. A.    11 Secheron Road, Hobart.

1918      Finlay, G. W.    Baskerville, Campbell Town.

1918      Fletcher, C. E.    Education Department, Hobart.

1909      †*Flynn, T. T., D.Sc.    Ralston Professor of Biology, University of Tasmania.

1921      Flounders, A.    102 Patterson Street, Launceston.

1921      Forward, J. R.    Mechanics' Institute, Launceston.

1890   L   Foster, H., Lt.-Col.    Merton Vale, Campbell Town.

1905   L   Foster, J. D.    "Fairfield," Epping.

1921      Fox, Miss.    Ladies' College, Launceston.

1918      Gatenby, R. L.    Campbell Town.

1908      †*Giblin, Major, L. F., D.S.O., B.A.    Government Statistician, Davey Street.

1918      Gillett, Henry.    "Wetmore," Ross.

1920      Gillies, J. H.    Macquarie Street.

1918      Gould, J. W.    Tramways Department, Hobart.

1907      Gould, Robert.    Longford.

1921      Gepp, T. A.    Hydro-Electric Department, Deloraine.

1921      Grace, W. L.    91 High Street, Launceston.

1905   L   Grant, C. W.    High Peak, Huon Road.

1921      Hall, E. L.    38 Lyttleton Street, Launceston.

1913      Hardy, G. H.    C/o Australian Museum, Sydney.

1918      Harrap, Lt.-Colonel, G.    Launceston.

1921      Harris Miss Ila.    Studio, Findlay's Buildings, Launceston.

1921      Harris, Dr. R. E.    73 Cameron Street, Launceston.

1921   L   Harvey, David Hastie.    "Manresa," Lower Sandy Bay, Hobart.

1902   C   Haswell, William, M.A., D.Sc., F.R.S., F.L.S.    The University, Sydney, N.S. Wales.

1913      Hawson, Edward.    "Remine," 174 Argyle Street, Hobart.

1919      Hay, Rt. Rev. R. S., D.D., Bishop of Tasmania. Bishopscourt, Hobart.

1921    Heritage, J. E.   76 Frederick Street, Launceston.

1921    Heyward, F., F.R.V.I.A.   43 Lyttleton Street,
Launceston.

1915    Hickman, V. V., B.Sc.   "Burnham," Mulgrave
Crescent, Launceston.

1919    Higgins, Dr. P.   Campbell Town.

1913    Hills, Loftus, M.B.E., M.Sc.   Government Geologist of Tasmania, Launceston, Tasmania.

1921    Hill, A. H.   143 Charles Street, Launceston.

1914    Hitchcock, W. E.   Moina, Tasmania.

1921    Hogg, W.   Public Buildings, Launceston.

1918    Hogg, G. H., M.D., C.M.   37 Brisbane Street,
Launceston.

1921    Horne, George, V.D., M.A., M.D., Ch.B.   63
Collins Street, Melbourne, Vic.

1921    Horner, A. G.   16 York Street, Launceston.

1921    Hudspeth, R., Parliament Street, Sandy Bay.

1921    Hughes, J.   Public Buildings, Launceston.

1909    °Hutchison, H. R.   1 Barrack Street, Hobart.

1920    Hytten, T.   "Eltham," Bathurst Street, Hobart.

1913    Ife. G. W. R., LL.B.   Summerhill Road, Hobart.

1918    Irby, L. G.   Conservator of Forests, Forestry Department, Hobart.

1898    °Ireland, E. W. J., M.B., C.M.   Launceston General Hospital.

1918    Innes. H. S.   C/o *Mercury* Office, Launceston.

1919    Jackson, George A.   79 Collins Street, Hobart.

1906    °Johnson, J. A., M.A.   Principal of Phillip Smith
Training College, Hobart.

1921    Johnson, J. D.   142 St. John Street, Launceston.

1921    Judd, W., M.A.   College Street, Launceston.

1921    Keating, Senator J. H.   Senate Commonwealth
Parliament.

1921    Keid, H. G. W.   Geological Survey Office, Launceston.

1911    Keene. E. H. D.   Tantallon, Tarleton.

1910    Kermode, R. C.   Mona Vale, Ross.

1918    °Kermode, Lewis, B.A.   Birkdale, Lancashire,
England.

1913    Knight. J. C. E.   "Windermere," Claremont.

1918    Knight, C. E. L., B.Sc.   Claremont.

| Year | | |
|---|---|---|
| 1919 | | Knight, H. W. National Mutual Buildings, Macquarie Street, Hobart. |
| 1919 | | Leahy, F. T. C/o Electrolytic Zinc Company, Risdon. |
| 1887 | | †Lewis, Sir Neil Elliot, K.C.M.G., M.A., B.C.L., LL.B. "Werndee," Augusta Road, Hobart. |
| 1919 | | °Lewis, A. N., M.C. "Werndee," Augusta Road. |
| 1912 | | †Lindon, L. H., M.A. "The Lodge," Park Street, Hobart. |
| 1900 | | Lines, D. H. E., M.B., Ch.B. Archer Street, New Town. |
| 1921 | | Listner, J. Parker. Leslie House School, New Town. |
| 1875 | C | Liversidge, Professor Archibald, M.A., LL.D., A.R.S.M., F.R.S., F.I.C., F.C.S., F.G.S., F.R.G.S. "Fieldhead," Coombe Warren, Kingston, Surrey, England. |
| 1921 | | Littler, F. M. 65 High Street, Launceston. |
| 1912 | | †*Lord, Clive E., Curator and Secretary of the Tasmanian Museum, Hobart. "Cliveden," Sandy Bay. |
| 1921 | | Lord, Chester. "Mellifont," High Street, Sandy Bay. |
| 1921 | | Lord, Raymond. "Handroyd," 6 Franklin Street, Hobart. |
| 1921 | | MacCabe, W. B. Clarence Point, West Tamar. |
| 1919 | | Mackay, A. D., B.Sc., M.M.E. 4 Fawkner Street, South Yarra, Vic. |
| 1912 | | McAlister, Miss M. K. Holebrook Flats, Holebrook Place. |
| 1893 | | *McAulay, Alexander, M.A., Professor Mathematics in the University of Tasmania. The University, Hobart. |
| 1921 | | McGowan, W. Superintendent of Reserves, Launceston. |
| 1921 | | McClinton, Dr. R. 70 St. John Street, Launceston. |
| 1921 | | McInytre, Dr. W. Keverall. 37 Brisbane Street, Launceston. |
| 1902 | C | *Maiden, J. H., I.S.O., F.R.S., F.L.S., Director of the Botanic Gardens, Sydney, & Government Botanist of N.S.W. Botanic Gardens, Sydney. |
| 1918 | | Mansell, A. E. Melton Mowbray. |

| | |
|---|---|
| 1918 | Martin, Brig.-General W., V.D. Launceston. |
| 1913 | Mather, J. F. 1 Mt. Stuart Road, Hobart. |
| 1921 | Masters, A. H. A.M.P. Chambers. Launceston. |
| 1893 | *May, W. L. Forest Hill, Sandford. |
| 1921 | Meston, A. L., B.A. State High School, Launceston. |
| 1909 | Millen, Senator J. D. Roxburgh, Newstead. |
| 1907 | Miller, Lindsay S., M.B., Ch.B. 156 Macquarie Street, Hobart. |
| 1921 | Miller, W. D. & W. Murray Ltd., Launceston. |
| 1921 | Miller, R. M. State High School, Launceston. |
| 1894 L | Mitchell, J. G. Parliament Street, Sandy Bay. |
| 1921 | Monds, C. F. 4 Adelaide Street, Launceston. |
| 1911 | Montgomery, R. B. Davey Street. |
| 1918 | Murdoch, Hon. Thomas, M.L.C. 55 Montpelier Road, Hobart. |
| 1921 | Murdoch, Ronald. "Marathon," Lower Sandy Bay. |
| 1921 | Morris, E. Sydney, M.B., Ch.M., D.P.H., Chief Health Officer, Tasmania. 3 Montague Avenue, New Town. |
| 1921 | Muschamp, Rev. E. Holy Trinity Rectory, Launceston. |
| 1882 | Nicholas, G. C. "Cawood," Ouse. |
| 1918 | Nicholls, Sir Herbert, Kt., Chief Justice of Tasmania. Pillinger Street, Queenborough. |
| 1910 | Nicholls, H. Minchin, Government Microbiologist, Dept. of Agriculture, Hobart. Macquarie Street, Hobart. |
| 1919 | Nicolson, Norman. "Streanshalh," Campbell Town. |
| 1921 | Nye, P. B. Geological Survey Office, Launceston. |
| 1917 | Oldham, N., J.P. New Town. |
| 1921 | Oldham, W. C. 39 George Street, Launceston. |
| 1919 | Oldmeadow, H. E. R. "Lowes Park," Woodbury. |
| 1920 | Orr, Dr. Hubert. Campbell Town. |
| 1921 | Padman, R. S. 56 St. John Street, Launceston. |
| 1921 | Patten, W. H. 59 Cameron Street, Launceston. |
| 1921 | Parker, R. L. 81 St. John Street, Launceston. |
| 1908 | Parsons, Miss S. R. 190 Davey Street, Hobart. |

Year of
Election.

1888  C  Pearson, W. H., M.Sc., A.L.S.  18 Palatine Road, Withington, Manchester, Eng.

1902  †°Piesse, E. L., B.Sc., LL.B.  39 Broadway, Camberwell, Vic.

1910  Pillinger, James, 4 Fitzroy Crescent, Hobart.

1918  Pitt, Frank C. K.  "Glen Dhu," The Ouse.

1919  Pitt, C. F.  Campbell Town.

1908  Pratt, A. W. Courtney.  "Athon," Mt. Stuart Road, Hobart.

1921  Reid, A. McIntosh.  Geological Survey Office, Launceston.

1921  Reid, W. D.  Public Bulidings, Launceston.

1921  Reynolds, John.  Knocklofty Terrace, Hobart.

1919  Riggall, Captain A. Hortin, D.S.O.  Tunbridge.

1919  Robinson, J. Moore-.  Librarian and Publicity Officer, Chief Secretary's Department, Hobart.

1921  Rolph, W. R.  *Examiner & Weekly Courier* Office, Launceston.

1919  Rowland, E. O.  Secretary Public Service Board, Hobart.

1884  †°Rodway, Leonard, C.M.G., Government Botanist of Tasmania.  Macquarie Street, Hobart.

1913  Ross, Hector, Sheriff of Tasmania.  Macquarie Street, Hobart.

1921  Savigny, J.  21 York Street, Launceston.

1896  Scott, R. G., M.B., Ch.M.  172 Macquarie Street, Hobart.

1921  Scott, H. H.  Curator of the Victoria Museum, Launceston, Tas.

1921  Sharland, M. S. R.  C/o *The Mercury* Office, Hobart.

1892  C  °Shirley, John, D.Sc., Principal Teachers' Training College, Queensland.  "Cootha," Bowen Hills, Brisbane.

1921  Shields, Hon. Tasman, M.L.C.  13 Patterson Street, Launceston.

1901  Shoobridge, Canon G. W.  3 Molle Street, Hobart.

1921  Shoobridge, Hon. L. M., M.L.C.  "Sunnyside," New Town.

1921  Simson, L.  3 St. George's Square, Launceston.

1917  Slaytor, C. H., F.I.C.  Misterton, Doncaster, England.

O

LIST OF MEMBERS.

1901 C   Smith, R. Greig, D.Sc.   Linnean Hall, Elizabeth
             Bay, Sydney.

1921      Smithies, F.  34 Patterson Street, Launceston.

1919      Snowden. Colonel R. E.  "Minallo," West Hobart.

1896 L  *Sprott, Gregory, M.D., C.M.   Macquarie Street,
             Hobart.

1921      Spurling, S., Jnr.  Brisbane Street, Launceston.

1919      Stevenson, Miss F.   "Leith House," New Town.

1896 L   Sticht, Robert, B.Sc., E.M., Mt. Lyell Mining and
             Railway Co. Ltd.   Queen Street, Mel-
             bourne.

1921      Strike, R. J.   Town Hall, Launceston.

1913      Susman, Maurice.   88 Murray Street, Hobart.

1920      Swindells, A. W.   141 Campbell Street.

1907      Tarleton, J. W.  Sandy Bay.

1918      Taylor, Walter E.   Elboden-Street, Hobart.

1920      Taylour, W. H.  Equitable Buildings, Melbourne.

1920      Taylour, Harold.   Equitable Building, Mel-
             bourne.

1921      Thomas, P. H.   "Woolton," Mowbray Heights,
             Launceston.

1892 C  *Thompson, G. M., F.L.S.   Dunedin, N.Z.

1921      Thompson, Dr. L. Grey.   Patterson Street, Laun-
             ceston.

1918      †Thorold, C. C., M.A.   The  Hutchins  School,
             Hobart.

1921      Tymms, Dr. A. O.   18 York Street, Launceston.

1921      Wakefield, F. W.   Forestry Dept., Geeveston,
             Huon.

1918      Walch, Percy.   King Street, Sandy Bay.

1901 C   Wall, Arnold, M.A.  Professor of English Lan-
             guage & Literature in Canterbury College,
             Christchurch, N.Z.

1913      Wardman, John.   Superintendent of the Botani-
             cal Gardens, Hobart.

1918      Waterhouse, G. W., B.A., LL.M., Cantab.  Messrs.
             Ritchie & Parker, Alfred Green & Co.,
             Launceston.

1918      Watt, W.  The Observatory, Hobart.

1921      Waterworth, A. G.  State School, Glen Dhu.

1918      Weber, A. F.   Lands Department. Hobart.

---

# ANNUAL REPORT
## 1921.

In accordance with Rule 39, the Council present a Report of the proceedings of the Society for 1921.

### The Council and Officers.

The Annual Meeting was held on 14th March, 1921, and the following members were elected as the Council for 1921:—Rt. Rev. Dr. R. S. Hay, Dr. A. H. Clarke, Dr. W. L. Crowther, Major L. F. Giblin, Messrs. W. H. Clemes, W. H. Cummins, J A. Johnson, and L. Rodway.

At a meeting of the Society, held on Monday, 11th April, Mr. J. Moore-Robinson was elected a member of the Council.

During the year Ten Council Meetings were held, the attendance being as follows:—Major Giblin 9, Mr. Johnson 9, Dr. Clarke 8, Mr. Rodway 8, Dr. Crowther 7, Mr. Clemes 7, Mr. Cummins 6, Mr. Moore-Robinson 6, Rt. Rev. Dr. Hay 4.

The Council, at its first meeting, made the following appointments:—

Chairman of Council: Dr. A. H. Clarke.

Standing Committee: Dr. Clarke, Major Giblin, and Mr. Rodway.

Editor of Papers and Proceedings: Mr. Clive Lord.

Hon. Treasurer: Mr. L. Rodway.

Secretary and Librarian: Mr. Clive Lord.

Trustees of the Tasmanian Museum and Botanical Gardens: Dr. Clarke, Dr. Crowther, Messrs. Clemes, Cummins, Johnson, and Rodway.

### *Farewell to Dr. A. H. Clarke.*

Dr. A. H. Clarke, who has been Chairman of the Council of the Society and also Chairman of Trustees of the Tasmanian Museum and Botanical Gardens for many years, retired from these positions at the end of the year, as he is retiring from practice, and proposes to live at St. Helens, on the East Coast. In view of the valuable services rendered by Dr. Clarke, the Council and the Trustees arranged a farewell entertainment, which was held on 12th December, and at which the President of the Society, His Excellency the Governor, presided. Members of the Council were thus able to express their appreciation on behalf of the Society for all that Dr. Clarke had done for it, and also to wish him every success in his new sphere.

### *Meetings.*

During the year one Special and ten ordinary Meetings were held. The details concerning papers read and lectures delivered will be found in the Abstract of Proceedings.

### *Membership.*

Mainly owing to the formation of the Northern Branch of the Society, the membership roll shows a considerable increase. Many of the members did not join until late in the year, and the Society will not reap the full benefit of the increased membership until next year. The roll at the end of the year showed four honorary members, eleven corresponding members, nine life members, and two hundred and seventeen ordinary members.

### *Obituary.*

It is with regret that the Society has to record the death of the following members during the past year:—

T. Bennison, of Hobart (elected 1900).

Hon. C. E. Davies, M.L.C. (elected 1884).

A. J. Taylor, Librarian of the Tasmanian Public Library (elected a member in 1887).

## REPORTS OF SECTIONS

### *Psychology and Education Section.*

Six meetings were held during the year, and were well attended.

Officers—L. F. Giblin, Chairman; T. W. Blaikie, Hon. Sec.

A series of papers on "The Examination System" were read and discussed; the subjects and contributors being:—

"To what extent do examinations test the work of Education?"  S. R. Dickinson, M.A.

"Inspection v. Examination."  T. W. Blaikie.

"Intelligence Tests as a substitute for Examinations." Dr. Morris Miller.

"To what extent can examinations be modified to meet present needs?"  L. F. Giblin.

"The Testing of Adult Education."  L. Dechaineux and J. A. Johnson, M.A.

### Historical and Geographical Section.

The Historical and Geographical Section was first formed in 1899, but has been in recess for many years.  During the 1921 Session an effort was made to revive the Section, and a meeting was held on September 2nd, the following members being present:—Dr. W. L. Crowther, Messrs. H. S. Baker, J. W. Beattie, W. F. D. Butler, G. W. R. Ife, Clive Lord, and J. Moore-Robinson.

During the year the following meetings were held:—

September 2nd.  Section reconstituted.  Officers elected: Chairman, W. F. D. Butler.  Secretary, J. Moore-Robinson.

September 15th.  Inspection of Mr. J. W. Beattie's Historical Museum.

October 26th.  Lecture, "A Voyage from V.D.L. to England in 1839."  By Dr. W. L. Crowther.

# BRANCH REPORTS

## NORTHERN BRANCH.

### REPORT, 1921.

A preliminary meeting of those interested in the formation of a Northern Branch of the Royal Society was held in the Mechanics' Institute, Launceston, on the 11th May. At this meeting it was decided to draw up a circular, to be distributed to all who were thought to be interested, with the object of convening a public meeting to see what support the conveners could expect.  This meeting was finally held on 10th June, and there was a large attendance, Mr. W. R. Rolph being in the chair.  A resolution that a Northern Branch be formed was moved by Mr. Loftus Hills, and seconded by Mr. F. Heyward.  The necessary office-bearers and committee were elected, the following gentlemen consenting to act:—Dr. G. H. Hogg, Rev. J. W. Bethune, Dr. C. W. Atkinson, Messrs. H. H. Scott, Loftus Hills, F. Heyward, G. W. Waterhouse, F. M. Littler, W. D. Reid. Secretary and Treasurer, Mr. J. R. Forward. Mr. G. W. Waterhouse was subsequently elected chairman. This meeting decided to record its appreciation and thanks to Mr. Rolph for his work leading to the formation of a Northern Branch of the Society.

The inaugural meeting was held on 27th June, when the President of the Society, His Excellency the Governor, presided. There was also present a delegation from the Council consisting of Mr. L. Rodway, C.M.G., (Vice-President), Dr. Crowther, Mr. J. Moore-Robinson, and Mr. Clive Lord (Secretary). At this meeting a lecture on "The Application of Science on the Western Front" was given by Mr. Loftus Hills, M.Sc., Government Geologist. The following lectures have been given during the session:—

June 27. "The Application of Science to Warfare on the Western Front." By Loftus Hills, M.B.E., M.Sc.

July 22. "The Application of the Stereoscope to Science." Mr. H. H. Scott.

August 13. "Glimpses of Evolution." Dr. W. K. Gregory.

September 21. "What Astronomy Teaches about the Sun." A. T. Kirkaldy.

October 21. "The Emotions and James' Theory." R. O. M. Miller, B.A.

November 28. "Wonderful Java." H. D. Flanagan.

In addition there were two public meetings held under the auspices of the Branch in the interests of a National Reserve in the Cradle Mountain-Lake St. Clair area.

Mr. G. W. Waterhouse presided at all of these meetings. The Committee have much pleasure in recording a successful session. The membership numbers 63.

## ROYAL SOCIETY OF TASMANIA

### RECEIPTS AND EXPENDITURE, 1921. GENERAL ACCOUNT

| RECEIPTS. | | £ | s. | d. |
|---|---|---:|---:|---:|
| Government Grant in Aid of Printing | | 100 | 0 | 0 |
| Special Grant in Aid of Printing A.A.A.S. Papers | | 100 | 0 | 0 |
| Subscriptions— | | | | |
| Current—169 at £1 1 0 | | | | |
| Arrears—3 at 1 1 0 | | | | |
| Advance—3 at 1 1 0 | | 183 | 15 | 0 |
| Payments for use of Society's Room | | 10 | 0 | 0 |
| Sale of Publications | | 15 | 18 | 0 |
| Miscellaneous | | 15 | 15 | 3 |
| | | £425 | 8 | 3 |
| Dr. Balance, 1921 | | 69 | 19 | 4 |
| | | £495 | 7 | 7 |

| PAYMENTS. | | £ | s. | d. |
|---|---|---:|---:|---:|
| Dr. Balance Brought Forward | | 50 | 6 | 6 |
| Salaries | | 33 | 10 | 0 |
| Papers and Proceedings— | | | | |
| 1920 (Part) £97 13 3 | | | | |
| 1921 (Part) 206 15 6 | | 304 | 8 | 9 |
| Expenses of Meetings | | 28 | 9 | 0 |
| Library and Insurance | | 18 | 19 | 6 |
| Light and Fuel | | 2 | 4 | 2 |
| Lantern and Operator | | 3 | 10 | 0 |
| Postages and Petty Cash | | 16 | 17 | 0 |
| Northern Branch | | 19 | 5 | 0 |
| Miscellaneous | | 17 | 2 | 6 |
| Bank Charges | | 0 | 15 | 2 |
| | | £495 | 7 | 7 |

## MORTON ALLPORT MEMORIAL FUND ACCOUNT, 1921

| RECEIPTS. | £ s. d. | PAYMENTS. | £ s. d. |
|---|---|---|---|
| Interest Received from Perpetual Trustee Co.— | | Balance Brought Forward ... ... ... ... | 9 14 10 |
| 5 Per cent. on £200 War Loan.. £10 0 0 | | Cr. Balance, 1921 ... ... ... ... | 0 0 2 |
| Less Trustee Co. Commission.. 0 5 0 | | | |
| | 9 15 0 | | |
| | £9 15 0 | | £9 15 0 |

£200 was raised by Public Subscription in 1878 to establish a Memorial to the late Morton Allport. The Fund is invested in the name of the Perpetual Trustees, Executors, and Agency Co. of Tasmania Ltd., and the income is used for the purchase of Books for the Library of the Society.

I have compared the Receipt Book, Vouchers, and Bank Book with items particularised in the Cash Book, and found them to be correct.

R. A. BLACK,
Hon. Auditor.

11th January, 1922.

L. RODWAY,
Hon. Treasurer.

CLIVE LORD,
Secretary.

# ROYAL SOCIETY OF TASMANIA, NORTHERN BRANCH

## STATEMENT OF RECEIPTS AND PAYMENTS, 1921

| | £ | s. | d. | | £ | s. | d. |
|---|---|---|---|---|---|---|---|
| To Donation toward Inaugural Meeting .. .. | 5 | 0 | 0 | By Expenses of Meetings .. .. .. .. .. | 5 | 9 | 0 |
| ,, Pro Rata Refund on Subscriptions Paid .. | 14 | 0 | 0 | ,, Lantern Slides .. .. .. .. .. .. .. | 2 | 0 | 0 |
| | | | | ,, Printing and Stationery .. .. .. .. | 4 | 13 | 9 |
| | | | | ,, Lanternist .. .. .. .. .. .. .. | 1 | 10 | 0 |
| | | | | ,, Sundry Accounts .. .. .. .. .. .. | 2 | 8 | 2 |
| | | | | | £16 | 0 | 11 |
| | | | | Balance in Savings Bank, 31/12/21 .. | 3 | 4 | 1 |
| | £19 | 5 | 0 | | £19 | 5 | 0 |

J. R. FORWARD,

Hon. Secretary Northern Branch.

17th January, 1922.

# INDEX

# PAPERS & PROCEEDINGS

OF THE

# ROYAL SOCIETY

# OF TASMANIA

FOR THE YEAR

# 1921

(With 30 Plates and 5 Text Figures)

ISSUED 28th FEBRUARY, 1922

PUBLISHED BY THE SOCIETY

The Tasmanian Museum, Argyle Street, Hobart
1922

*Price: Ten Shillings*

# Papers and Proceedings

of the

# Royal Society of Tasmania

———

## BACK NUMBERS

A limited number of copies are available for purchase. Prices, etc., can be obtained on application to the Secretary.

# ROYAL SOCIETY OF TASMANIA

## PAPERS AND PROCEEDINGS, 1921

## CONTENTS

Wholly set up and printed in Australia by Davies Bros. Ltd., at "The Mercury" 22 773     Office, Macquarie Street, Hobart, Tas., 1922.

www.ingramcontent.com/pod-product-compliance
Lightning Source LLC
Chambersburg PA
CBHW020507270326
41926CB00008B/770